Hacking Life

<strong> Ideas Series

Edited by David Weinberger

The <strong> Ideas Series explores the latest ideas about how technology is affecting culture, business, science, and everyday life. Written for general readers by leading technology thinkers and makers, books in this series advance provocative hypotheses about the meaning of new technologies for contemporary society.

The <strong> Ideas Series is published with the generous support of the MIT Libraries.

Hacking Life: Systematized Living and Its Discontents, Joseph M. Reagle Jr.

The Smart Enough City: Putting Technology in Its Place to Reclaim Our Urban Future, Ben Green

Hacking Life

Systematized Living and Its Discontents

Joseph M. Reagle Jr.

The MIT Press
Cambridge, Massachusetts
London, England

This book was set in Stone Serif Medium by Westchester Publishing Services. Printed and bound in the United States of America.

Library of Congress Cataloging-in-Publication Data

Names: Reagle, Joseph Michael, author.
Title: Hacking life : systematized living and its discontents / Joseph M.
    Reagle Jr.
Description: Cambridge, MA : MIT Press, [2019] | Series: Strong ideas |
    Includes bibliographical references and index.
Identifiers: LCCN 2018028561 | ISBN 9780262038157 (hardcover : alk. paper)
Subjects: LCSH: Technological innovations--Social aspects. | Self-help
    techniques--Social aspects. | Quality of life. | Lifestyles.
Classification: LCC HM851 .R432 2019 | DDC 303.48/3--dc23 LC record available
    at https://lccn.loc.gov/2018028561

10 9 8 7 6 5 4 3 2 1

To Mom—who taught me my first hack of tying shoes

Contents

Acknowledgments

All of us have a little life hacker in us. I have a fair amount. My thinking strongly tilts toward the rational style. When I write, I work in chunks, separated by breaks. To keep myself accountable, I track my daily words written and hours on task. I don't like clutter and do like to keep things organized. I've struggled with health concerns and the health care system. I use typing-break timers and an unusual keyboard. When I feel a cold coming on, I take a zinc lozenge—even though I suspect it is a placebo. I am far from gregarious, and at big gatherings I create challenges for myself, such as introducing myself to three strangers. I am an anxious person and find levity in Marcus Aurelius and calm in a decade-plus mindfulness practice. I am also a white male with a computer science degree: true to type, so far. However, I don't track much else and have no desire or expectation of uploading myself into a computer. If forced to choose between Soylent (soy-based), Huel (oat-based), and MealSquares (brownie-like), I prefer Huel, but would much rather have a peanut-butter-and-jelly sandwich.

I took on this project to better understand life hacking given that I find it both compelling and, at times, concerning. What I learned is the focus of this book, but I don't conclude that this self-help for the digital age is wholly helpful or harmful, or even novel. It's more complicated than that, as are the stories of those who share the hacking mind-set.

I extend my thanks to those who shared their motivations, practices, and hesitations in hacking life. Most were enthusiasts, but this doesn't mean they were without their own questions and concerns. Indeed, so much of life hacking is an experiment. I apologize that a few the people I spoke with don't appear in the following pages, but my discussions with them still informed my understanding and writing; this includes Jon Cousins, Maggie Delano, Awais Hussain, and others who wished to remain anonymous.

Between my sources and those who read drafts are those who answered factual questions or reviewed sections of prose. These are people whom I followed online or in print and who helped me get closer to getting their stories right. This includes Danny O'Brien, Danny Reeves, Bethany Soule, Richard Sprague, Gina Trapani, Tynan, Amy Webb, and Nick Winter. Thank you.

Most importantly, there are those who helped me with the manuscript itself.

David Weinberger is the editor of the Ideas Series at the MIT Press, and he provided invaluable feedback toward the book's development. I'm a fan of his books, so I am lucky to have had his help crafting this book's focus and prose. David has shown me many kindnesses over the years, and it was a joy to collaborate with him—we also both write in Markdown. I am thrilled to be part of this series and to have this book published in print and online under a Creative Commons license. Gita Devi Manaktala, editorial director at the MIT Press, patiently answered my many questions. Michael Harrup and Kathleen Caruso were thorough copyeditors. Other folks at MIT Press who also helped include Kyle Gipson, Gabriela Bueno Gibbs, Judy Feldmann, Victoria Hindley, Sean Reilly, and Michael Sims. I am sure there are others.

I am indebted to a handful of scholars. I don't think anyone usually enjoys reading PhD dissertations, but I read Matt Thomas's excellent "Life Hacking: A Critical History, 2004–2014" with rapt attention. Alongside Joey Daoud's 2010 documentary, *You 2.0—A Documentary on Life Hacking*, Thomas's work is an early and important treatment of this topic. Thomas also gave me feedback on my initial efforts. Natasha Schüll read the whole manuscript and also helped with a suggestion toward the title of the book. Rebecca Jablonsky reviewed the introduction and chapter on health hacking. Meryl Alper, my office neighbor at Northeastern University, kindly shared her expertise and sources on cognitive diversity. Bess Williamson shared her work on the importance of the disability community's history of hacking. Benjamin Hunnicutt corresponded with me about ancient and medieval notions of procrastination. I also received useful feedback from anonymous peer reviewers.

Thanks also to the friends who shared their time with me. Valerie Aurora and Noam Cohen read the whole manuscript and, among other things, independently pushed me to be more rigorous about hacker ethics. Alex

Censullo, a former student, also read it all and noted a number of rough spots needing refinement. Amy Gilson made good suggestions on the chapter on relationships.

Finally, Nora Schaddelee read drafts of each chapter. I can only hope my bread baking provides some sort of redress. I'm also grateful when Casper reminds it's time for a computer break—with a nudge to my calf to shepherd me along.

1 Introduction

Mark Rittman's home is a web of sensors and control. Filaments of data pass between his house, his body, and the server in his garage. Door, motion, and temperature sensors monitor his environs. His iPhone and health band monitor him. Everything is logged for analysis, and controlling the lighting, temperature, and music is as easy as a request to Siri. With the addition of his latest gadget, the iKettle, Rittman hoped to ask Siri for a cup of tea. Better yet, he wanted to add the kettle to an automated morning routine: when the health band on his wrist noticed he was awake, it could alert the house to turn up the heat and lighting downstairs and have the kettle ready for when he got out of the shower. Unfortunately, Rittman had a hard time getting the gadget online, as he tweeted to the thousands following his saga: "3 hrs later and still no tea. Mandatory recalibration caused wifi base-station reset." When he did get it online, the kettle did not work with his other devices: "To get my iKettle to actually work with Siri I had to hack this integration together myself." He continued to tweet about this process, and when he finally succeeded, his story went global, starting with a report in *The Guardian*: "English man spends 11 hours trying to make cup of tea with Wi-Fi kettle technology."[1]

This project exemplifies the hacker mind-set: an enthusiastic—sometimes excessive—fascination with the workings of systems. But let us imagine another hacker who did not persevere on the technical front. Harper buys the iKettle on sale and, after tinkering with it over a couple of weekends, concludes that it's hopeless. Worse yet, the receipt has gone missing. Fortunately, there is recourse to a different sort of hack: Harper remembers a post on the site *Lifehacker*, "How to Return Nearly Anything without a Receipt."[2] Harper opts for the last-ditch effort and waits a few more weeks until after Christmas to return the kettle. Even though there may be long lines, stores tend to be more lenient then.

Rittman, a big data analyst and self-tracker, pulled off his hack because he understood the technical systems underlying home automation. Harper pulled off the no-receipt hack because of an understanding of a different system: the dynamics of the shopping season. These two hacks are indicative of how, in the past ten years, the notion of hacking as a quick or clever fix to a technical system has been applied to all aspects of life. Life hackers track and analyze their meals, finances, sleep, work, and headaches. They share tips on how to efficiently tie shoelaces, pack luggage, find dates, and learn languages.

All of this might surprise those who associate hacking with criminals in hoodies hunched over green-type terminals, but it's in keeping with the word's origins. Sixty years ago, model railroad enthusiasts at the Massachusetts Institute of Technology (MIT) used *hack* to describe a quick fix to "The System," the web of wires and relays under the train platform. Hackers are drawn to exploring, building, and manipulating such systems.

Today, life hacking sits at the intersection of technology, culture, and larger concerns about work, wealth, health, relationships, and meaning. It is the manifestation of the *hacker ethos*, an individualistic and rational approach of systematization and experimentation.[3] For instance, some "biohackers," as they call themselves, are experimenting with "Strategies for Engineered Negligible Senescence." This name for life extension oozes confidence—it only makes "SENS," after all. With the continued proliferation of technology, especially apps and connected sensors, this hacker ethos is appearing in many areas of our life that have never been engineered or hacked before. In addition to extending life, there are systems for increasing productivity, achieving material contentment, maximizing fitness, and finding romantic partners and pleasing sexual ones.

Some of this might seem a bit weird or extreme. Plenty of critics have pointed out life hacking's pretensions and excesses. Yet the critics, too, have their excesses. One journalist describes the life hacker favorite *Getting Things Done* as "a holy book for the information age [that] is turning stressed-out worker bees into members of an unlikely new cult obsessed with keeping an empty inbox."[4] Calling enthusiasts a "cult" is catchy, but it's also hyperbolic. We have all experienced moments of being overwhelmed by work and email. And what do these *enthusiasts*—a perfectly good word—and *Getting Things Done* have in common with a cult? No one claims the book is "holy" or inerrant. The author is neither semidivine nor especially charismatic. Readers are not required to abandon alternatives, recruit newcomers, or isolate themselves from friends and family.

Life hacking is an approach to life and a type of self-help. It has strengths, to which I am sympathetic given my own geekiness, and weaknesses, about which I have concerns. Yet these concerns are not because life hacking is alien and cultish. Rather, they arise *because* of its relevance: we can all use some help as our lives become increasingly governed and structured as systems.

The term *cult* distracts us from the more interesting question: What does life hacking tell us about life well lived in the twenty-first century? We will see that life is increasingly like the iKettle, a complicated system. And to succeed, like Rittman, we must dedicate ourselves to mastering its rules.

Life Hacking Geeks and Gurus

A hacker is popularly understood as someone who breaks into computers: those who exploit system weaknesses for ill-gotten gain. Yet for those familiar with the term, it means something different. Yes, hackers often have a technical affinity. And like the model railroad enthusiasts at MIT, they do like to understand and explore systems. But for most hackers, a *hack* means a novel solution or fix, which is often shared. This includes clever fixes that are good enough and increments toward perfection.

Although sharing tips is not novel—recall Hints from Heloise—the term *life hacking* emerged among a handful of technically inclined writers in 2004. In February of that year, Danny O'Brien proposed a "life hacking" session at the O'Reilly Emerging Technology Conference in San Diego, California. O'Brien, a writer and digital activist, noted that "alpha geeks" are extraordinarily productive, and he wanted to speak "to the most prolific technologists about the secrets of their desktops, their inboxes, and their schedules."[5] The idea caught on. Within the year Merlin Mann launched *43 Folders*, named for a way of organizing future tasks via folders, and Gina Trapani started *Lifehacker*, a site that remains popular today. Tim Ferriss took the practice mainstream with his 2007 best seller *The 4-Hour Workweek: Escape 9–5, Live Anywhere and Join the New Rich*.[6] Although Ferriss does not make much use of the *life hacker* term—he sees himself as a self-experimenter in *lifestyle design*—his books and podcast make him its most famous practitioner.

Lifestyle design is an accessible label for those who want to reach an audience beyond those who identify as hackers—or even know what *hacking* means. Other labels speak to different areas of focus. Minimalists seek to pare down and live more simply, a goal often facilitated by technology. Pickup artists use systematic techniques and behavioral hacks to further their sexual interests.[7] And those who focus on tracking their lives, such as steps taken or foods eaten, might identify with the Quantified Self movement. I consider all of this life hacking because of the shared enthusiasm for improving life via a systematic approach. This includes small tips, like how to peel an onion without crying, and weightier suggestions, like how to find contentment.

It's not a coincidence that the term *life hacking* emerged a few years after Richard Florida's 2002 book *The Rise of the Creative Class*. Why do some regions in America do well relative to others? Florida argues that metropolises with the "3Ts" (technology, talent, and tolerance) correlate with growth. This growth is driven by workers who create "new ideas, new technology, and creative content," including artists, engineers, writers, designers, educators, and entertainers. Members of the creative class, about 30 percent of the American workforce, "engage in complex problem solving that involves a great deal of independent judgment."[8] They accept or prefer flexible work even if it exceeds the bounds of the 9-to-5 workweek, are less concerned with dress and formality, and identify more with their profession than with their employer. Most relevant to life hacking, they feel that working too much is better than counting the minutes before the end of the day. And they tend to complain of too little time rather than too much work. Life hackers are the systematizing constituency of the creative class.

Among self-identifying life hackers, many are true to type, but there are, of course, individual differences. I've followed and spoken to many enthusiasts, online and in person, and even as they differentiate themselves—not all biohackers associate with the Quantified Self, for example—they have something in common. Even those who prefer the label *self-experimenter* or *lifestyle designer* share the life hacker ethos. They are rationally inclined individuals fond of systems and experimentation—whatever differences, distancing, and distinctions also exist.

One distinction that can be drawn among life hackers is between *geeks* and *gurus*. I make this distinction because most life hacking critiques focus on prominent personalities, especially Ferriss. Yet as important as he is, Ferriss is not a typical life hacker. He is a guru, someone who sells lifestyle advice and his role as its vendor. Even if *guru* is not always flattering, I do not use it as an insult. Pragmatically, *guru* is more concise than *self-help author, life coach*, or *lifestyle designer*. Analytically, it designates those who offer and are looked to for guidance. A recent documentary about self-help author Tony Robbins is subtitled *I Am Not Your Guru*.[9] But he *is* a guru: he and Ferriss are professional advice givers. The question, then, is, What assumptions underlie their advice, and is that advice sound and worth what they charge?

Geeks, on the other hand, are enthusiasts looking to fix their foibles and improve their quality of life. For example, later in the book we will meet a relationship hacker who shared her dating spreadsheet template so others could use or improve it. Many geeks similarly share their hacks and experiments—such is the nature of their enthusiasm—but few desire or manage to become professional writers and lifestyle coaches.

Gurus do deserve scrutiny. They court publicity and argue others should pursue a course of action premised on unspoken assumptions and financial gain.[10] The former attracts our attention; the latter deserves it. Even so, we should not lose sight of life hacking as a subculture of those sharing tips and tools for a better life.

Practical Philosophy, Self-Help, and Systems

You, one among many, can be a success with the right attitude and actions. To learn how, you need only consult some of the 45,000-plus self-help titles in print. Most Americans do just that, and the market for this genre is worth more than $500 million—$10 billion when audio, videos, infomercials, and personal coaching are included.[11]

Life hacking is the latest chapter in the history of self-help, and as the meaning of success has changed, so has the advice given. Do we succeed by being open to divine intervention, as in the 1890s? By following the examples of those who had grown rich, as in the self-help classics of the 1930s? Or by adopting the secrets of the alpha geeks, who thrive amid today's information glut? As Steven Starker writes in his history of the genre, self-help books "reflect their sociocultural context, revealing something of the needs, wishes and fears of individuals of their period."[12] And as the author of a *New Yorker* profile of Ferriss quipped: "Every generation gets the self-help guru that it deserves."[13]

Just as life hacking is a recent instance of self-help, both are continuations of what is now being called "practical philosophy." Unlike academic philosophy, practical philosophy is focused on *what* is worthwhile in life and *how* to realize it.[14] It's a life philosophy. Stoicism and Confucianism are ancient practical philosophies. Life hacking is a contemporary one. For example, you can be productive (what) by limiting the time you spend on email to a certain time of the day (how).

Self-help is a practical philosophy, steeped in American culture. As Starker writes in *Oracle at the Supermarket: The American Preoccupation with Self-Help Books*, "American individualism, I believe, is the wellspring from which nearly all self-help materials flow." Self-help, he continues, is a manifestation of "American opportunism, self-reliance, and determination to succeed."[15] More recently, a cultural critic writing for *New York* magazine notes that "strains of self-help culture—entrepreneurship, pragmatism, fierce self-reliance, gauzy spirituality—have been embedded in the national DNA since Poor Richard's Almanack."[16] Although Scotsman Samuel Smiles's lucrative *Self Help* (1859) was the first book to use the term, self-help joins apple pie as a European import that is now inexorably linked with America.

Life hacking is now a slice of the self-help pie. Before moving on to new ventures, Gina Trapani published three books of hacks culled from *Lifehacker*. Ferriss has compiled five best-selling books, maintains a popular blog, and hosts a widely listened to podcast, all under the 4-Hour brand. Half a dozen authors have published works on minimalism, including *The 100 Thing Challenge* and *Everything That Remains*.[17] There are also many smaller life hacker titles that don't reach the mainstream audience. Still, despite being published via independent presses or as e-books, they receive dozens of reviews on Amazon. I have even come across a life hacking magazine in my grocery store checkout and in a television show, *Hacking the System*, on National Geographic.

Life hacking is a continuation of American self-help for geeks, which has gone mainstream. The values of "American individualism," of being "pragmatic" and "entrepreneurial," and of having an "endless ability to overcome obstacles" are all core to life hacking. Life hackers add a systematizing mindset, willingness to experiment, and fondness for tech; this befits a world of far-flung digital networks, a world of systems and gadgets.

Some might find life hacking, like self-help, difficult to take seriously. It spans from small tricks, which can be dismissed as trivial, to lifestyle design, which can be likened to a refashioning of the same old "S.H.A.M."—the title of a book critical of the "Self-Help and Actualization Movement."[18] Yet this reach is what makes life hacking interesting: there is an underlying ethos of systematizing that embraces both mundane hacks and life's larger pursuits.

Entrepreneur Paul Buchheit, Google employee number 23, lead developer of Gmail, and coiner of Google's early motto "Don't be evil," believes that hacking is an "applied philosophy" of life. He writes that "wherever there are systems, there is the potential for hacking, and there are systems everywhere. Our entire reality is systems of systems, all the way down." Granted, "not everyone has the hacker mindset (society requires a variety of personalities)," but those with this mind-set are the ones who "transform the world" across industry, governance, and even religion. For Buchheit, "hacking is much bigger and more important than clever bits of code in a computer—it's how we create the future."[19]

Buchheit's belief is provocative, simplistic, and totalizing—like many self-help premises. And as Starker observes, it's easy for the critic of such beliefs to be dismissive, to respond with a "shake of the head, momentary sneer, superior smile, and benign neglect." Nevertheless, "the self-help book is a firm part of the fabric of American culture, too pervasive and influential to be ignored or lightly dismissed, and certainly worthy of investigation."[20] The same is true of life hacking.

Life Hacking's Shades of Gray

The power of hacking, for Paul Buchheit, resides in the fact that every system is governed by two sets of rules: the perceived rules of how things are thought to work and the actual rules of reality. He believes that "in most complex systems, the gap between these two sets of rules is huge. Sometimes we catch a glimpse of the truth, and discover the actual rules of a system. Once the actual rules are known, it may be possible to perform 'miracles'— things which violate the perceived rules." So for example, a computer hacker can exploit the gap between how a program is supposed to behave and the reality of a buffer overrun. Of course, "hacking isn't limited to computers."[21]

Computer hackers are often discussed using a trope from old Western movies: white-hat hackers fortify system weaknesses arising from this gap and black hats maliciously exploit them. Gray hats are in between: they might break into a system without permission but cause little to no harm. Harper's holiday return of the kettle is a light shade of gray. As Rittman and others discovered, getting the kettle's Wi-Fi to work is not easy. Returning it without a receipt bends the rules but doesn't seem so bad. What if Harper had instead used the same technique to return the gadget to a different store at full price?

Harper would then have defrauded the second store and walked away with more cash than the original sale price. That would be a darker shade of gray.

Lifehacker's "How to Return Nearly Anything" post appeared as part of its annual Evil Week leading up to Halloween. The *Lifehacker* editors write that such posts, although "a bit tongue-in-cheek," reflect that "knowledge is power, and whether you use that power for good or evil depends on you. Sometimes evil is justified, or sometimes it can help you fight evil. Learning to crack passwords teaches you security practices. A better understanding of lying and manipulation earns you the ability to detect such tactics (or use them in situations in which it's actually the lesser of two evils)."[22] This rationale sounds almost Machiavellian. It also evinces a technically inclined and individualistic mind-set—not surprising. However, whether something is good or evil depends on more than the individual. To understand this, replace the moral absolutes with an alternative question: To what degree is a life hack harmful or beneficial, and to whom? We'll return to this question often.

The no-receipt hack is obviously self-interested. But it's not harmful if Harper returns the kettle to the same place where she bought it and at the same price. What if everyone used this hack? This question is an instance of Immanuel Kant's *categorical imperative*: do only that which you would want everyone to do. The first case of returning an inoperable kettle at the original place and price is innocuous. However, if everyone used this no-receipt hack to return discounted products at full price, the world would be worse off for it. Beyond the theft, stores would in turn adopt less flexible return policies, harming other shoppers as well.

Kant's categorical imperative expands the scope of moral consideration beyond the individual. We can ask if a hack is *universal*: Does it continue to work if everyone does it? And is it *beneficial*: Is the world then a better place?

Consider the real-life case of "Bob," a developer at Verizon, who was caught outsourcing his own work to a firm in China.[23] Many American workers, including software developers, face the anxiety of having their jobs outsourced overseas. Bob outsourced his work but kept his job. He paid the Chinese one-fifth of his salary and spent his days browsing the web and watching cat videos. He turned a corporate practice to his own advantage, hacking the system. Bob's hack was clever, and I read his story with some delight. He was also dishonest and a liability because he gave outsiders access to his company's systems; I understand why he was fired. Yet was he taking advantage of a workforce reality or complicit by adopting the strategy himself? He was doing both. This was a darker life hack. Clearly, Bob's hack was self-interested. Also, his hack wasn't universal. It worked only because it was singular and surreptitious. It also had the potential to harm others. His dishonesty put his employer at risk. It doesn't survive Kant's scrutiny because we would not wish such dishonesty to be universal.

There are also life hacks that can *unintentionally* harm the hacker and others. Consider the parallel between productivity hacking and cosmetic surgery. At the individual level, cosmetic surgery is a type of self-enhancement that can improve quality of life. It can go also wrong, making things worse. Or surface enhancements can provide temporary respite from deeper needs, leading to a cycle of interventions that never satisfy. It is hard to claim, universally, that cosmetic surgery is good or bad for all individuals. The same is true of life hacking. And this becomes further complicated when we think about the social implications of self-enhancement. Enhancement's impetus is often social, and when undertaken, it pushes standards increasingly higher—driving contentment further out of reach.[24] One person's enhanced beauty can make others feel uglier.

Similarly, some productivity hacks work well. Prioritizing tasks, rather than overscheduling, is key to a productive day. Some hacks won't work. Drinking lots of water and holding your urine is supposed to make you more focused but is more likely to be distracting. And like some surgeries, there are hacks that can make things worse or that will never satisfy. Overscheduling is a mistake, and superproductivity will never be enough. Finally, enhanced productivity accelerates the demands placed on everyone, including the productive.

These are the shades of gray of our *digital age*, a moment of far-flung interactions, ubiquitous devices, and unsettled science; a moment in which we can work remotely, outsource chores, and track and experiment with every indicator of life, from heart rate to emails sent. By considering cases like Bob's, we can identify the values inherent in *what* is thought to be worthwhile and the efficacy and consequence of *how*.

Nominal, Optimal, and Near Enemies

As with computer hacking, there are useful, useless, and harmful life hacks, with nebulous boundaries between. By exploring these boundaries, we can better understand the challenges of the new millennium. In an economy that prizes immediacy and flexibility, how do we manage time? In a culture that values autonomy and self-reliance, how do we motivate ourselves? In a world in which material excess is now as much a problem as deficiency, how do we relate to stuff? In a period of increasing uncertainty but ubiquitous monitoring, how do we know what really works? When others are within a finger's reach on our devices, how ought we to connect and relate to one another? When we realize that nothing, even the most clever hacks, will save us from uncertainty and loss, how do we find meaning in life?

Technology-related criticism speaks to these questions, usually by pitting opposing sides against one another, creating heroes and villains, rather than productive conversation. We can do better, in part, by asking open questions without forgone conclusions.[25] Take arguments about Facebook's effects on users' well-being, for example. Rather than simply concluding that Facebook makes people depressed or that it gives the depressed social support, we should ask about the different ways different people use Facebook. Similarly, rather than asking if life hackers are visionaries or cultists, we can make distinctions among practitioners and among practices.

Just as I distinguish between geek and guru hackers, I distinguish between nominal and optimal hacking. Among engineers, to say that something is *nominal* means that it is within the expected range. If the power at my electrical outlet is between 114 and 126 volts (120 volts±5 percent), it is nominal. I use this term instead of *normal* because the latter is loaded. To return to the cosmetic surgery parallel, what does a *normal* nose look like in a multiethnic world? There can be different normals in different contexts. At the same time, within a single context, normal tends toward a privileged ideal. What does a normal nose look like as rhinoplasty becomes common? We can ask the same question about being productive or healthy. The ideal becomes ever narrower: social norms affect what individuals want and vice versa.[26]

Nominal permits me to temporarily put aside issues of normalcy and draw a distinction between it and *optimal*, at or exceeding the leading edge. Their difference is related to intention, one of *keeping up* versus *surpassing*. Take swimming: whereas the nominal hacker wants to be a good enough swimmer to safely enjoy the water, the optimal hacker wants to be the best at racing upstream. This difference is like that between reconstructive and cosmetic surgery or between therapy and enhancement. The distinction between nominal and optimal hacking, though, can be seen in every domain of life.

The earliest example of life hacking I can recall is of nominal health hacking: John Walker's *The Hacker's Diet*. Walker founded the company behind AutoCAD, an engineering and drafting program still used today. As the 1980s came to a close, Walker was concerned that he had grown out of shape and overweight. Because he was an engineer, he decided to "approach weight loss as an engineering problem. I studied the human body the way I'd tackle a misbehaving electronic circuit or computer program: develop a model of how it works, identify the controls that affect it, and finally adjust those controls to set things aright." His engineering approach worked. In less than a year, "under my own direction and without any drugs or gimmicks," he went from 215 to a fit 145 pounds—nominal.[27] His *Hacker's Diet*, first posted online in 1991, was the go-to resource for many internet users over the next decade and a half.

Ray Kurzweil, on the other hand, is an optimal health hacker. Google hired the well-known futurist in 2012 to contribute to its artificial intelligence efforts. He takes hundreds of vitamins and supplements a day, and the recent septuagenarian believes his efforts have taken nearly thirty years off his biological age. By hacking his health, he expects to reach the moment, a few decades away, when biological life need not end and a fully digital life is possible—and preferable. Less grandiose optimal hacks include cognitive enhancements, maniac workweeks, and Casanova-like seduction.

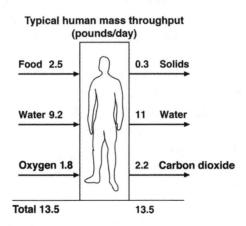

Figure 1.1
John Walker, "Human Mass Throughput," in *The Hacker's Diet*, 2005, http://www.fourmilab.ch/hackdiet/e4/rubberbag.html.

I will argue in this book that life hacking, especially the optimizing type, is associated with a type of tunnel vision. Life hacking can be like donning a set of horse blinders so as to block out distractions and focus attention on personal goals. This means, however, that with their vision fixed on the horizon, hackers can be naive to the people and circumstances on their periphery. The more optimal the hacking, the more narrow and distant the vision tends to be.

Still, I am not condemning life hacking. Life hackers' strengths *and* weaknesses are two sides of the same coin. Dining out with a meticulous self-tracker might be tiresome, but her well-informed restaurant recommendations could be excellent. This insight is also related to the trope of the double-edged sword. A scheduling app might enable you to squeeze more into your day, which, at the end, leaves you feeling more stressed and anxious. Life hackers' weaknesses of character are their sources of strength, and their gadgets are double edged.

If life hackers' strengths and weaknesses are two sides of the same coin, what of the coin's edge? For this, I borrow an analytic tool from Buddhist philosophy: the near enemy. Virtues, like compassion, often have an obvious opposite, like animosity; this is known as the *far enemy*. There are also sentiments that masquerade as virtues: pity as compassion, dependence as love, indifference as equanimity. These are *near enemies*. In the following chapters, I identify near enemies in the domains of work, wealth, health, relationships, and meaning. No one wants to be incapable or incompetent, but being efficient is not the same as being effective. We decry materialism, but being precious about minimalism is not the same thing as living unfettered. No one likes being sick, but compulsively checking health statistics is its own sort of illness. We hope we are beloved, but continuous connectivity and sexual conquest will not save us from alienation. There is no greater virtue than wisdom, but Wisdom 2.0 falls short.

As much as life hacking promises, it obscures. The hope that a robotic kettle will shave a few minutes off a busy morning can all too easily eclipse the simple pleasure of a cup of tea.

2   The Life Hackers

I never expected to see anything about life hacking at the grocery store. But there, among the tabloids in the checkout line, was "the most useful magazine you will buy this year": *The Practical Guide to Life Hacks*. This fifteen-dollar glossy had articles on how to love your job, twenty-six household tips to save money, a sixty-second fitness regime, and the secrets of happy families. The content of the magazine was not that different from that of *Martha Stewart Living*, sitting next to it. Self-help has long been a staple of the checkout line. But "life hacks" next to candy bars? How had this happened?

In the 1958 horror movie *The Blob*, a gelatinous space-born terror grows in size and danger with each person consumed. Just as some critics liken self-improvers to members of a cult, others liken the genre itself to a creeping horror—a characterization I also disagree with. In an article about how "self-help publishing ate America," one critic writes that this "plague of usefulness" has "infiltrated and commandeered other fields in its drive to reproduce."[1] In his critical history of life hacking, Matt Thomas calls it a "technologized" and "colonizing" type of self-help, with a "rapacious" need to "apply the logic of the computer to all human activity": "once it has colonized one domain, it looks for another to take over."[2] Even the grocery store is not safe.

It is easy to imagine life hacking as a fast-growing tumor on the omnipresent blob of self-help. Even so, this image fails us when it comes to understanding the character of life hacking, which is not a colonizing plague. Life hacking is, instead, the collective manifestation of a particular human sensibility, of a *hacker ethos*.

In the hacker's sight, most everything is conceived as a system: it is modular, composed of parts, which can be decomposed and recomposed; it is governed by algorithmic rules, which can be understood, optimized, and subverted. There are boring systems, which hackers seek to automate and outsource, and interesting systems, which are novel and require creativity. Hackers like their gadgets, so setting up a new Wi-Fi kettle, even if it takes hours, can be more interesting than putting the kettle on every day. Similarly, experimenting with meal-replacing nutrition shakes can be more interesting than making lunch. Because life hackers are fond of systems, and everything can be seen as a system, they bring a surprising amount of enthusiasm and optimism to bear on many facets of life.

Life hacking did not spread because people were ingested or colonized. Rather, those who hack came to the fore, and they now have more opportunities to design their lives and our world according to their shared ethos—for better and worse. This ethos is individualistic, rational, experimental, and systematizing. As such, it's well suited to this moment of far-flung digital systems. *The Practical Guide to Life Hacks* is evidence of life hacking's relevance—even if the term itself is faddish. To get a better sense of the hacker ethos, let's consider those most responsible for the emergence of life hacking: those who coined the term, popularized the practice, took it mainstream, and exemplify the lifestyle.

Alpha Geeks and Authorpreneurs

In February 2004, Danny O'Brien, a writer and digital activist, was one of the many tech enthusiasts converging on San Diego for the O'Reilly Emerging Technology Conference. However, O'Brien was not as interested in technology as he was in technologists' habits. In the description for his life hacking session, he wrote that "alpha geeks" are extraordinarily productive, and he wanted to understand their secrets. He asked participants to share "the little scripts they run, the habits they've adopted, the hacks they perform to get them through their day." Given how they benefit from these hacks, he wondered, "Can we help others do so, too?"[3]

O'Brien defines a hack as "a way of cutting through an apparently complex system with a really simple, nonobvious fix."[4] This is in keeping with the term's origins, which originated from MIT's Tech Model Railroad Club in the 1950s, specifically within the Signals and Power (S&P) subcommittee responsible for the electronics underneath the train platform. As Steven Levy writes in his history of computer hackers, the "S&P people were obsessed with the way The System worked, its increasing complexities, how any change you made would affect other parts, and how you could put those relationships between the parts to optimal use."[5] By 1959, the club had developed enough jargon that it issued a dictionary, which defined a *hacker* as someone who "avoids the standard solution."[6] This affinity for understanding and tinkering with systems, often by way of unconventional approaches, continues today. Often, hacking entails the bending, or breaking, of implicit rules and expectations.

Life hacking was born amid the crosscurrents of software developers and writers, a segment of the creative class. These are both professions in which practitioners are sometimes evaluated by the number of lines or words written. Such jobs also require a fair amount of self-discipline. It is difficult to focus on writing code or prose when so many digital distractions are at hand. And in 2004, with the resurgence of the online economy and faltering of print journalism, developers and writers were increasingly working independent of large corporations and mastheads. Nearly every developer of an app must play the part of an entrepreneur. Similarly, authors must increasingly play the role of what *The Economist* calls the "authorpreneur": they must be their own publicists, game the best-seller lists, and do speaking tours.[7] Today, they must also blog and podcast.

Cory Doctorow, one of the attendees of O'Brien's session, fits the authorpreneur mold. Doctorow, like O'Brien, has worked for the Electronic Frontier Foundation, a nonprofit civil liberties group based in San Francisco. He is also a longtime contributor to the popular blog *Boing Boing*. And he is a successful science fiction author who often releases his works under a Creative Commons license; this permits readers to freely read and make copies of his books. Borrowing an aphorism from tech publisher and conference convener Tim O'Reilly, Doctorow has made books freely available "because my problem isn't piracy, it's obscurity.... Because free ebooks sell print books." Doctorow even made this logic the premise of his first novel in 2003: *Down and Out in the Magic Kingdom*.[8] The book's protagonist lives in a world in which necessities are freely available. The distinguishing feature of life is "whuffie," a real-time measure of social reputation, which is tracked and accessed via a brain implant. In such a world, whuffie determines relative rank, such as who gets a table in a crowded restaurant, and it's instantly visible to everyone.

Doctorow exemplifies the authorpreneur, developing a significant following through his blogging at *Boing Boing*, fiction writing, activism, and San Francisco Bay Area connections—even if he was born in Canada and eventually left San Francisco for London and then Los Angeles. He was also an early promoter of life hacking. Doctorow was on the conference committee of the 2004 Emerging Technology Conference and posted his notes from the life hacking session. A few months later, in June, when O'Brien and Doctorow were in London for another conference, Doctorow again took notes at the life hacking discussion and posted them to *Boing Boing*. Doctorow had introduced *Boing Boing* readers—myself included—to life hacking, and he would also lend his "whuffie" to one of the first blogs dedicated to the topic.

43 Folders and Getting Things Done

In September 2004, Merlin Mann, an "independent writer, speaker, and broadcaster," launched the blog *43 Folders*. Before this, Mann had been a web developer, project manager, waiter, courtroom exhibit designer, and "enthusiastic but unprofitable indie rock musician"—among other things. And for the past decade, Mann has done most of what he does "in front of a MacBook in the western third of San Francisco."[9] Mann's eclecticism, his fondness for Apple products, and his affinity with the Bay Area are common among early life hackers.

Mann named *43 Folders* after a paper-based way of "tickling" one's memory to complete tasks, using twelve monthly and thirty-one daily folders. (Twelve plus thirty-one equals forty-three.) This old-school, nondigital way of organizing tasks is described in David Allen's 2001 book *Getting Things Done* (GTD), a source of inspiration to many life hackers. In his brief minutes of the first life hacking discussion in San Diego, Doctorow listed *Getting Things Done* as the top recommended reading for nascent life hackers. As soon as Mann saw Doctorow's notes, "I knew I was with my people. I had been using GTD enthusiastically for a couple months at that point and immediately saw a bunch of common ground."[10]

Allen's *Getting Things Done: The Art of Stress-Free Productivity* proposes a system wherein the incomplete tasks occupying your mind are captured and processed: they are prioritized, quickly dispatched (completed or trashed), or planned and substantively engaged. Stress is mitigated by way of an algorithm.

If the life hacking wave crested in 2004 with O'Brien's neologism, Allen's 2001 book served as its motivating current. The book was discussed and recommended at O'Brien's first life hacking session and inspired the name

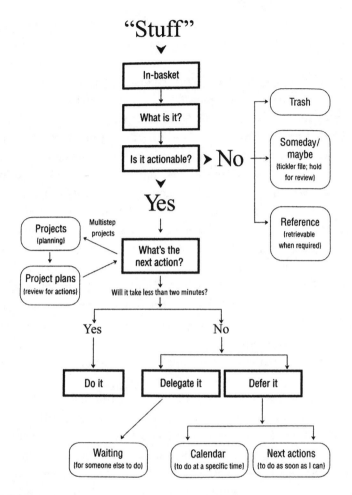

Figure 2.1

Processing workflow diagram from David Allen, *Getting Things Done: The Art of Stress-Free Productivity* (New York: Penguin, 2001), 32.

and much of the content of Mann's *43 Folders*. And although Allen never mentioned hacks, he did speak of tricks: "the highest-performing people I know are those who have installed the best tricks in their lives." Like a computer, people have inputs and install tricks. GTD, then, is a system for processing "all of the me 'inputs' you let into your life" so that your brain is released from the obligation to worry about them. Allen would later comment that geeks were early adopters of his system because they "love coherent, closed systems, which GTD represents."[11] Mann agreed and considered GTD "geek-friendly" for eight reasons, one of which is that "geeks love assessing, classifying, and defining the objects in their world"; life hacking was really just "a superset of GTD."[12]

At *43 Folders*, some of Mann's most popular early posts included "Getting Started with 'Getting Things Done,'" "Introducing the Hipster PDA" (using index cards and a binder clip), and "Hack Your Way out of Writer's Block." In 2008, Mann wrote that "in no small measure, it was Cory Doctorow's surpassingly generous linking and encouragement that shot my crummy little site to its cruising altitude.... Cory will have my deepest gratitude for using his considerable whuffie to almost singlehandedly put *43 Folders* on the map."[13]

In the following year, Mann joined with O'Brien to pursue the emerging life hacking phenomenon, but their efforts were short-lived. They cohosted a life hacking session at the 2005 Emerging Technology Conference and collaborated on a life hacking column for the new O'Reilly magazine *Make*. They also planned to write a book on the topic for O'Reilly's "Hacks" series. (Tim O'Reilly's publications and conferences were important venues for early computer hackers, and he was equally encouraging to the young maker and life hacking communities.)

Ironically, O'Brien and Mann never completed any books about life hacking.

O'Brien turned his attention toward digital activism and looks upon his early life hacking efforts with good-natured chagrin. In a 2010 interview, he conceded that he could be considered the "absent father of life hacking" because "I am such an alcoholic of systems.... I have tried them all and nothing works." And he appreciates the irony of failing to write the book: his Electronic Frontier Foundation biography reads "it has been nearly a decade since he was first commissioned to write a book on combating procrastination."[14]

Four years after the launch of *43 Folders*, Mann expressed dissatisfaction with the superficiality of life hacking blogs and "'productivity' as a personal fetish or hobby."[15] In the following year, he announced he had a contract to write a book about "inbox zero," his notion of ruthlessly keeping one's inbox empty. Yet his posting at *43 Folders* was flagging, and this book, too, was never published. In a rambling essay in April 2011, he confessed that "my book agent says my editor (who is awesome) will probably cancel My Book Contract if I don't send her something that pleases her ... today. Now. By tonight. Theoretically, I guess ... uh ... this." Apparently, "this" did not please her, and his last post to *43 Folders* was in October 2011. Like O'Brien, Mann describes his relationship with life hacking as troubled: "I'm not doing this because I'm great; I'm doing this because I'm terrible. I sometimes describe myself as feeling like a drunk in the pulpit, where if I don't get there and talk and try to share what's working for me, I could end up back on the bottle."[16] Today, Mann continues to be a jack of many creative trades. He still writes, even if he no longer updates *43 Folders*, and offers his services as a productivity consultant. Otherwise, he spends much of his time as a contributor to geeky podcasts.

The life hacking mantle would have to be picked up by someone else.

Lifehacker and the Rational Style

Writing the first book of life hacks would fall to Gina Trapani, who also lived in California, though she now resides in Brooklyn. She describes herself as a "[software] developer, founder, and writer"—in keeping with the authorpreneur mold—and she launched *Lifehacker* in January 2005.

Trapani recalls that the idea for the website was "hatched back in late 2004" following what "Danny O'Brien cooked up earlier that year." She saw Doctorow's notes on *Boing Boing*, so "without Danny and Merlin, *Lifehacker* would have never happened. I owe both of these guys a huge debt of gratitude for their articulation of a concept that I literally launched a writing career upon."[17] In short order, *Lifehacker* became the most popular and successful purveyor of life hacking tips. Its early posts were a little more diverse than those of *43 Folders* and included "Dishwasher tips," "Soporific songs," and "Windows keyboard shortcuts"—not something the Mac-centric Mann would touch. Three books based on material from the blog followed in 2006, 2008, and 2011.

Just as it was on *43 Folders*, GTD was an early topic at *Lifehacker*, and Trapani was fond of Allen's notion of "tricks." Her first book was entitled *Lifehacker: 88 Tech Tricks to Turbocharge Your Day*, and her last book began with the quote from Allen about his respect for "those who have installed the best tricks in their lives."[18] In 2009, she handed editorship of the website over to a collaborator and returned to start-up life and writing code rather than prose.

Life hacking appeals to Trapani because she has "a very systematic way of looking at life." Computer programs automate things, and in life hacking, she observes, "you kind of reprogram the way that you perform tasks, to make them a little faster and a little more efficient." And once you have found an optimized routine, it only makes sense to share so others can "benefit from this and experience a system that another person has already tried." This systems-oriented thinking is core to the life hacker ethos, as Trapani explains: "technically minded people have this very strong focus on making sense of the world and making things systematic and methodical."[19] There is some empirical evidence for this claim.

Psychologists speak of a *cognitive style* as a way of taking in and processing data; it's a persistent personal attribute that is seen in patterns of thinking and behavior. Two different cognitive styles are often discussed: *systematic* (rational/analytic) and *intuitive* (associative/experiential).[20] Intuitive thinking tends toward a larger, holistic view and relies upon the integration of intuition, feelings, and context. Systematic thinking seeks patterns and makes use of rules.

For those who enjoy Sudoku, part of the pleasure is discerning a puzzle's internal logic and patterns. Among Sudoku fans, some of these patterns have evocative names, like the "X-Wing," "remote pairs," and "avoidable rectangles." But for newcomers, these patterns are unnamed: they are subtle brain tingles trying to emerge into consciousness. Not surprisingly, a study has found that among new players, those with the systematic cognitive style improved with experience, unlike their intuitive peers. Two other studies have found an association between the systematic/rational style and computer students and hackers.[21]

Among life hackers, this mind-set has even become a matter of advocacy. When I was learning about productivity and nutrition hacking, I followed discussions at LessWrong, an online community dedicated to "refining the art of human rationality." There I also learned about the Center for Applied Rationality, a small Bay Area nonprofit that offers workshops on cognitive biases so that we can begin "patching the problems" of human thinking. ("Patching" is a term for fixing buggy software.) There's even a book, *Algorithms to Live By: The Computer Science of Human Decisions*, that advocates approaching personal and social concerns the same way computer scientists think about and solve their challenges.[22]

It's not unreasonable to ask if this systematic style is associated with gender or autism. In a 1993 *Wired* article, Steve Silberman characterized autism as the "geek syndrome." Given that autism is partially hereditary, Silberman asked if the concentrations of geeky folk in places like Silicon Valley meant that the genetics that contributed to their brilliance could, in subsequent generations, become debilitating. Subsequently, a controversial researcher has concluded that autism is the manifestation of a masculine hypersystemizing brain.[23]

The geek syndrome hypothesis is a contentious one, among both researchers and the public. It intersects with debates about gender difference and essentialism, cognitive difference and disability, and questions of identity and culture. In 2016, Silberman returned to the topic in *NeuroTribes: The Legacy of Autism and the Future of Neurodiversity*.[24] Silberman describes the history of autism diagnosis and treatment, its association with early geek culture, its emergence in popular awareness, and the rise of parent and autist advocacy. In the intervening twenty-three years between his *Wired* article and *NeuroTribes*, Silberman realized that the geek syndrome is more complicated than he originally conceived.

I will return to how self-help culture is often gendered, but for the present, it is clear that the systematic style of thinking is central to life hacking, especially to the woman who succeeded in popularizing it. For Trapani, a life hack is a "systematic way to get something done in your life, whether that's on your computer...or folding your socks."[25]

The 4-Hour Workweek and Lifestyle Design

Although *Lifehacker* remains paramount, with more than a million monthly readers, dozens of life hacking sites exist. The content aggregator AllTop lists recent articles from about eighty life hacking sites including the blogs *Zen Habits, Life Optimizer*, and *Unclutterer*. Most of these sites are small, personal undertakings and not the sole occupations of their creators. Ironically, the person who made a career out of life hacking and took it mainstream does not often use the term.

Tim Ferriss is the author of a handful of *New York Times* best sellers, an investor (in the likes of Uber, Facebook, and Twitter), the creator of a top blog and podcast, and someone often included in annual lists of the innovative and powerful. Rather than describe himself as a combination of an author and entrepreneur, he prefers to list how others have described him. For example, his "About" page claims that "*Newsweek* calls him 'the world's best guinea pig,' which he takes as a compliment."[26] I can find no such description on *Newsweek*'s part, though a *Newsweek* book review did say that "Ferriss's willingness to be a guinea pig produces some fascinating results."[27] Similarly, Ferriss often attributes to the *New York Times* the quote that he is a cross between famed businessman Jack Welch and a Buddhist monk. This appears, however, to be from a 2011 profile in which Ferriss is described as "positioning *himself* somewhere between Jack Welch and a Buddhist monk."[28] In addition to being an author, experimentalist, and entrepreneur, he has a knack for self-promotion.

His first book, *The 4-Hour Workweek*, made Ferriss famous. In it, he speaks to those disenchanted with the hope of finding a dream job or getting by until retirement. Ferriss argues that by being clever, his readers can enjoy life now. The goal of the titular four-hour workweek is to "escape 9–5, live anywhere, and join the new rich," to "free time and automate income." This is accomplished by limiting drudgery and maximizing effectiveness.

One way to free up time is to personalize the practice of outsourcing. If companies can do it, why not us? Ferriss writes that "becoming a member of the NR [new rich] is not just about working smarter. It's about building a system to replace yourself."[29] Such a system includes creating an absentee business and outsourcing tasks to "virtual assistants," who can be hired for as little as a few dollars an hour in the Philippines and India. It is fitting that most of Ferriss's chapter on outsourcing is a reprinting of A. J. Jacobs's *Esquire* article on the topic; Ferriss outsourced his writing about outsourcing. This is common in Ferriss's books, which are collages of his own experiences, recommendations, lists of resources, interviews, and excerpts from others.

With drudgery dispatched, Ferriss coaches his readers on how to be effective in what they do want to do. The four-hour approach is to *deconstruct* an activity into its key steps, *select* the critical steps, *sequence* them in an optimal order, and create *stakes* to increase accountability and motivation. For example, in *The 4-Hour Workweek*, he claims he won the 1999 US Chinese kickboxing championship via this method. Before weigh in, he lost twenty-eight pounds in eighteen hours through dehydration, allowing him to compete in a lighter weight class. He also exploited a technicality: a contestant who steps off the platform three times is disqualified. After rehydrating, he used his weight to push the "poor little guys," three weight classes below him, out of the ring. He writes that he won all his matches by technical knockout—though his exploitation of the rules annoyed the judges. Ferriss committed to becoming a champion; he deconstructed the tournament (especially the rules for disqualification) and selected and sequenced the steps of water weight loss and gain. He applies this same approach in all of his work, including the thirteen episodes of his 2015 television series *The Tim Ferriss Experiment*, in which he attempted to quickly master the guitar, attracting women, car racing, jujitsu, parkour, and poker.

As noted, to be a successful authorpreneur, you must be an advocate for yourself. In this, Ferriss has excelled. When *Wired* asked its readers to vote for the biggest self-promoter of 2008, Ferriss's fans led him to win "by a land-slide." In a *New Yorker* profile of Ferriss, a professional publicist praised him as "the smartest self-promoter I know."[30] In an interview a couple of years later, Ferriss disagreed with this characterization—he thought his friend and magician David Blaine was superior—but he still took it as a compliment.

The anecdote of how Ferriss determined his first book's title and jacket design offers a good example of this savvy self-promotion. Ferriss created a Google AdWords campaign for each of the six possible titles he had in mind, including *Broadband and White Sand* and *Millionaire Chameleon.* He then bid on related searches, so that when people searched for "401k" or "language learning," they would see one of his titles. In the course of a week, and for less than $200, Google told him that *4-Hour Work Week* was the title that the most users clicked on. On the low-tech side, he printed dust cover designs and placed them on books in the new nonfiction racks at a nearby bookstore. He then sat nearby and watched which covers tended to draw the most attention. This anecdote shows moxie, and its retelling—including on *Boing Boing* by Doctorow—is its own form of promotion.

Ferriss displays the opportunism, self-reliance, and determination of an American self-help guru, even if he calls it "lifestyle design." For example, he portrays the genesis of *The 4-Hour Workweek* as a consequence of a nervous breakdown from running his brain and performance-enhancing supple-ment business. Inspiration was born of desperation. Even so, his proposal for *The 4-Hour Workweek* was rejected by dozens of publishers, but he persevered and published three best sellers under the 4-Hour moniker. Yet the recep-tion of the third one, *The 4-Hour Chef,* was a deep disappointment. Barnes & Noble refused to carry it given that it was published by Amazon. This failure then set the ground for his next success, of taking a break and experiment-ing with podcasting. He now reaches more people through his podcast than through his best-selling books. Ferriss capitalizes on the American fondness for bootstrap stories, and he has not yet exhausted his own. He has also taken to sourcing such stories from others; his favorite question to ask of the suc-cessful is "How has a failure set you up for a later success?"

Ferriss embodies the values of American self-help, especially the pursuit of success. However, he is different from the other life hackers in this chap-ter. He is not a computer geek and readily acknowledges his lack of techni-cal chops. This contributes to his mainstream success. We will later see that when it came to hacking dating, he didn't code a solution to the problem, he outsourced it. While others developed software to game OkCupid or created a spreadsheet for calculating romantic potential, he simply delegated the task of selecting and scheduling dates to overseas teams. Ferriss is as obsessed with experimentation and systems as anyone in this book, and he can speak about these topics to a nontechnical audience.

Life Nomadic and *Superhuman*

In September 2013, Tynan, a minor geek celebrity who uses his first name only, announced, "My friends and I bought an island." The appeal in such a purchase, he observed, is that "an island is like your own little country, with complete control of everything within its borders." Unfortunately, "cheap islands are in far away inconvenient spots, and the close islands are all crazy expensive." Hence, the idea remained a fantasy until a friend sent him a listing for an island in eastern Canada. It turns out that many of these are "cheap AND close." Soon after Tynan's post, a story at *Gawker* declared that his achievement was the fulfillment of "one of the most-cherished fantasies of libertarian geeks everywhere." The news was also a topic of conversation at Hacker News, a tech and entrepreneurship site, and Reddit, which has a forum dedicated to the establishment of its own self-sufficient island. The author of the *Gawker* article concluded: "Now that Tynan and his crew have succeeded where Reddit Island failed, I think it's fair to say he is officially King of The Tech Geeks."[31]

I would not go so far to label Tynan as "king of the tech geeks," but he is a life hacker exemplar. Tynan is involved in most every domain I address in this book. This is a bold claim, since so many life hackers are true to type: tech savvy, travel happy, and pursuing unusual paths to success in life. Even so, my claim is substantiated by even a brief biography.

Like many life hackers, Tynan did not take school seriously. His efforts in high school were half-hearted, and this attitude persisted into college. In 2000, as a sophomore, he dropped out to pursue a different path toward wealth, friendship, and love. He took up gambling and joined a group of young men systematizing seduction.

Tynan's gambling operation consisted of online confederates taking advantage of casino weaknesses. For example, casinos sometimes offer limited promotions that give a player a slight edge over the house, such as a

1 percent loyalty program on a slot machine. Tynan and his peers would pool their resources to extract, at scale, as much profit as possible. At the height of his operation, Tynan rented an office, hired employees, kept accounts, and paid taxes; he had to work only ten to twenty hours a week to make easy money. As a young man in his twenties, he had a nice house, a Rolex, and a Mercedes-Benz S600.

This came to an end when, in 2006, their scheme was detected and their funds were confiscated. Even if otherwise legal, casinos and banks don't like gamblers playing loose with accounts and money. Tynan lost hundreds of thousands of dollars, which he accepted with a surprising degree of calm. He decided that despite what had been an incredibly profitable endeavor, he didn't enjoy it anymore and that he had learned that while he liked money, he didn't need to chase it. He hoped, instead, to focus on his other goals, to "become fully polyphasic" (i.e., sleeping only in short periods throughout the day), put fifteen pounds of lean muscle on his thin frame, become a well-known rapper, and "Find and date one incredible girl OR date several great girls."[32]

This latter goal of dating amazing women speaks to the main source of Tynan's fame, as a member of Project Hollywood. This group of pickup artists, living in Dean Martin's former mansion, was portrayed in Neil Strauss's best-selling 2005 book *The Game*.[33] (Strauss is also a friend of Ferriss's and makes appearances on his podcast and television show.) In the book's drama-filled pages about masculine exultation and dissolution, Tynan is referred to as "Herbal"—his "rapper name," a variation on "Ice Tea," and appropriate to his later obsession with tea.

After the collapse of Project Hollywood, Tynan turned his attention to living with as few encumbrances as possible, to traveling the world, and to writing about it all. He traded in his house and Mercedes to pursue the *Life Nomadic*—the title of one of his Amazon books. For much of his adult life, his main "base" was a recreational vehicle (RV) in San Francisco—the subject of another book, *The Tiniest Mansion*.[34] When he wants solitude, he retreats to inexpensive ocean cruises. Cheap tickets can be had on out-of-season return trips, and the food and facilities are free. There, Tynan can focus on work: writing self-published self-help books, developing a blogging platform, and most recently, developing the site Cruise Sheet, which helps others find cheap cruises. And as he still plays poker occasionally, cruise ships have plenty of weak players with money to lose.

Although he appreciates periods of solitude, relationships are key to many of Tynan's schemes—be they gambling, seduction, or buying an island—and making friends is a topic of his book *Superhuman Social Skills*.[35] Tynan finds his lifestyle of few possessions, frequent travel, focused work, and global friendships far preferable to an office job. When his RV was still his main base, he wrote: "I would honestly rather be, I mean, I guess I am kind of homeless when you think about it, I'm living [in an RV] at a Gas station but I'd rather be like, legitimate homeless than honestly have a hundred thousand dollar a year consulting job or something horrible like that." This lifestyle means that he has few obligations: "you really are free, you can really do what you want to do."[36]

The hacker ethos touches every facet of Tynan's life. He is enthusiastic: "If it seems too good to be true, drop everything and check it out."[37] And he utilizes systems, whether to make money, pick up women, or automate his home. At his most developed base in Las Vegas, his smart phone wakes him, his curtains open automatically, and as he brushes his teeth, his agenda for the day is displayed on the forty-inch LCD embedded within the mirror. His home secures, vacuums, heats, and cools itself. Many of his books have the word *superhuman* in the title because, as he observes, "you can often achieve results that look superhuman just by setting up lots of easy systems."[38] It takes some work to set them up, but once you do, they save you time, money, and focus. Proficiency with such systems means that Tynan lives a version of masculine fantasy: one filled with "great girls," rewarding work, and world travel.

More so than anyone else, Tynan exemplifies life hacking, even if the others portrayed here had more to do with its emergence. O'Brien coined the term, Mann and Doctorow popularized it, Trapani commercialized it, and Ferriss took it mainstream. These life hackers, and tens of thousands of others, share an ethos of individualism, rationality, systematization, and experimentation. Although this self-help's ascendancy might appear to be like that of a tumor on a colonizing blob, it is the manifestation of a personality that thrives in the digital age. But this does not mean life is therefore easy or that hacks always work. After all, O'Brien championed hacking productivity, but his book about procrastination has yet to be written.

3 Hacking Time

In the spring of 2016, the radio program and podcast *Freakonomics* concluded its self-improvement month with special guest Tim Ferriss, "a man
whose entire life and career are one big pile of self-improvement." The final
question for Ferriss was speculative: If you had a time machine, when and
why would you go? After being excused from an obligation to assassinate
a historical tyrant, Ferriss said he'd like to have drinks with Ben Franklin.
Ferriss appreciated Franklin's enthusiasm, his contributions across many
fields, and for being "a bit of a merry prankster and a bit of a showman."[1]

Franklin and Ferriss do have a lot in common. Both are self-help authors:
Franklin by way of his *Poor Richard's Almanack* and Ferriss by way of his books,
blog, and podcast. Ferriss even likens his books on effectiveness, fitness, and
learning to Franklin's trinity of desired attributes, of being "healthy, wealthy
and wise."[2] Franklin is considered by some the first scientific American,
exploring and testing the world around him. Ferriss thinks of himself as a
guinea pig, exploring and testing his own body and abilities. And both are
famously associated with a concern for productivity and time. Franklin is
known for scheduling every hour of his day—"time is money" after all—and
Ferriss is known for limiting his drudgery to four hours a week.

Franklin and Ferriss are also the target of common criticisms. Both
have been chided for their showmanship. In Paris, Franklin's charm was
the basis of insults from the British ambassador and contempt from John
Adams, his American colleague. Even if the British were propagandizing
and Adams was an envious prig, their complaints sprang from a kernel
of truth. Ferriss's showmanship, too, has been a topic of complaint. One
entrepreneur characterized Ferriss's early efforts as aggressive, spammy, and
alienating in a post entitled "5 Time Management Tricks I Learned from
Years of Hating Tim Ferriss."[3]

Other critics complain about the character of Franklin and Ferriss's productivity. Mark Twain, sire of the ornery Tom Sawyer, cursed Franklin's maxims
for the suffering they inflicted on the young. Twain's revenge was to coin his
own adage and facetiously attribute it to Franklin, just to confuse things:
"Never put off till tomorrow what you can do day after tomorrow just as well."
In turn, one critic asks if Ferriss's "ideology of achievement" is nothing more
than a "framework for hilarious and pathetic self-delusion, and a distraction
from the real substance of life"?[4] Most substantively, scholars see privilege in
Franklin's ethic of work and in Ferriss's ability to limit it to four hours a week.
Franklin was prolific, but he gave little thought to how his wife, Deborah
Read, made it possible for him to live such a productive life. He was also able
to delegate much drudgery to his enslaved personal servants—before becoming an abolitionist later in life. In turn, Ferriss has accomplished a lot in his
four-hour workweeks but only by outsourcing his tedious tasks to virtual
assistants.

Franklin and Ferriss are bookends to centuries of effort toward self-
improvement. They are archetypal American men. Franklin was representa-
tive of a type of colonial American, as Ferriss is of a Silicon Valley one. They
also provide a starting point for considering life hackers' seeming obsession
with time and what they may take for granted when they seek to make the
most of it.

Time Thrift

Historian E. P. Thompson argues that European history can be divided into
two orientations to work: task and time. In the task orientation, people
worked through a cycle of chores corresponding to periods of the day. In
the morning, the farmer put the goats to pasture and milked the cows. By the
end of the day, the chickens were back in the roost. Time was not a thing to
be spent or saved, and there was less of a division between "work" and "life."

The time orientation arose with the emergence of industry: work was now
piecemeal and part of a larger process. Work was dependent on the synchronization of labor, and the clock enabled the coordination of a distributed
market, from the weaving of cloth to its shipment on the afternoon train.
Thompson observes that it did not take long for the necessity of coordination to become an ideology of "time thrift": "Puritanism, in its marriage
of convenience with industrial capitalism, was the agent which converted

people to new valuations of time; which taught children even in their infancy to improve each shining hour; and which saturated people's minds with the equation, time is money." To those accustomed to working on the clock, the older task orientation "appears to be wasteful and lacking in urgency."[5]

Such was the case for Frederick Taylor and Frank and Lillian Gilbreth, founders of "scientific management" at the beginning of the twentieth century. Taylor believed that managers, with the help of experts, ought to optimize the efficiency of workers with the aid of a stopwatch. Famously, he optimized the routine of men carrying pig iron and tripled their output—though historians question the rigor of his methods and veracity of his claims. In turn, the Gilbreths are known for their time and motion studies. In one of their filmstrips—viewable on YouTube—a Remington typist works next to a spinning chronometer. Under the tutelage of Frank Gilbreth, the typist improved her technique and won a typing competition on behalf of her employer. Such demonstrations won the influence of Taylor and the Gilbreths among the management class and beyond—even as they feuded between themselves. The Gilbreths' efficient household was even the source of the popular books *Cheaper by the Dozen* (1948) and *Belles on Their Toes* (1950), coauthored by two of their twelve children.[6]

Although Frank Gilbreth coached the fastest typist in the world, he was frustrated with the limitations of the QWERTY keyboard, infamous for its longevity despite its inefficiency. QWERTY was designed to keep the keys of early machines from jamming, rather than increasing the comfort and speed of the typist, and Gilbreth proposed an improved keyboard. His suggestion eventually inspired the development of a simplified keyboard by August Dvorak in 1936. With the Dvorak keyboard, commonly occurring letters and sequences are easily typed from the home keys. The only folks that I know of who use these keyboards are hacker-types, including Tynan and Matt Mullenweg, founder and CEO of WordPress.

Today's creative class is largely beyond the synchronization required by industrial capitalism. Yes, people do still have milestones and deadlines and sometimes make use of shared calendars and scheduling services like Doodle. Even so, accomplishing a single task in a specific moment is less important than juggling multiple tasks at all times. This leads journalist Nikil Saval, author of an extensive history of the workplace, to think of life hacking as Taylorism 2.0. Saval concedes that life hacking "started out as a somewhat earnest response to the problem of fragmented attention and overwork—an attempt to reclaim some leisure time and autonomy from the demands of boundaryless labor. But it has since become just another hectoring paradigm of self-improvement." He grants that in life hacking, there's no one looking over our shoulders with a stopwatch. We are, ostensibly, trying to help ourselves. But something else happened along the way. We surrendered our autonomy to "a stratum of faceless managers, in the form of apps, self-administered charts tracking the minutiae of eating habits and sleep cycles, and the books and buzzwords of gurus."[7] And the internalized manager isn't really faceless; it is our own face exhorting us to be *Smarter Faster Better*—the title of a recent book about "the secrets of being productive in life and business."[8] Other critics observe that productivity gains rarely go to the workers, though the latter do accrue anxiety and a sense that they are somehow to blame.[9]

Yet shouldn't people be free to experiment with ways to improve their lives? Unlike those working in call centers and warehouses, where the vise of managerial monitoring grows ever tighter, the hacker still has some freedom of movement. If people can make an informed decision, they will no doubt realize some things work for them and some things don't. We will see life hackers who, in time, temper their enthusiasm and realize their pursuit of "productivity porn" is counterproductive. We will also see life hackers who quit their high-pressure jobs, sell all their belongings, and choose to travel the world with nothing other than what is in their backpacks. But before that, how is it that self-help and life hacking suggest we boost productivity?

"Schedule Your Priorities"

We should be excused for thinking that life hacking is obsessed with efficiency and time: Ferriss's 4-hour workweek sounds as if it is about managing time. However, Ferriss chose this title because it tested well on Google AdWords, not because it was the best reflection of the book's content.[10] In *The 4-Hour Workweek*, Ferriss stresses *effectiveness*, "doing the things that get you closer to your goals," over *efficiency*, "performing a given task (whether important or not) in the most economical manner possible." Of course, "Efficiency is still important, but it's useless unless applied to the right things." In this view, "Being busy is a form of laziness—lazy thinking and indiscriminate action."[11] You can *efficiently* paddle a boat in circles, but the *effective* boater is efficient and purposeful.

This distinction between efficient and effective is a powerful insight, but it is not novel: self-help repeats itself every couple of decades. Before Ferriss's book, the best-known productivity self-help book was Stephen Covey's *The 7 Habits of Highly Effective People*, first published in 1989. The title mentions effectiveness rather than efficiency, and Covey's stance is captured in his oft-quoted aphorism: "The key is not to prioritize what's on your schedule, but to schedule your priorities."[12] That same year, Richard Koch published the best seller *The 80/20 Principle: The Secret of Achieving More with Less*.[13] In both, efficiency without priorities is a near enemy of effectiveness. Efficiency appears to be a virtue but can become a vice.

Even Alan Lakein, author of the 1973 classic *How to Get Control of Your Time and Your Life*, asks: "Please don't call me an efficiency expert. I'm an effectiveness expert." Why? Because "making the right choices about how you use your time is more important than doing efficiently whatever job happens to be around."[14] Again, much like Ferriss, he criticizes those engaged with the trappings of efficiency. The overorganized person is always making, updating, and losing lists; the overdoer is always busy and has no time to assess value; the time nut only manages to make himself and others anxious.[15] In this view, efficiency is only a means toward effectiveness.

How, then, can we be effective? Lakein recommends that readers carefully consider and articulate their life goals, then prioritize them into three groups, with the bulk of the day spent pursuing the most important. Given that we are easily distracted and wander away from high-value work, Lakein dedicates most of his book to "how to get back after you've escaped."[16] Many of these techniques are implemented in Lakein's appendix, "How I Save Time." (Effectiveness advocates do muddle their case by slipping into time-saving language.) Without any preamble, Lakein lists sixty-one techniques for enhancing productivity. Some techniques focus on effectiveness: "#23 I always plan first thing in the morning and set priorities for the day." Others focus on efficiency: "#52 I write replies to most letters right on the piece of paper." If you replaced the word *paper* with *email* throughout his list, it would easily be recognized as a list of life hacks, thirty years before the coining of the term. And technique #47, "I delegate everything I possibly can to others," foreshadows Ferriss's outsourcing.

The importance of prioritizing can be traced back to the very first productivity consultant, Ivy Lee. The story goes that in 1918, Lee was summoned by Bethlehem Steel magnate Charles M. Schwab to improve the productivity of Bethlehem's executives. Lee asked for nothing up front. He needed only fifteen minutes with each executive and, after three months, would accept whatever Schwab thought his advice had been worth. Lee explained his approach to each executive: at the end of the day, write down and prioritize tomorrow's six most important tasks; tomorrow, work through the tasks and repeat the exercise at the end of the day. After the three months, Schwab was so satisfied that he wrote Lee a check for $25,000 (worth more than $400,000 today).

Subsequent productivity self-help, including life hacking, is a series of variations on Lee. Each day (1) identify, review, and prioritize goals, (2) plan the consequent tasks, and (3) make progress on those tasks. For example, in *7 Habits* Covey distinguishes between important and urgent priorities. Though Covey does not cite Eisenhower, the former president is famous for his quip about the problems he faced: "The urgent are not important, and the important are never urgent." (Another good Eisenhower quote is that "plans are worthless, but planning is everything.") Covey fashions a matrix from these two variables and encourages his readers to spend more time on important but not urgent issues ("quadrant IV"). He agrees with Lakein on the importance of delegation, which Covey believes is "perhaps the single most powerful high-leverage activity there is."[17]

Turning a prioritized goal into a doable task is helped by clear specification. A classic rubric is that the goals should be SMART: specific, measurable, assignable, relevant, and time delimited. Additionally, tasks are more likely to be done when distractions are minimized and when we start small. It also helps to have a system for staging tasks. Life hackers are especially keen on what they refer to as "workflows." As I noted earlier, David Allen's 2001 tome *Getting Things Done: The Art of Stress-Free Productivity* was an inspiration to the founding life hackers. At GTD's core is a system for processing "stuff," which Allen defines as "anything you have allowed into your psychological or physical world that doesn't belong where it is, but for which you haven't yet determined the desired outcome and the next action step." In GTD, stuff is collected, processed, organized, reviewed, and completed; this is facilitated by moving tasks between various buckets, such as *incoming*, *someday*, *now*, or *waiting*. Allen warns that "as long as it's still 'stuff,' it's not controllable."[18]

As anyone who has experimented with managing their "stuff" knows, jotting it down and making a plan does help. This insight alone makes productivity self-help worthwhile, and it may be related to what is known as the "Zeigarnik effect," which is the mind's tendency to remember and return to incomplete or interrupted tasks. Legend has it that Bluma Zeigarnik's 1927 research on this was inspired by a waiter in a café. The waiter had a remarkable memory for the orders of active tables but quickly forgot them when the table was cleared. Zeigarnik took her hypothesis into the lab and found that subjects who were interrupted had a better chance of recalling a task than those who completed it. Social psychologist Roy Baumeister suggests that GTD helps reduce the Zeigarnik effect: "uncompleted tasks and unmet goals tend to pop into one's mind," and this can be stressful, especially if there are too many.[19]

GTD isn't the only workflow. More often than not, life hackers adopt methods they use at work. *Personal Kanban* was inspired by Toyota's just-in-time production system. Tasks are written down on sticky notes and placed in one of three columns, the first of which is the To Do column. The second column is for Works in Progress (WIP), which should be limited to a few focused items. Upon completion of a WIP item, it's moved to the Done column. To Do items are then reevaluated, and one of them is moved to the WIP column.[20] Similarly, folks adapt software development frameworks, like the "scrum" agile methodology, to their own lives. This, too, often entails moving sticky notes about on a whiteboard.

Naturally, life hackers freely tweak these systems to their own tastes. Gina Trapani, founder of *Lifehacker*, uses a simplified GTD of three lists: next, projects, and someday/maybe. Although there are plenty of sophisticated apps for GTD, she manages it via a simple text file, synchronized via Dropbox, and edited in an app she developed named todo.txt. To keep things really simple, entrepreneur Alexandra Cavoulacos coined the 1-3-5 rule. As in the other systems, you write down a "comprehensive list of everything you have to do." Then, on any given day, you work to "accomplish one big thing, three medium things, and five small things." Before leaving work for the day, you "define your 1-3-5 for the next day, so you're ready to hit the ground running in the morning."[21] This is simple, has built in prioritization, and takes advantage of the fact that it's easier to get a good start on the day when there is a small, identified, or incomplete task awaiting you in the morning.

Life hackers' concern with and distinction between effectiveness and efficiency is not novel. Cavoulacos's "1-3-5" method is not very different from Ivy Lee's a century ago. What is different is their borrowing of systems for managing technical projects at work and bringing them home. They also like to experiment, be it with weird sleep patterns or getting slapped in the face.

Polyphasic Sleep

In addition to traveling back in time to meet Ben Franklin, people fantasize about controlling it: if only we could slow down the precious moments or fast-forward through the more annoying ones. Most pressingly, what if we could have more time in the day? This is the premise of Nancy Kress's 1993 speculative fiction *Beggars in Spain*.[22] In a not-too-distant future, ambitious parents bestow the genetic gift of sleeplessness upon their children. As the genetically modified children mature, a divide emerges between the sleepers and sleepless. Whereas ordinary people continue to spend much of their lives unconscious, the sleepless can study, practice, and work throughout the night. This seems unfair to many sleepers, who impose restrictions upon the sleepless. An ice skater is banned from the Olympics because her daily twelve hours of practice give her an unfair advantage. Resentment and fear widen the rift, and after violence, many of the sleepless retreat to their own enclave, first on Earth, and then in an orbiting space station. The title of the book is based on a debate among the sleepless. Just as a sleeper might ask what she owes to a beggar in another country, what do the sleepless, the most productive segment of humanity, owe to the sleepers of Earth?

We are far from genetically eliminating sleep, but life hackers try by other means, namely, polyphasic sleep. Most people are monophasic, sleeping overnight; some are biphasic, sleeping in two sessions with an intermission in between—it appears this was the natural pattern before the invention of artificial light. Polyphasic sleep is something else altogether. It is an attempt to increase waking hours by splitting sleep into short naps *throughout* the day. In *The 4-Hour Body*, Ferriss asks if giraffes need only 1.9 hours of sleep, why not humans? Given that the "most beneficial phase of sleep" is the one to two hours of REM (rapid eye movement), is there a way to "engineer things" so we "shave off" the six or so hours of less productive sleep?[23] It can be done. WordPress founder Matt Mullenweg wrote most of the code for the blogging platform while napping forty minutes every two-and-a-half hours. Pickup artists Neil Strauss and Tynan experimented with polyphasic sleep during Project Hollywood. They only made it through the first seven days—the first ten of which are supposed to be hardest. On a second attempt, Tynan managed four-and-a-half months of twenty-one wakeful hours on the Uberman cycle of fifteen-minute naps every two hours.

Although they continue to use their Dvorak keyboards, Mullenweg and Tynan's sleep engineering could not be sustained. Mullenweg ended his experiment, and the most productive year of his life, when his schedule proved incompatible with that of his new girlfriend. Tynan stopped because it was disruptive to others' schedules, and he figured he didn't really need the extra time.

Cultural critic Jonathan Crary argues that we are now confronted with a "24/7" time orientation, one that is indifferent to our needs and "against which the fragility of human life is increasingly inadequate." In *24/7: Late Capitalism and the Ends of Sleep*, Crary laments that our sleep is encroached upon by the tendrils of online work and consumption: screens delay our slumber as we email coworkers and shop on Amazon. The life hacker's dream of polyphasic sleep is an attempt to acquiesce. However, no one does it for long. Even a bachelor will eventually find it incompatible with ordinary life and that missing a nap unsettles his sleep schedule and thinking. As Crary concludes, "Sleep cannot be eliminated. But it can be wrecked and despoiled."[24]

Additionally, we are not giraffes.

"Quadrupled My Productivity"

In 2012, Maneesh Sethi finally managed to go viral. The blogger behind *Hack the System* paid someone to slap him when he was not being productive. Granted, much of the attention he received was incredulous, but the stunt served as a fulcrum. It was the culmination of efforts to promote himself, like Ferriss, as a lifestyle design entrepreneur. And it launched him on his future course of developing a gadget that was shocking—literally. His story also provides a case study for concerns about exploitation.

Four years earlier, in 2008, Sethi had been a student at Stanford when he read Ferriss's *The 4-Hour Workweek* (4HWW). Sethi found it so inspirational that within hours of finishing it, he bought tickets to Buenos Aires because, as he put it, "I realized that by following Tim Ferriss's ideals I'd be able to do what I wanted to do."[25] He took leave from school and set about becoming a 4HWW guru by creating an absentee business, traveling the world, taking on extraordinary challenges, and teaching others how to do the same. When, in 2009, Ferriss called for "real-world lifestyle design case studies," eighteen people submitted videos showing how 4HWW had changed their lives for the better. Ever the hype man, Sethi's video began with a still picture of himself doing a push-up on the back of an elephant; this was part of a project he documented at Tumblr: "I travel to exotic locations, find exotic animals, and do pushups upon them."[26]

Sethi portrayed himself as a "digital nomad": all that he owned could fit in his backpack. Additionally, he created what Ferriss called a "passive income" business. Whereas Ferriss learned he could manage his supplement business from afar, Sethi, like many, turned to Google's AdSense. Say you have a great web page about doing push-ups; AdSense can pay you to place an ad from a protein shake company, for example, on *your page*. (This is different from AdWords, wherein advertisers pay to have an ad placed on *Google's search page*.) The company gets visibility for its product, you get money, and Google takes a cut. Once Sethi automated his system, he needed only a few hours a week to find terms for which Google had ads but for which there was not much good content. He then paid others to create web pages with content related to those terms and lived off the ad revenue from that outsourced content. It is fitting that AdSense, a favored source of passive income for life hackers, was prototyped, while he was at Google, by Paul Buchheit, the hacker who sees reality as a "systems of systems, all the way down."

Sethi did not win Ferriss's contest, but buoyed by the exposure on Ferriss's blog, Sethi started his own, *Hack the System*, and announced a crowdfunding campaign that contributed $5,000 toward getting a small school in rural India online. This crowdsourced philanthropy also follows the Ferriss mold. In Ferriss's thirties, he began using his birthday for philanthropy. In 2010, his friends and fans raised more than $100,000 toward sending students in high-need public schools on field trips.

Ferriss held another 4HWW contest, in 2011, with the reward being a "scholarship" to Ferriss's upcoming $10,000 Opening the Kimono seminar on how to develop and promote online content. ("Opening the kimono" was resurgent tech industry jargon from the 1990s; fortunately, the creepy expression was put down again in 2014 when Forbes included it in its list of "most annoying business jargon."[27]) In this video submission, Sethi declared he did not need to work at all; his income was "completely passive and completely outsourced": "4-hour workweek, screw that, I'm living a 0-hour workweek lifestyle and I'm teaching tons of people to do the same."

He included two awkward video testimonials about his lifestyle coaching. Next up, he wanted to redefine miniretirement by engaging in ninety-day lifestyle experiments. "Next year, I'm going to live on a desert island, alone, with just a Swiss Army knife and a satellite internet connection." But right now, he was working on becoming a famous deejay in Berlin. Sethi did this, to his satisfaction, using "The Sex Scandal Technique" of Kim Kardashian: do something provocative and get famous fast. Rather than developing deejay skills, making connections with promoters, and working up the ladder, he and a partner threw their own monthly parties: "Within just a few weeks of throwing these parties, we got to host Tim Ferriss live in Berlin. Our party brought in hundreds of people from countries all around the world."[28]

Of course, like Ferriss, Sethi wasn't really working just four (or zero) hours a week or even "semi"-retired. And it's questionable whether having Tim Ferriss fans at your party makes you a famous deejay. He was traveling and enjoying himself, but he was also hustling as a lifestyle and marketing guru. Sethi was reaching for the success that Ferriss achieved—as well as that of his older brother, Ramit Sethi, author of *I Will Teach You to Be Rich*.[29] He worked on promoting self-help best sellers including Ferriss's *The 4-Hour Chef* (in which he is mentioned) and books about diet and a "hormone cure" for women. And famously, in 2012, he "hired a girl on craigslist to slap [him] in the face" when he got distracted by Facebook.

> I'm looking for someone who can work next to me at a defined location (my house or a mission cafe) and will make sure to watch what is happening on my screen. When I am wasting time, you'll have to yell at me or if need be, slap me. You can do your own work at the same time. Looking for help asap, in mission, near 16th mission BART. Compensation: $8/hour, and you can do your own work from your computer at the same time.[30]

Sethi claimed the gimmick quadrupled his productivity, and his analysis on his blog charted the improvement. Yet even with outsourced willpower costing less than minimum wage, shouldn't a gadget be able to do something similar for less?

In 2014 Sethi announced Pavlok, a wristband that delivers "tiny jolts" of "Pavlovian conditioning" so as to break its users of bad habits. It was a popular idea, which raised $283,927 (508 percent of its initial goal) on Indiegogo. Traditionally, people use rubber bands on their wrists to snap themselves out of unwelcome thoughts or habits. A rubber band, pulled and then released, snaps you. Pavlok zaps you. Although rubber bands are virtually free, Sethi believed the $200 gadget was worth it. Pavlok "integrates with sensors, friends, and GPS to keep you on track with your goals." It could zap you when you raise your hand to your mouth (for nail biters or snackers), when you visit your favorite fast-food place, or when you spend too much time on Facebook. Additionally, as a result of teaching an online course about breaking bad habits, Sethi claimed "about 5% of people who try to quit a habit cold-turkey succeed in quitting the habit for good. About 25% who used a rubber band succeed. And, about 55-60% of users who used Pavlok succeeded."[31]

Sethi promoted Pavlok in every way available to Ferriss's "new rich" entrepreneurs, appearing in newspapers, on podcasts, and in blogs; the gadget was even lampooned on *The Colbert Report*, a useful barometer of popular attention. An especially valuable opportunity was a 2016 appearance on ABC's entrepreneurial reality show *Shark Tank*, where his pitch was not well received. Sethi was called a con man by one of the judges and much worse after he refused a deal from the most sympathetic investor; he was accused of being there solely to promote his product rather than make a deal for additional funding. This complaint of self-interested behavior is not uncommon among life hacking hustlers like Ferriss and Sethi.

We'll continue with motivation hacking in earnest in the next chapter, but this gloss of Sethi sets the stage for returning to our question about Ben Franklin's productivity at the start of this one. What do life hackers take for granted when they seek to make the most of their time? More pointedly, when does life hacking tip over into exploitation?

Privilege and Exploitation

In Sethi's 2012 "Sex Scandal Technique" post about how to "achieve any goal, instantly (and party with Tim Ferriss)," he chided his peers for their entitlement: if you believe that because you went to college, worked hard, got good grades and a degree, if you think this means you deserve a job, you are mistaken. There are millions of people in similar circumstances. He asked: What makes you special? Additionally, people overseas will hustle much harder, for much less, than any American college graduate.

> Let me tell you a story about one of my employees in the Philippines. I hired Klarc to help me build a habit: at 10:00 every day, he would call me and remind me to floss my teeth.

One day, at 10:32, I received a Skype message. "Excuse me Mr. Maneesh Sir (Klarc always called me sir, even though I asked him not to), I'm so sorry I'm late. We were hit by a hurricane, and the whole village has no electricity! I had to run 8 miles to the next village so that I could call you!"

Would you run 8 miles to remind me to floss? I was paying Klarc $2 / hr (but gave him a hefty bonus after this incident). What are you doing to make yourself so valuable [that an] employer would pay 10–20x that amount?[32]

Sethi's answer, naturally, was to "hack the system": "The shortest path to a goal is not by doing what everyone else is doing. It's often by doing the EXACT opposite." To become a deejay in Berlin, he threw his own parties. To raise his own profile, he started a podcast and interviewed better-known life hackers.

Yet in the same article in which Sethi lectures others about the "fallacy of entitlement," he speaks of paying a Filipino to remind him to floss. It is commendable for people to strive for efficiency, and should they go too far, they have an opportunity to reevaluate their goals and priorities toward effectiveness. Yet just as Ben Franklin's productivity was dependent upon the elided labor of his wife and slaves, the outsourcer is dependent on the labor of others.[33] For jobs that are local, labor will be performed by those in the "gig economy," like Uber drivers, who have flexibility but few benefits, and many of whom will soon be displaced by automation. For jobs that can be done remotely, this labor will be undertaken by those overseas who might be desperate for income. To respond to that desperation with honest, if menial, work could be virtuous. Ferriss has noted that "there are people I have outsourced to in India who now outsource portions of their work to the Philippines. It's the efficient use of capital, and if you want the rewards of a free market, if you want to enjoy the rewards of the capitalist system, these are the rules by which you play."[34] But when is it exploitative? When are the rules unfair? Such is the double-edged sword of automation and globalization.

The premise and promise of the systems embraced by life hackers is one of effectiveness, of freedom and flexibility. To appropriate outsourcing from corporations for this personal use is a hack, but one that also inherits corporations' ethical lapses. As kind and accommodating as Sethi might be, was Klarc free to skip a day and help his family after the hurricane, to keep his own time rather than exchange it for two dollars? Or was his family so dependent on his wage that Klarc had little choice but to run eight miles to remind Sethi to floss? Similarly, in the United States, the presumption is that workers have a choice between a steady job and the flexibility of gig work, but increasingly such work is done by those already at the margins and who have little choice.[35] In turn, productivity hackers sometimes seem to be cheerleading for things that will be abused by corporate regimes. Four years after Sethi launched a wristband said to correct bad habits, Amazon patented something similar for warehouse employees who reach for the wrong item. Amazon's proposal, thankfully, doesn't include a zapper, but there is an unsettling, even if coincidental, reciprocity between those who can choose a regime for themselves and those who can require it of others.

To look at the faces of life hackers, one usually sees white, smart, and technically inclined men with degrees from good colleges. This isn't always the case: some like Trapani are women, some like Sethi are of color, and among the technically inclined, dropping out of a good college is its own accreditation of merit. Silicon Valley billionaire Peter Thiel offers a $100,000 fellowship to young people to skip or drop out of college and "build new things instead of sitting in a classroom." But critics need not reach far to characterize Silicon Valley "know-it-alls" and life hacking gurus as privileged white dudes who overlook others' circumstances.[36]

Getting Things Done is a useful system for remaining productive, for focusing on what's important, and lessening anxiety. Nonetheless, I better appreciate the assumptions inherent in this method thanks to a talk by Heidi Waterhouse on "life-hacking for the rest of us." Waterhouse, a "technical writer, crafter, and working mother," notes that GTD assumes you are the master of your environment, that others do not control your schedule—that you can even delegate tasks—and that you do not have external dependencies like elder or child care. Her preferred system, Unfuck Your Habitat (UfYH), is productivity hacking, but with fewer assumptions, which are often related to gender and class. UfYH is much more fitting for those who want to do something useful in the few minutes after a teleconference and before taking the kids to school.[37] You might not be able to make the kitchen spotless in that time, but you might be able to clear out the dish rack so as to make washing some dishes later that much easier.

For critics, GTD and productivity hacking are individualistic responses to collective problems: in the guise of self-realization and entrepreneurialism, workers seek to escape the 9–5 rut by way of those on the lower rungs. A lucky few do ascend the ladder, but everyone that remains must either serve as a replaceable rung, perhaps in a call center, or continue to climb while parroting the buzzwords of *freedom* and *flexibility*.[38] Perhaps Sethi's payment of two dollars an hour is a fantastic wage in rural Philippines and Klarc is a successful entrepreneur in his own context, but perhaps not, and this concern is rarely raised.

These critiques of privilege and exploitation don't completely damn productivity hacking. Although gurus do focus on the wealthy, such as in Ferriss's $10,000 Opening the Kimono event, most life hacking advice is accessible to those who can access the web or a library. Also, aside from the gurus, most life hackers are ordinary geeks attempting to improve their lives. Recall that the term *life hacking* arose among attendees at a tech conference *sharing* tips. This is commendable, as are Waterhouse's and others attempts to expand the scope of life hacking to "the rest of us." More diversity among life hackers should lead to better hacks.

It isn't that life hacking is inherently flawed, only that, until now, it has been too bound to its demographic legacy, something that emerged at a tech conference in California. Alice Marwick, an astute scholar of Silicon Valley culture, writes that Ferriss and his peers "are successful because they uphold the values of the tech community (passion, success, self-improvement, meritocracy) and don't criticize or interrogate any of those values; they reinforce the 2.0 sense of itself as uniquely special, smart, and revolutionary." That is, Ferriss "universalizes a wealthy, white man's experience as a workable method for others" and his get-rich-quick techniques "can only be pursued by a few people before becoming unsustainable; not everyone can game Google AdWords."[39] Similarly, Sethi seems disdainful of those not willing or able to "hack the system" as he does, but the system would be trashed if everyone did so. Exotic animals would go extinct should everyone attempt push-ups on their backs.

Given that hacking seeks to exploit or contravene systems, to bend the rules, the ethical hacker should be careful to hack the system, not the other people caught up in it. Computer hacking has a rich history of ethical concern.[40] We should similarly ask if a life hack is universal (can everyone do it) and beneficial (beyond the lone hacker)? But such considerations are largely missing among life hackers. Ferriss is provocative. He titled his post on his experiments with outsourcing relationships "Mail Your Child to Sri Lanka or Hire Indian Pimps: Extreme Personal Outsourcing."[41] He's also pragmatic. Outsourced tasks should be time consuming and well defined. But he and Sethi say little on how to outsource without exploiting others. Simply put, even privileged geeks have as much a right to self-help and happiness as anyone else, but what do they owe others?

Beggars in Spain

In Nancy Kress's speculative world in which the sleepless ask what they owe the sleepers, much of the discourse is shaped by a philosophy known as "Yagaiism." Kenzo Yagai, an inventor of an inexpensive cold-fusion power generator, believed that a person's worth is based on what they could do well and that their only obligation was to abide by their agreements. As Yagai's energy technology reshaped the world, so did his philosophy. A wealthy industrialist was a believer and opted to have one of the first sleepless children, hoping his daughter Leisha would be able to do well. As he explained to her: "People trade what they do well, and everyone benefits. The basic tool of civilization is the contract. Contracts are voluntary and mutually beneficial. As opposed to coercion, which is wrong."[42] Nonetheless, as Leisha matured, she remained uncertain about Yagaiism—and fond of some sleepers—despite many of her sleepless friends' arguing for secession. Although Leisha might kindly give some change to a panhandler, her sleepless friend Tony asked, What if there were a mob of them? He asked:

> "What do you owe the beggars then? What does a good Yagaiist who believes in mutually beneficial contracts do with people who have nothing to trade and can only take?"
> "You're not—"
> "*What*, Leisha? In the most objective terms you can manage, what do we owe the grasping and nonproductive needy?"
> "What I said originally. Kindness. Compassion."
> "Even if they don't trade it back? Why?"[43]

As Kress wrote in her preface, she wanted to explore the long-range effects of an increasingly polarized society, between the productive and nonproductive, and to work though her understandings of Ayn Rand, a proponent of individual excellence, and the ideas in Ursula Le Guin's 1974 novel *The Dispossessed: An Ambiguous Utopia*. Kress reached her own conclusion near the end of the book, in the voice of Leisha: "what the strong owe beggars is to ask each one why he is a beggar and act accordingly. Because community is the assumption, not the result, and only by giving nonproductiveness the same individuality as excellence, and acting accordingly, does one fulfill the obligation to the beggars in Spain."[44]

The parallels between *Beggars in Spain* and criticisms of productivity hacking are striking. Consider the coupling between Yagai's transformative technology and his philosophy. I doubt Kress anticipated this, having published her story in 1993, but the internet's own development had a similar cultural coupling: many prominent hackers and entrepreneurs were influenced by libertarianism and Ayn Rand's philosophy of objectivism.[45]

Paul Graham, a famed computer programmer, hacker essayist, entrepreneur, and venture capitalist, sounds as if he could be a Yagaist. In a 2004 essay he wrote that those who are best at something "tend to be far better than everyone else" and that technology serves as a lever, exaggerating this further. Accordingly, in a modern society it's natural for there to be a gap in income just as there is a "gap between the productive and the unproductive." As long as it's the result of creating value, rather than corruption or coercion, "increasing variation in income is a sign of health." And being *relatively* poor isn't so bad in a rich society: "If I had a choice of living in a society where I was materially much better off than I am now, but was among the poorest, or in one where I was the richest, but much worse off than I am now, I'd take the first option."[46]

Graham's take on being poor in a superwealthy society is rational, but it isn't economically plausible or psychologically generalizable. Graham is wealthy, and it's difficult to conceive of a society in which everyone else is better off than he is. Additionally, research shows that people feel discontent in the face of inequality independent of their own absolute income.[47] Coincidentally, this was a significant theme in Cory Doctorow's *Down and Out in the Magic Kingdom*, mentioned in the last chapter.

Graham has a deserved reputation for insight into the hacker mind-set and culture. In his collection of essays on hacking, he explains that the term *hack* can be used for fixes that are clever or kludgy because "ugly and imaginative solutions have something in common: they both break the rules."[48] When life hacking is used to break the rules of our collective systems for personal advantage, little thought is given to those who are affected. Indeed, those left behind may be employed, literally, for menial drudgery by those clever enough to have just escaped it. But what of improving the system itself? Life hacking, simply, has little to say about this. Although life hacking practices could make one a more effective advocate for social improvement, life hacking's focus is on hacking, above all, the self.

4   Hacking Motivation

On a lovely summer day, I headed to San Francisco's Presidio Park for a picnic unlike any other I have attended. The small gathering was for fans of the motivation app Beeminder, and Nick Winter, author of *The Motivation Hacker*, was the special guest. Winter is the "founder/hacker" behind Skritter, an app for learning Chinese characters, and CodeCombat, a platform that gamifies learning to code. It's clear that despite being someone who sometimes spends *many* hours in front of a computer, like Ferriss and Tynan, he isn't content with the skinny-nerd stereotype. Winter's webpage features a picture of him doing a single-arm handstand: he's wearing a Google T-shirt, thin-soled "five-finger" shoes—also preferred by Tynan—and a surprisingly serene expression for someone who is upside down (figure 4.1). When I met at him at the picnic, he was wearing the same nonshoes and tossing a Frisbee.

The Motivation Hacker is a lab report of self-experimentation and a tutorial on how to maximize motivation. Winter's goal had been to write the book in three months "while simultaneously attempting seventeen other missions." Among other things, he wanted to learn to skateboard, try skydiving, learn three thousand new Chinese characters, go on ten romantic dates with his girlfriend, hang out with a hundred people, run a four-hour marathon, and "increase happiness from 6.3 to 7.3 out of 10." Most importantly, he had to finish developing Skritter.[1] Winter was inspired to take on these challenges after reading a post on *LessWrong*, a community blog dedicated to "refining human rationality."

The *LessWrong* post was itself a summary of Piers Steel's *The Procrastination Equation: How to Stop Putting Things Off and Start Getting Stuff Done*.[2]

Figure 4.1
Nick Winter doing a handstand, 2013, http://www.nickwinter.net/. Used with permission.

Steel is a professor of organizational dynamics who suggests that the extent of our motivation can be understood as an equation:

$$\text{motivation} = \frac{\text{expectancy} \times \text{value}}{\text{impulsiveness} \times \text{delay}}$$

That is, if you want to motivate yourself, make sure your goal is achievable and of value while minimizing distractions and the delay before receiving a reward. For example, imagine you want to motivate yourself to start work on a new chapter in your novel. Begin by writing for just twenty-five minutes, followed by a five-minute break. This is achievable, and you know from experience the hardest part is getting started for the day; you will have begun what Steel called a "success spiral." You also want to limit distractions and see an immediate reward. So you disable your network connection and reward yourself with a small treat, like a grape, at the end of the twenty-five minutes. Upon reading the *LessWrong* post, Winter was "excited to see if these techniques, designed to fix low motivation, could be used to hack high motivation to absurd levels."[3]

It is fitting that Winter's inspiration happened by way of an online rationality forum. It is especially galling for the rationally minded to fail to do what is in their own best interest. But failing to do the right thing has long been frustrating. The ancients called it *akrasia,* the Greek word for lacking self-control. And methods to overcome *akrasia* are as ancient as the temptations themselves. In Homer's epic *The Odyssey,* Odysseus had his sailors plug their own ears and bind him to his ship's mast so he could hear the Sirens' song. The sailors were to row past, unable to hear the bewitching call nor their captain's pleas to steer toward the deadly rocks. Accordingly, commitments, like burning a bridge so there is no retreat, are sometimes called "Ulysses pacts," substituting Odysseus's Roman name. Centuries later, in his letter to the Romans (7:14–17, New Life Version), Paul lamented: "I don't really understand myself, for I want to do what is right, but I don't do it. Instead, I do what I hate." His solution was to make himself a servant of his God, rather than remain a slave to his own sinful nature.

Thomas Schelling, a Nobel laureate in economics, was a more recent theoretician of *akrasia.* Schelling is most well known for his application of game theory to global conflict and cooperation. In 1978 and 1980, he published two lesser known articles about the games people play with themselves to manage internal conflicts.

> Sometimes we put things out of reach for the moment of temptation, sometimes we promise ourselves small rewards, and sometimes we surrender authority to a trustworthy friend who will police our calories or our cigarettes. We place the alarm clock across the room so we cannot turn it off without getting out of bed. People who are chronically late set their watches a few minutes ahead to deceive themselves.[4]

Schelling felt that self-control was an important subject and proposed a complementary field to economics. Just as *economics* comes from the Greek terms for *household* and *management, egonomics* would be the art and science of *self-management*. There was no shortage of cases: How do we manage our counterproductive fear, anger, sloth, addictions, and other unwanted behaviors? Just as we manage our dysfunctional scratching of poison ivy by trimming our nails and wearing mittens to bed, we need similar "tricks" for the rest of life. Much like David Allen's use of the term *tricks* decades later in *Getting Things Done*, this was life hacking in all but name.

Amusingly, the most likely emblem of effective self-management is that of a tomato—though perhaps the Pavlok wrist zapper, discussed in the last chapter, will take its place. In the 1980s Francesco Cirillo created a workflow, the "Pomodoro Technique," after a tomato-shaped kitchen timer he had in college. (*Pomodoro* means *tomato* in Italian.) The idea is to think about your task, work for an interval, typically twenty-five minutes, and take a short break when the time is up. If you are distracted by an errant thought ("I wonder if Sally returned my email?"), simply write it down for later and continue on task. After you do a few of these, you can take a longer break. Like a lot of productivity hacking, this seems to be about time management. But it's actually a psychological tool, a self-management tool, an egonomics tool. Its users claim it improves focus, boosts motivation, improves the ability to estimate task duration, strengthens resolve in the face of complex tasks, and lessens anxiety about taking them on. I use a similar time-boxing method and find much of this to be true for me. As Stephen Covey wrote in *7 Habits*, "'Time management' is really a misnomer—the challenge is not to manage time, but to manage ourselves."[5]

At the book's outset I observed that life hacking is a phenomenon of the digital age. We live in a culture in which the creative class is expected to be self-reliant but in a moment in which distraction is omnipresent. Motivation hacking is offered as a solution, as a means of coping or even excelling. We will see that some of its suggestions are useful but that many are oversold.

More importantly, we'll see just how much work managing the self can be and that it's possible to still feel that it fails to suffice.

The Science of Motivation

Life hackers drink from the well of popular science. They read best sellers and watch TED talks about the behavioral basis of willpower and good habits. This coincides with the boom in social-science-based self-help since 2010, including Steel's *The Procrastination Equation*. The term *egonomics* never caught on, but Schelling's questions have—in a big way.

In the last chapter we met Roy Baumeister, the prominent social psychologist who suggested a connection between GTD and the Zeigarnik effect. He's best known for his "ego depletion" theory, popularized in the book *Willpower: Rediscovering the Greatest Human Strength*. His theory is that we have a limited reservoir of willpower, which is linked to blood sugar: "As the body uses glucose during self-control, it starts to crave sweet things to eat—which is bad news for people hoping to use their self-control to avoid sweets."[6] Because willpower can be fickle, Baumeister and his coauthor suggest that a good way to resist temptation is to structure your life to avoid it in the first place.

The motivation hacker also needs to build constructive habits. *The Power of Habit: Why We Do What We Do in Life and Business* suggests that to create a habit, you need a cue (to trigger the brain), routine (to make it automatic), and reward (to establish those routines). *Smarter Faster Better: The Secrets of Being Productive in Life and Business*, by the same author, suggests you make use of SMART goals (specific, measurable, assignable, relevant, and time delimited), but within the frame of a larger "stretch" goal, otherwise you might suffice with trivial goals.[7] Coming up with effective goals is also a topic of *Rethinking Positive Thinking: Inside the New Science of Motivation*.[8] As is common with this genre, the best seller *Grit: The Power of Passion and Perseverance* was complemented by a popular TED talk.[9]

All of this popular social science is further complemented by the hype of *gamification*, which applies game design elements, like scores, leaderboards, and achievement levels, to things like learning and fitness. And the self isn't the only target of this literature. So-called growth hackers make use of the same techniques to increase sales of their products and services. In one book, a former game designer suggests hooking consumers on products by employing the same cycle of cues, routines, and rewards used in building personal habits.[10]

These are the works that life hackers take lessons from. They use the motivation equation, set smart goals, develop good habits, persevere, and gamify. They then add their systematization and fondness for technology. These influences are manifest in Winter's attempt to hack his "motivation to absurd levels" when completing his Skritter app.

In *The Motivation Hacker*, Winter writes of a moment when his work on the app had stalled: "I want desperately to finish the app, but I couldn't make myself do the work. I had more bugs than ever...and I could see that the iPhone app was many months away. Expectancy and Value were low, Impulsiveness and Delay were high, and my motivation was gone."[11] He realized that if he wanted to finish, he would have to design an approach using the motivation equation. He began with success spirals, setting an easily achievable number of hours dedicated to working on the app every day. Early successes increased the *expectancy* that he could achieve his goals. Importantly, he specified these goals in terms of effort, not outcome. To do otherwise courts failure because we have little control over what happens in the world. Focusing on inputs rather than outputs lessens disappointment, and the motivation hacker is primed to try again.

Winter also realized he had been spending too much time fixing bugs, which was a low-*value* task. He knew that he'd "like fixing bugs more" when it helped users, so he focused on completing the features so he could do the initial "alpha release" to users; this was higher in *value* and decreased the perceived *delay* to the next milestone. Finally, to limit his *impulsiveness* he reserved his most productive time in the morning for app development and otherwise time-boxed email and other distractions (e.g., check email only after lunch).

Winter's motivation hacking worked. He tracked the time spent on task and made a game of beating his running daily average. He was getting "more done per hour, and had more fun doing it" the longer he worked each day. So he decided to be ambitious and see how many hours he could work in a single week. In the previous two months, he had averaged nine hours a day, but in this concentrated week, he managed twelve, yielding 87.3 hours in total. To further lessen his impulsiveness, Winter recorded and posted a time-lapse video of both his screen and his face. By telling his friends he was going to do this, he created a commitment that he did not want to fail. It also curbed his impulsiveness, since he didn't want others to see him wasting time visiting distracting websites. In doing this, he achieved absurd levels of productivity while not losing track of his other goals. In addition to working 87 hours, he had been social five times, averaged 125 pull-ups a day, and was sweet to his girlfriend 100 percent of the days tracked. Subsequently, he conducted the same weeklong experiment with his CodeCombat project and "clocked in at 120.75 hours."[12]

Productivity Porn

When I read Winter's post about working 120 hours in a week, I was dismayed and intrigued. My dismay was shared by the first commenter to the post: "What, are you an idiot? My goal this week is to see if I can go five days without urinating. What kind of sense does this make? There are surely better things you can do than see if you can work yourself to death, no?"[13] I was intrigued because Winter so clearly relished the experiment. He averaged 17.25 hours of work a day, with 6.38 hours for sleep and 22 minutes for eating. Yet the well-being indicators he assiduously tracks had been high: his average happiness was 7.03/10 ("awesome!"), his energy was 6.64 ("high for me"), and his health was 5.33 ("5 is 'okay'"). The other handful of commenters appreciated the experiment and insights gained. Programming can be meditative, and you can do a lot with focus and motivation. They asked questions about his approach and how he made the video. Winter was also warned to "enjoy it while it lasts"; such focus becomes more difficult with age, especially with children. (He has since had two children, something I return to in a subsequent chapter.)

Winter has clearly hacked his productivity, but others are rarely—if ever—so successful. Lesser hackers wonder if their tinkering is just another type of procrastination. And we ought to ask, How much of this is based on sound science?

Many a life hacker is fond of the aphorism, often attributed to Abraham Lincoln, "If I had five minutes to chop down a tree, I'd spend the first three sharpening my axe." There is little evidence that Lincoln said this, but *Lifehacker* echoed the claim in 2011:

> Lincoln, who was a skilled woodcutter before becoming one of the most important presidents in US history, probably meant this both literally and figuratively. Inefficient tools waste your energy. It's better to spend the majority of your time

finding and cultivating the best tools for any task....Applied to indoor jobs, "sharpening your axe" may include things like setting up email filters, using text expansion, and installing productivity software. Furthering your education, eating right for better brain power, and otherwise sharpening your most important tool—your mind—also will help you work more efficiently.[14]

Although this sentiment is used to justify the hours life hackers spend on their systematizing, experimentation, and tweaking, many appreciate that this can waste more time than it saves. Merlin Mann, creator of *43 Folders*, joked about the lure of "productivity pr0n" (pornography in internet slang) as early as 2005: "It is a tongue-in-cheek term often used lovingly by its avid—even obsessive—consumers. It often implies the awareness that not all productivity pr0n leads to actual productivity....In any case, many friends of *43 Folders* (including its author) will readily confess to their productivity pr0n addiction."[15] By 2008, this loving sentiment had turned bitter: Mann had become disillusioned with the superficiality of life hacking. Consequently, he committed to cutting back on what he termed "half-finished, half-useful, half-ideas that I both make and consume" and instead "do all of it better."[16] By the end of the year, he had reduced his posting to *43 Folders* and ceased it altogether in 2011.

More recently, Heidi Weiss, a technical writer, mother, and blogger, called this predilection "process fondling." In a 2015 talk about life hacking "for the rest of us" (i.e., women, parents, and caretakers), Weiss spoke about applying software workflows to her life, especially her hobby, "agile crafting," which brings "agile principles to the needle arts." She warned that "if you spend more than an hour a day reading about time management, you have failed."[17] This has even been the topic of an XKCD comic (figure 4.2), popular among geeks, that charted, within a five-year time frame, "How long can you work on making a routine task more efficient before you're spending more time than you saved?"[18]

The Reproducibility Crisis

Clearly, "sharpening the axe" can be a way of procrastinating. Instead of chopping wood, we experiment with novel methods and materials for improving the blade. But do we know that any particular gadget or method for sharpening actually works? As with self-help in general, we should not be surprised to learn that some claims are short of well founded. For example,

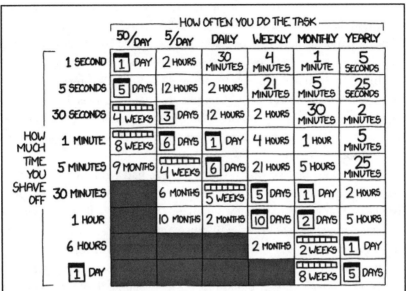

Figure 4.2
Randall Munroe, "Is It Worth the Time?," XKCD, 2013, http://xkcd.com/1205/.

could holding your urine, as was farcically suggested earlier, actually boost productivity? *Lifehacker* thinks so, based on a trawl of questionable research. "The Best Body Hacks to Boost Your Productivity at Work," recommends that you "put your thumb in your mouth and blow to reduce stress," "chew gum or coffee stirrers for added focus," and "use your right ear for important conversations." Most notably, "control your bladder to control impulsive decisions"; that is, take a big drink of water before a meeting so that the determination not to wet yourself will spill over.[19]

That post is an example of a larger problem with contemporary research, its reporting, and the self-help suggestions based on it. Consider the recent hoax study that concluded that eating chocolate accelerates weight loss. The study had real subjects (only fourteen), a typical methodology (subject to false positives), and a statistically significant result (with minuscule effects), and it was published by a rigorous peer-reviewed journal (so says the publisher).[20] This was a weak study best ignored, but many news sites reported the finding as fact, revealing problems with scientific rigor and journalistic vetting.

To gauge the extent of this problem, a number of efforts are being made to reexamine well-regarded and classic studies. The Reproducibility Project, a collaboration of hundreds of researchers, repeated one hundred studies from top-tier psychology journals and managed to reproduce the results of just thirty-five. Another approach, the Replicability-Index, uses meta-analysis to combine existing studies' data so as to reveal spurious findings. This happens to include Roy Baumeister's famed ego-depletion theory of motivation, though Baumeister remains convinced his methods and conclusions about blood-sugar are sound.[21]

The reformers believe that researchers have had too much freedom to steer work toward statistically significant results. A *p*-value represents the likelihood that a novel finding would happen by chance alone—5 percent is a typical upper threshold for significance. Yet this value is meaningful only in the context of testing a single hypothesis, *not* of fishing for results across many variables. For example, the chocolate study took eighteen measurements from fifteen people: blood protein levels, cholesterol, sleep quality, weight, well-being, etc. By trawling for results across eighteen measurements, the researchers had a 60 percent chance of finding something that looked significant at the 5 percent level. Whether researchers inadvertently fool themselves or purposefully trick their peers, the practice is known as *p-hacking*, appropriately enough.

The problem of p-hacking is compounded by journals' publishing only novel findings. For every remarkable result (e.g., "chocolate accelerates weight loss"), there are many unpublished studies that find the opposite but are never published. This publication bias distorts our understanding of the world and contributes to baseless self-help advice.

One way forward is for researchers to register their hypotheses and methods before any data are collected. This limits researchers' degrees of freedom in shaping the analysis. Additionally, even negative findings should be published so as to prevent publication bias.

Until these reforms become the norm, researchers are in fraught waters, especially when they give advice to the public. The authors of *Grit* and *Rethinking Positive Thinking* have both been criticized for making unwarranted but "science-y" claims in pursuit of the self-help market.[22]

This concern has even caused a split between two coauthors. In one of the most popular TED talks ever, "Your Body Language Shapes Who You Are," Harvard Business School Professor Amy Cuddy spoke of her research, with Dana Carney and Andy Yap. She began her talk with "a free no-tech life hack and all it requires is that you do this: change your posture for two minutes." Cuddy and her coauthors had found that "power posing," taking a confident posture, for two minutes increases confidence, risk taking, and testosterone, decreases cortisol, and improves how one is perceived in "stressful evaluative situations," like a job interview. This shows that "our bodies change our minds, our minds change our behavior, and our behavior changes outcomes." The "no-tech life hack" is to not just fake it until you make it, "but fake it until you become it." Cuddy asked the audience to share her message with others, especially those with the least resources, power, and privilege, "because it can significantly change the outcomes of their lives."[23]

Cuddy's talk and subsequent book were popular successes, but attempts at replication by those who wanted to build on the research yielded poor results. A few years later, Dana Carney, Cuddy's coauthor, took the unusual step of explaining why she no longer taught, researched, or spoke to the public about power poses. The failed replications and her understanding, in hindsight, of the work's weaknesses led Carney to conclude that the effect was not real. As Carney did much of the data collection and analysis, she was able to frankly disclose the many mistakes she and her colleagues had made. In their research design, the testosterone effect may have been the result of winning a small prize rather than posture. In their analysis, they ignored data, selectively removed outliers, and reported only the statistical tests that showed significance (i.e., they engaged in p-hacking). In response, Cuddy conceded that although the most rigorous attempt at replication—a registered study— failed to find the behavioral and physiological changes, it confirmed subjects' reports of *feeling* more powerful; the behavioral and physiological changes "are secondary to the key effect" and the subject of continuing research.[24] However, people's self-reports are notoriously unreliable. Subjects often report what they want to believe. Had the change in feeling been the only finding, it would not have merited a TED talk, life hack, or new self-help regime.

Part of the problem might be the attempt to reach the TED stage. In 2012, the TED organization was forced to issue a warning about the increase of pseudoscience at TEDx events. In 2015, comedic writer Will Stephen gave a compelling-sounding talk that began: "I have absolutely nothing to say whatsoever. And yet, through my manner of speaking, I will make it seem like I do—like what I am saying is brilliant. And maybe, just maybe, you will feel like you've learned something."[25] This parody echoed a debate from a few years prior in which TED was criticized for offering solutions that were little more than placebos: they were "middlebrow megachurch infotainment" that offered overly simple, inspirational but ineffectual, solutions.[26] The same critique has been leveled at life hacking and Tim Ferriss specifically. The author of one prominent profile notes that sections of Ferriss's books "sound like an Onion satire of a TED talk," and another characterizes his speech as that of the "*Wired*-reading app-happy nerdpreneurs" and his prose as "a combination of northern Californian lingo (Ferriss is often 'super psyched') and TED Talk jargon."[27]

A lot of life hacking advice is based on published research. Unfortunately, much of this work is of questionable quality. Worse yet, there is a lot of "woo," what skeptics call bogus beliefs dressed up in science's trappings, and life hackers are not immune to its allure. Fortunately, the current tumult means that science remains capable of improving. The life hacker must then be savvy to the differences between phony science, weak science, and rigorous science—listening with both ears.

Odyssean Goal Tracking

As a hacker and developer of learning apps, Winter naturally made use of an app in his efforts to be absurdly productive. There are hundreds of apps that provide goal tracking, graphing, habit building, daily inspirational quotes, and even hypnosis. Such apps have become especially popular with the addition of social and gaming features. You can now join group challenges (nearby or virtually) and receive encouragement and coaching. You can also connect your goals with role-playing. In Habitica, eat junk food and your character loses health points, do ten push-ups and it gains gold and experience points. Winter used Beeminder, which describes itself as "Odyssean goal tracking," referencing the myth of Odysseus bound to his ship's mast. Beeminder asks you to bind yourself to a set of increasing monetary penalties. Forget to floss your teeth? You just lost your $5 and are now on the hook for $10, then $30, $90, $270, and more.

Beeminder is not the only such app—StickK is a popular alternative from Yale economists—but it is the geekiest. Beeminder and StickK both receive the money their users forfeit for broken commitments—StickK allows users to specify a different beneficiary, but even then the company still gets a cut. This seems odd at first, but it was not troubling to the users I spoke to: they saw it as paying for a useful service.

Beeminder is the product of Danny Reeves and Bethany Soule. Reeves has a doctorate in computational game theory, and he subsequently worked on incentive systems at Yahoo. Soule has a master's degree in machine learning and often "speaks publicly about her crazy Quantified Self life-hackery."[28]

Beeminder is intended for "akratics," those who want to do something that is achievable but are unlikely to follow through. Many life hackers speak of a difficulty in motivating themselves to floss their teeth, and this is a perfect Beeminder goal: it's of value *and* definitely doable, whereas becoming an astronaut is valuable but unlikely. Beeminder uses penalties to motivate its users to achieve their desirable and doable goals, just as Schelling suggested decades ago. Consider the example of A. J. Jacobs, the author who outsourced his life and otherwise turns yearlong experiments into best-selling books, like reading the *Encyclopedia Britannica* and living biblically. As part of his *Drop Dead Healthy* experiment, he decided to kick his dried mango habit—despite their "veneer of being healthy," they are "really just orange-colored sugar."[29] He wrote a check to the American Nazi Party and told his wife to mail it should he ever eat another dried mango. Jacobs succeeded, and Beeminder uses a similar aversion to losing money encapsulated within a web service.

Upon creating a goal, Beeminder creates a path of daily milestones called "the yellow brick road." The idea is that a long-term goal is more likely to be achieved if you take baby steps toward it. Every time you "derail," or step off your road, you pay a quickly increasing penalty. The road can be flat (floss your teeth at least once a day) or increasing (go from writing three hundred to a thousand words a day). Beeminder is structured to offer "meaningful commitment with maximal flexibility." The commitment becomes "meaningful" with the increase of the penalty: $5, $10, $30, $90, $270, $810, and $2,430. (The most anyone ever paid has been $810.)

The flexibility is in specifying how quickly your milestones ramp up: "Beeminding means committing to keep your datapoints on your yellow brick road, but the steepness of the road is under your control, with a one-week delay." The week delay, which Beeminder calls the "akrasia horizon," keeps you from the immediate temptation of adjusting your goals downward: "it's the time horizon beyond which you can make rational decisions, undistorted by akrasia." And the penalty schedule is chosen so that you reach your "motivation point" as quickly as possible, such that "you'll never waste more than half of the amount that eventually motivates you to stay on track."[30]

Sean Fellows, a software engineer I met at the Beeminder picnic, used the app for a number of ordinary tasks like watering his plant, exercising, calling relatives, brushing his dog, and sending photos to his mother's digital photo frame. Fellows most appreciated Beeminder's integration with IFTTT (IF This Then That), which allows users to write recipes that integrate different services and devices. For example, your phone can automatically tell Beeminder if you've gone to the gym (via geolocation), called your father (via the dialer app), exercised (via the accelerometer), and completed urgent tasks (via the todo app). Fellows managed to mind his goals with modest pledges, never having paid more than $30. And, true to type, he had a bunch of scripts and a Beeminder goal for managing his Beeminder goals.[31]

Winter has used Beeminder as a goal tracker, without penalty, and a motivator, with large penalties. As noted, the motivation equation worked well for Winter when launching Skritter. The launch date was a hard deadline, Winter's finances were at stake, and he likes to code. He didn't set a pledge amount for this goal, but he still used Beeminder to track his efforts. Winter initially set a modest goal and managed to increase his app development time from 1.3 to 2.7 hours per day. This showed he could improve, but it wasn't enough, so he increased the goal to 5 hours a day. For the first three months of the Beeminder goal, he "skated the edge" of derailment, as he was "never more than a day's work away from failing."[32] In time, his use of the motivation equation created a success spiral, and he easily exceeded his target.

Other goals required the possibility of losing money. When I expressed my concern to Winter about being a workaholic and the oddness of setting social and girlfriend goals, he conceded that doing work was his "natural state, so adding Beeminders for everything else is what I do to avoid doing too much work and not getting balance ... it's dangerous to focus only on, say, work productivity, because you can definitely make yourself into a work monster."[33]

One of the unnatural goals for Winter was to go skydiving, and he requested that the folks at Beeminder set a $7,290 penalty for failing to follow through. Surprisingly, this isn't all that unusual. Short-circuiting the usual schedule, which starts at $5, to a higher penalty is a feature available to premium members of the service. Not only did this increase Winter's motivation, it lessened his anxiety about jumping out of a plane. He pledged thousands of dollars, paid for the skydiving tickets on a specific date, told all his friends and colleagues, and wrote about it in a draft of the book: "Now that I've pre-committed far more than necessary, I'm so sure that I'm going to successfully jump out of the plane that I'm not afraid anymore. I'm excited."[34] In the end, he didn't like it and has no desire to jump again, but he had successfully insulated himself against any anticipatory wobbling of will. For Winter, if it comes down to willpower, you haven't sufficiently hacked your motivation. Beeminder provides a mechanism for folks like Fellows and Winter to do just that. People could cheat and falsify their data to avoid a penalty, but Beeminders are self-selecting: they do not want to mess up their tracking data—they often use automated devices (like a Withings scale or Fitbit)—and they want to continue to benefit from the service. Yes, Beeminder does make money when you fail at your goals, but as the Beeminder website says: "we make you fail *less!*"[35]

The Rat Race

Is Nick Winter's 120-hour workweek a harbinger of a troubling future? His maniac week was a personal challenge undertaken by a hacker with significant autonomy, but what might it mean for others? He tested motivational hacks on himself, but what does it mean when employers come to expect maniacal motivation from workers forced to compete among themselves? Captive rats racing through a maze easily comes to mind.

The notion of the rat race stems from psychological experiments in the early part of twentieth century. Most famously, beginning around 1929, Robert Tryon and his students began breeding a diverse group of rodents into lineages of "bright" and "dull" maze runners. Those that avoided previously encountered dead-ends were interbred, as were those that fared poorly. In one study, Tryon wanted to test the role of nature and nurture, so he let some dull mother rats foster bright pups and bright ones foster dull pups. The difference in the data was stark: nature (genetics) trumped nurture (fostering).[36]

Incidentally, a few decades later, Robert Rosenthal and a colleague noted that this experiment was not blinded: Tryon and his students knew which rats were which. Rosenthal asked his students to replicate the study, telling them he would provide bright and dull mice. In truth, Rosenthal randomly assigned mice to the two groups. Still, surprisingly, the purportedly quick group did better. He suggested this was because the students had biased the results, perhaps by favoring those thought to be bright.[37] This parallels the reproducibility problems I alluded to earlier and is a further lesson regarding how easy it is to fool ourselves.

As early as the 1950s the "rat race" appeared in popular culture as a way to speak of the exhausting pursuit of success at the behest of an unseen force. Is productivity hacking complicit in accelerating the pace? To answer this, we have to distinguish between the rat, the race, and the guru.

There have long been complaints about the configuration of the capitalist maze. In its most recent form—which different critics refer to as late, new, digital, or cognitive capitalism—imbibing the self-help tonic only perpetuates the anxiety it purports to quench. This is Micki McGee's argument in her 2005 book about America's self-help culture, *Self-Help, Inc.* The anxiety is the consequence of "our culture's fantasy of a disengaged, masterful, rational, and controlling self that creates the possibilities for endless and futile self-improvement." Self-help gurus foster this anxiety by "conjur[ing] the image of endless insufficiency," which leads workers "into a new sort of enslavement: into a cycle where the self is not improved but endlessly belabored."[38]

Although McGee makes no mention of the life hacker, her fantasy self-improver sounds like a good fit. Appropriately, in his critical history of life hacking, Matt Thomas concludes that "hacking is offered up as the solution to the overarching anxiety provoked by the networked age." As such, it is a "technologized form of self-help" in which we seek to "master ourselves using technology, make do with less, ignore structural conditions, forget about the past, and work, work, work to make ourselves more productive like good little robots."[39] For critics, motivation hacking is another station on the robotic assembly line. And gurus' promises of greater effectiveness and efficiency yield only increased austerity and enslavement.[40]

Modern life is challenging and often unjust; we do, also, live in an age of racing anxiety. Our possible responses are to be demoralized or cynical, to figure out a local fix, or to build a global alternative. Although gurus sell books on how to win the race, most life hackers are coping in their way by sharing local fixes to common problems. Most will, eventually, recognize the danger of "productivity porn" and "process fondling." Many life hackers recognize the importance of work/life balance—even if, like Winter, it means tracking social and relationship goals in an app. A few even reach for alternatives to our current social systems, though they tend to be far-fetched and high-tech, such as using bitcoin to distribute a universal basic income.

Granted, the digital age enables and rewards the hacker ethos, which can then become seen as the accepted path toward success. If you aren't hacking your motivation, you will be left behind. It is, therefore, valuable to ask if life hacking techniques are really useful, if this path is for everyone, and if there is a bigger fix. However, it is difficult to fault those attempting to keep up in the rat race, especially if it's through a maze that they enjoy running.

Winter did take things to an extreme. And for a few, this is a natural way to see and live in the world. If he wants to challenge himself to jump out of a plane, so be it. And Winter likes work, he likes coding. He concedes most people do not like working so much, but "perhaps more of them would if they filled the entire week up with exactly the stuff they wanted to work on." (After all, the real goal of the four-hour workweek is to spend time on what you value.) Even though it seems like "an eccentric, atypical thing to enjoy... others do enjoy the focus of the maniac work period... whether it's a week or just a weekend."[41] This group includes Beeminder cofounder Bethany Soule, who emulated Winter's "maniac week," posting her own time-lapse video, when her husband and cofounder took the kids to Canada for a week. Even though it was not as "epic" as Winter's week, Soule says she "got a lot out of this, enjoyed it more than my average work week, and intend to do it again. It'd be great to experiment over the summer with more nontraditional work-hour arrangements with Danny. Maybe trade weeks of intense work with weeks of vacation or something."[42]

For those like Winter and Soule, smart entrepreneurs who largely enjoy their work, productivity hacking is a way of improving their work satisfaction and flexibility. Yet at the optimum or "maniac" level, hackers must take care to ensure that it coexists with relationships and family obligations. As we saw in the last chapter, even if polyphasic sleep yields more time in the day, it is difficult to reconcile its scheduling demands with the larger social world. Similarly, without care, boosting productivity, especially in pursuit of material success, can lead to imbalance and burn out—a topic of the next chapter.

Hackers seek shortcuts, sometimes toward unusual ends. Tynan, for example, has taken a different route than most: college dropout, professional gambler, pickup artist, software developer, author. He learned to type on the Dvorak keyboard and twice attempted polyphasic sleep. Despite living frugally, he throws away nickels and pennies. The few dollars he loses a year aren't worth the hassle.

Tynan also likes to travel, and for many years his home had wheels. Two of his books describe the philosophy and practice of his lifestyle, *Life Nomadic* and *The Tiniest Mansion: How to Live in Luxury on the Side of the Road*. In the first book, Tynan discusses the philosophy of living in a recreational vehicle: "Minimalism is essentially freedom from excess, and there are few lifestyles more minimalist than living in less than one hundred square feet of space in a vehicle. The mental clutter associated with rent payment, home maintenance, cleaning, vacuuming, and furnishing is gone."[1] In *The Tiniest Mansion*, Tynan addresses the practicalities of living in an RV, such as getting utilities and disposing of waste. And he's frequently asked if this lifestyle interferes with dating: "My one suggestion is to tell a story early on that indicates that you aren't forced to live in an RV as a last resort, but that you intentionally chose a freedom-laden minimalist lifestyle."[2]

Telling others, and ourselves, a compelling story about our life gives it meaning. This is true for life hackers and their relationship to possessions. When David Allen spoke of getting a handle on "stuff" in *Getting Things Done*, he was speaking of incomplete tasks that occupy the mind. Material stuff also occupies the mind. It takes work to get and keep possessions, no matter how productive or organized you are. Consequently, some life hackers embrace minimalism by limiting their possessions to the essential. And technology frees them to become digital nomads, taking their work, social networks, and entertainment with them wherever they go.

When life hackers discuss their relationship to stuff, they tell two stories. They talk about the gear that is essential and how they discarded everything else. In these stories *zen* often makes an appearance. This invocation connotes simplicity and a clean aesthetic, made famous by Steve Jobs at Apple. As a young man, Jobs studied Buddhism intensively. Even though he was not known for his compassion and seemed far from ego-less, Zen suited his aesthetic. (There is a famous picture of young Jobs sitting, cross-legged, on the floor under a Tiffany lamp, the only piece of furniture worthy of his otherwise empty mansion.) Not surprisingly, most life hackers favor Apple's aesthetic and products. The blogs *43 Folders*, *Zen Habits*, and *Minimal Mac* have dozens of posts about Macs. Tynan is the notable exception to the fanboy rule—even so, his 2012 his laptop of choice was the Asus *Zen*book Prime.

Even if the references to Zen are shallow, they show that life hacking transcends simple tips and tricks. The hacker ethos informs how hackers understand and approach larger issues, like material contentment, and hackers are happy to share their recommendations and philosophy with others. We can learn much about contemporary life via their stories and the questions they prompt. For example, what does it mean to choose "a freedom-laden minimalist lifestyle" in a society of unequal wealth, in which others have few choices? To address this question, we need to first understand a bit of life hacking's cultural history.

Gear Lists and the *Whole Earth Catalog*

One tenet of minimalism is that if you rely on a few things, they should be dependable. As Tynan writes in *Life Nomadic*, the "best way to enjoy what this amazing world has to offer is through limited but high-quality consumption."[3] A recurring story life hackers tell about their relationship to stuff is their search for good gear. *Lifehacker*, for example, showcases bags and workspaces filled with useful items. Individuals also post gear lists. Tynan has been doing so since 2008—frequently extolling the virtues of wool clothing.

A good online gear list has a common structure. Each item is accompanied by an image and personal reflection. Some lists are capped by images of all the items arranged next to each other and another of everything packed away. Links to Amazon allow authors to make commissions on their recommendations. Tynan's lists are excellent: "every product I recommend is the absolute best in its class; if it wasn't, I wouldn't be using it."[4]

Although gear lists have reached their apex online, there are historical antecedents. In *Walden* (1854), Henry David Thoreau listed the supplies and foodstuffs he used during his experiment of simple living—making him a favorite of life hackers.[5] Among the items he purchased and scavenged, Thoreau paid $8.03 (and one-half cent) for the boards he used for his cabin, which were repurposed from the shanty of an itinerant railroad worker. Tynan makes no mention of *Walden*, but his account parallels that of Thoreau. Tynan spent around $20,000 for a 1995 Rialta RV, which he fitted with granite countertops cut from a single $200 slab. In their retrofits, neither Thoreau nor Tynan cared about luxury per se. They sought value, which was best had via used items and elbow grease.

A more recent gear list precursor is the *Whole Earth Catalog*, first published in 1968. The *Catalog* recommended tools and books for those seeking self-sufficiency and a bigger picture. Its publisher, Stewart Brand, trained as a biologist at Stanford University and served in the US Army, but his most notable characteristic is his take on the world. In the few years preceding the catalog, Brand campaigned for NASA to release a photo of Earth from space, which would show humanity's interdependence. When they did so, he used the image as the catalog's cover art and talisman.

Beyond perusing online copies of the *Whole Earth Catalog*, the best way to appreciate Brand's interests is through Fred Turner's history, *From Counterculture to Cyberculture: Stewart Brand, the Whole Earth Network, and the Rise of Digital Utopianism*.[6] Turner discusses the influences of Norbert Wiener's cybernetics, Buckminster Fuller's "comprehensive designer," Marshall McLuhan's "global village," the USCO art collective, and the road- and acid-tripping Merry Pranksters. Brand fashioned his eclectic interests into a syncretic vision for human improvement, and he created spaces in which his vision could become a reality.

Despite being in the thick of the counterculture, Brand maintained a clean-cut look and deeply appreciated what he learned as an infantry officer. He had learned that with both soldiers and hippies, you have to make the best of what you have. His organizing abilities allowed him to play the part of countercultural entrepreneur by identifying nascent trends and giving them space and cohesion, as he did as a coorganizer of the 1966 Trips

Festival in San Francisco. This three-day show was the first mass event of the hippie movement and featured the Grateful Dead, LSD-spiked punch, and a psychedelic light show. Thousands attended.

The *Whole Earth Catalog* served as another space, in print, for those seeking an alternative way of living—long before anyone spoke of lifestyle design. The *Catalog's* subtitle was *Access to Tools*, and its criteria were pragmatic. Items should be useful, further self-sufficiency, provide good value, and be little known but easily purchased by mail. Its stated purpose was grandiose: "We are as gods and might as well get used to it." Power was shifting away from the formal institutions of schools, churches, corporations, and governments. The individual could now "conduct his own education, find his own inspiration, shape his own environment, and share his adventure with whoever is interested."[7] This individual sounds a lot like a life hacker.

Despite its name, the *Whole Earth Catalog* was not just a listing of gear. More often than not, items in the *Catalog* were ideas, and the idea that Brand was most taken with fifty years ago was that of systems. Each issue of the *Catalog*, published regularly between 1968 and 1972, had a section dedicated to "understanding whole systems"—the same motive that drives hackers today. Other sections of the *Catalog* could serve as categories at *Lifehacker*: Shelter and Land Use, Industry and Craft, Communications, Community, Nomadics, and Learning.

Life hackers share Brand's belief that ideas are powerful tools. This is best seen in Tim Ferriss's *Tools of Titans: The Tactics, Routines, and Habits of Billionaires, Icons, and World Class Performers*. Ferriss writes that "world-class performers don't have superpowers"; instead, "the rules they've crafted for themselves allow the bending of reality to such an extent that it may seem that way." His self-help promise is that his Titans "learned how to do this, and so can you."[8] If Brand's readers were gods, when given access to the right tools, Ferriss's readers could appear like Titans, pre-Olympian deities, when given the same. Although both men love gadgets, their most powerful tools are ideas, especially those about systems and the rules for taking advantage of them.

The "Californian Ideology" and *Cool Tools*

Stewart Brand was quick to recognize that "computers and their programs are tools," as he wrote in the first *Whole Earth Software Catalog* (1984).[9] Most importantly, PCs could be networked, and in 1985 Brand cofounded The

WELL (Whole Earth 'Lectronic Link), a San Francisco–area bulletin board system. Again, he played the part of countercultural entrepreneur. The WELL was the online home for many of those later known as the *digerati*, the authors and entrepreneurs who championed the online revolution. Yet despite talk of a revolution, Brand saw cyberspace as a continuation of 1960s counterculture. In a 1995 essay for *Time*, "We Owe It All to the Hippies," he claimed that the hippies had provided "the philosophical foundations of not only the leaderless internet but also the entire personal-computer revolution."[10] Not all hippies were as keen on computers as Brand, but he saw their antiauthoritarianism and appreciation of interdependent systems as fundamental to what followed.

Nine years later, in 2004, two European scholars lamented these same philosophical foundations. In a much-discussed essay, UK media theorists Richard Barbrook and Andy Cameron warned that "a loose alliance of writers, hackers, capitalists and artists from the West Coast of the USA have succeeded in defining a heterogeneous orthodoxy for the coming information age." They identified this "Californian Ideology" of the digerati as "an anti-statist gospel of cybernetic libertarianism: a bizarre mish-mash of hippie anarchism and economic liberalism beefed up with lots of technological determinism."[11] Theirs was an astute ideological vivisection, even if their call for a European alternative was feeble.

Whereas Stewart Brand bridged the counterculture of the 1960s with the cyberculture of the 1980s and 1990s, Kevin Kelly carried the torch of the Californian Ideology into the new millennium. Kelly was an editor of a number of *Whole Earth* publications in their later years and, with Brand, helped organize the first Hackers Conference in 1984 and launch The WELL the following year. In the 1990s, Kelly became best known as the executive editor of *Wired* and for his books about complex systems and the rules of the new economy. Tools, systems, and rules are his motifs.

One of the curious things about Kelly is that his reputation as a tech enthusiast is contrary to his old-timey facial hair: a beard without a mustache. This and his interest in the Amish seem at odds with someone who believes that human culture and machine intelligence are becoming a beneficent superorganism that he calls the "technium." But Kelly believes the Amish have an undeserved reputation as Luddites. Although they abstain from many modern devices, they are "ingenious hackers and tinkers, the ultimate makers and do-it-yourselfers and surprisingly pro technology."[12]

The Amish think carefully about their relationship to technology; they are minimalists with tried-and-true tools.

In 2000, Kelly returned to the *Catalog*'s mission by way of *Cool Tools*, a new way of sharing recommendations. He began with an email list for tools that "really work" and moved to a blog in 2003. A decade later he expanded *Cool Tools* to include a print book and podcast. *Cool Tools* solicits reviews of tools of any type, be it a literal tool, kitchen gadget, or useful book. Tools can be "old or new as long as they are wonderful." The site's philosophy is to "post things we like and ignore the rest"; it asks its readers to simply "tell us what you love."[13] Kelly has been joined at *Cool Tools* by Mark Frauenfelder, a colleague from *Wired*, cofounder of *Boing Boing* ("a directory of wonderful things"), and founding editor-in-chief of *Make*. (Recall that life hacking's founders, Danny O'Brien and Merlin Mann, had a column in *Make* in 2005 and 2006.)

Kelly and Frauenfelder's interest in wonderful things and cool tools is complemented by another manifestation of the Californian Ideology. In *maker culture*, artists, hackers, and crafters share their creations of utility and delight. This happens online, in print, or at a Maker Faire, a gathering of artists, builders, citizen scientists, hackers, and performers. Makers use their cool tools to create wonderful things.

Kelly considers all of this, especially life hacking, part of a legacy: "The *Whole Earth Catalogs* preached the hacker/designer approach to life starting in 1968, decades before this lifehacking became the norm. The Catalogs were a paper-based database offering thousands of hacks, tips, tools, suggestions, and possibilities for optimizing your life." More recently, Kelly cofounded the Quantified Self (QS), a topic of the next chapter. He remains resolutely optimistic about technology and systems. Kelly's long-standing pinned tweet is "Over the long term, the future is decided by optimists."[14]

Kelly's optimism is one of the many connections between the counterculture of the 1960s, the cyberculture of the 1980s and 1990s, and the life hackers of today. The recurrent theme throughout is that the world is constituted by systems, and tools are the means by which you operate within and upon those systems. In this vision, enthusiasts decide the future, when empowered with the right tools and free from institutional interference. As we saw in chapter 1, life hacking is a continuation of American self-help and extols the values of individualism, pragmatism, perseverance, and entrepreneurialism. Now we can see that life hacking is also a manifestation of the Californian Ideology, with a side of systematizing.

Even so, many life hackers are unfamiliar with this historical legacy. Although Ferriss read the *Catalog* as a kid, traveled with *Walden*, and has Kelly as a frequent guest on his podcast, there is scant evidence of this kind of recognition among others, especially ordinary fans of life hacking. But you need not understand all the past turns of a path in order to begin walking it. And hacking is as much a sensibility as it is a culture. Life hackers are attracted to a path of technology and making, of optimizing and optimism.

"Masculine, Entrepreneurial, Well-Educated, and White"

In his history of the *Catalog*, Turner notes that its audience was "masculine, entrepreneurial, well-educated, and white." While the *Catalog* celebrated self-sufficiency and community, "it avoided questions of gender, race, and class toward a rhetoric of individual and small-group empowerment."[15] Although Matt Thomas makes no mention of the *Catalog* in his critique, he sees life hacking in a similar light. Minimalism, specifically, is a "distinctly masculine consumer style" emerging from young white men's socioeconomic anxiety.[16]

These broad characterizations are true enough, but the history of hacking does include those beyond this demographic, though they tend to be overlooked because prominent life hackers select heroes like themselves and portray them in the best possible light. At the same time, they are unaware of the stories of those who are different. Fortunately, this can be mitigated, partially, with three short asides.

—

In an earlier chapter I noted how productivity hackers and Ben Franklin share an underappreciation of how productivity is dependent on the invisible work of others. In this chapter, we have encountered another life hacker hero: Henry David Thoreau. Again, the parallels are striking. Thoreau was a smart young man from a modest family wishing to experiment with simple living. He conducted his experiment on property owned by Ralph Waldo Emerson, a family friend, for two years, two months, and two days. (If he were alive today, he might have blogged about this as the "2-2-2 challenge.") He wrote up his experiences, documenting his few supplies and expenses and his reflections of living in a cabin next to Walden Pond. As such, Thoreau has been claimed as the first declutterer and original minimalist.[17]

Yet Kathryn Schulz, writing in the *New Yorker*, asks: "Why, given his hypocrisy, sanctimony, and misanthropy, has Thoreau been so cherished?" Walden Pond was hardly remote: a railroad was being built nearby. In fact, Thoreau bought the windows and boards for his cabin from the family of an Irish-immigrant railroad worker, whose home Thoreau described as a "compost heap." This family did not choose to live simply, they had to. Additionally, Schulz believes Thoreau cheated in the accounting of his minimalism. Concord was a twenty-minute walk away, and he visited it several times a week, "lured by his mother's cookies or the chance to dine with friends." His mother and sisters visited him weekly, usually bearing food. He glossed over these facts "despite detailing with otherwise skinflint precision his eating habits and expenditures." Thoreau never married, and he lived the rest of his life in his parents' boarding house. Schulz thinks *Walden* reads like a cross of *The 4-Hour Workweek* and a Calvinist sermon: "Thoreau denigrates labor, praises leisure, and claims that he can earn his living for the month in a matter of days, only to turn around and write that 'from exertion come wisdom and purity; from sloth ignorance and sensuality.'"[18]

In contrast to Schulz, others defend Thoreau.[19] He paid rent to his parents and helped support the family even if the women did his laundry, which was the typical division of labor at the time. He was opposed to war, as well as the oppression and enslavement of Native and African Americans. Thoreau's experiment took determination, and he wrote about it with thoughtfulness and skill.

Even so, when we draw aggrandizing connections to heroes of the past, we should not forget their shortcomings or, at least, the biases of their time. We will soon see criticisms of privileged minimalists, to which Thoreau's case also speaks. By focusing on those who choose to live simply, we can easily overlook the skills and stories of those who must do so.

—

Even before the *Catalog*, there was another publication dedicated to hackers and makers: the *Toomey J Gazette*, started in the 1950s. In its pages, dozens of people with disabilities shared their DIY hacks for making products more accessible and useful. In the 1968 issue, the editor of the Homemaking section included hundreds of tips from a survey of "cooking quads" (quadriplegics), which could also be of value "to many who were less disabled." Examples include handling a sink faucet with a spoon (see figure 5.1) or placing a

FAUCETING

- "I turn on the water by hitting the faucet handles."
- "I walk my fingers around the sink to the water faucets."
- "I tap faucets on and off with small hammer with long handle."
- "I use a long wooden spoon (A) with four nails in the bowl section. Wrap nails with electrician's friction tape."
- English booklets list both homemade and commercial models of tap turners:

(B) For a single bar tap, a groove whittled out of a cylindrical piece of wood.

(C) A tap turner made of a length of wood, a drilled hole, and two cup hooks.

Figure 5.1
Gini Laurie, "Homemaking Problems & Solutions," 1968, *Toomey J Gazette*. Used with permission from Post-Polio Health International.

damp dishcloth under a bowl to keep it in place while stirring.[20] Subsequent issues showed this community of hackers at the forefront of home automation and remote education and work. The community would be recognized more broadly in the 1980s, when poet and author Mark O'Brien joined as the disability editor for a couple of *Whole Earth* publications. Acknowledging this improves our understanding of history. It broadens the picture of what a hacker can look like. And such recognition can enhance the exchange and development of useful hacks across communities.

Beyond those who are overlooked because they are outside the mainstream, there is the matter of co-option. Frequently, a heralded innovation outshines precursors by virtue of a high-tech and masculine sheen. As one snarky columnist wrote of the 2017 boom in Bay Area coliving (i.e., having roommates in San Francisco): tech entrepreneurs often "find an existing service, privatize it, and claim to have 'reinvented it.'"[21] Similarly, an overheard comment, tweeted and then retweeted many times, is that "[San Francisco] tech culture is focused on solving one problem: What is my mother no longer doing for me?"[22] One of those things is feeding you. And when hackers came up with meal substitutes, they were lauded as innovative tech creators. But this spotlight gave others pause.

When San Francisco tech reporter Nellie Bowles attempted to explain Soylent to her mom, her mother responded, "Oh, you mean SlimFast?"

> I balked. No, Soylent is definitely tech, I explained, and it's on my beat. It has a minimalist label and comes in iterative versions like software (we're at Soylent 2.0). It has a young white male founder who philosophizes about it and connects it to broader themes of life efficiency and has raised $20m in venture capital funding on its promise of releasing us from the prison of food.[23]

However, after thinking about it, Bowles came to the conclusion that most Silicon Valley food innovation is "just rebranding what women have been doing for decades. There's nothing inherently different about Soylent from SlimFast at all. And yet SlimFast is low-brow, funny and a little sad. Soylent is cool, cutting-edge, brutally efficient and, here's the key word: innovative." Soylent's creator claims the company is not targeting medicinal use and SlimFast is not nutritionally complete. Rather, Soylent is an inexpensive, convenient, and fully nutritious breakfast or lunch replacement.[24] This might be true, but I know men who use Soylent, tweet and blog about it, though I've never seen any man do the same for SlimFast.

—

Kevin Kelly is always in search of useful tools, and in 2008 he cofounded a movement for "tools that help us see and understand bodies and minds."[25] The Quantified Self (QS) was created to allow creators and users of these tools to gain "self knowledge through numbers." Five years later, Amelia Greenhall, a San Francisco designer, announced the first QSXX meetup. QSXX was created as "a space for all the interesting, women specific QS conversations we want to have." Greenhall majored in electrical engineering as an undergrad and got involved in QS while a graduate student in public health. She described her first meeting to me as a "finding your people moment," and within a year she began organizing meetups herself.[26]

Greenhall noticed that after her meetups, a woman would inevitably approach her wondering if there was room for women-specific health topics? This prompted Greenhall to investigate: "There are 500 Show & Tell talk videos online. I couldn't find any on periods, yet women have probably been self-tracking this for, oh, somewhere around 100,000 years."[27] And so in 2013, she organized QSXX San Francisco, which would be followed by groups in Boston and New York. Women practitioners and scholars are more visible in this space than in life hacking as a whole. This is in part because of their efforts to have their long-standing interests and history in self-tracking recognized.

Despite this visibility, women continue to be overlooked. After Apple's 2014 announcement of its Health app, Greenhall and others were interviewed about how women are excluded from self-tracking apps. Apple's app could be used to track electrodermal activity, calorie and calcium intake, heart and respiratory rate—but not menstruation. Greenhall explains that "VC [venture capital] money goes almost exclusively to white men, and white men always get the same advice: 'The place to start looking for ideas is in the things you need.'"[28] The consequence of this is that the resulting products tend to be hobbled by stereotypes and naiveté. For example, Greenhall notes that not all women want to lose weight, some want to gain or maintain it, but many apps assume otherwise. Also, women are not as keen to share their location, weight, and sleep data with the world because of safety concerns. QSXX helps ensure a space remains among self-trackers for those who do not identify as male.

Others, in time, realize that the values that go along with the high-tech sheen are alienating, and they choose to step away. For example, in an essay in *The Atlantic*, an engineering professor wrote about why she no longer identifies as a maker: "The cultural primacy of *making*, especially in tech culture—that it is intrinsically superior to not-making, to repair, analysis, and especially caregiving—is informed by the gendered history of who made things, and in particular, who made things that were shared with the world, not merely for hearth and home."[29] The consequence of this, sadly, is that the dominant demographic associated with the story of hacking becomes self-perpetuating.

From Much to Minimal

Life hackers tell two stories about their relationship to possessions. If the first is about the gear and tools they find essential, the second is how they get rid of everything else. Joshua Millburn and Ryan Nicodemus are friends who became evangelists of this latter tale. By the age of thirty, despite their success, they were possessed by a "lingering discontent."

> We had achieved everything that was supposed to make us happy: great six-figure jobs, luxury cars, oversized houses, and all the stuff to clutter every corner of our consumer-driven lifestyles. And yet with all that stuff, we weren't satisfied with our lives. We weren't happy. There was a gaping void, and working 70–80 hours a week just to buy more stuff didn't fill the void: it only brought more debt, stress, anxiety, fear, loneliness, guilt, overwhelm, and depression. What's worse,

we didn't have control of our time, and thus didn't control our own lives. So, in 2010, we took back control using the principles of minimalism to focus on what's important.[30]

Their blog, *The Minimalists*, was sufficiently popular that in the following year, they quit their jobs and published *Minimalism: Live a Meaningful Life*, followed by an international book tour. They offered private mentoring and online writing classes to those who wished to follow their path. In 2012, they moved to a mountainside cabin in Montana—"the Thoreau thing with Wi-Fi."[31] For a time, they were a media sensation, telling their story to every outlet that authors aspire to reach. Every generation experiences insights anew. For those that grew up online, Millburn and Nicodemus had discovered a near enemy: if contentment is a goal, material wealth is no guarantee.

However, Millburn and Nicodemus are not the first of their generation to claim dissatisfaction, launch a blog, and attempt to parlay that into a self-help writing career. Leo Babauta established *Zen Habits* at the start of 2007 with a focus on productivity. At the end of the year, he followed with the e-book *Zen to Done: The Ultimate Simple Productivity System*. In 2009, just as *Zen Habits* was peaking in popularity, he began a new blog, *mnmlist*, which was also followed by a complementary book. His conversion from hacking productivity to minimalism was seen, a few years later, in his recommendation to *Zen Habits* readers that they "toss productivity out": there's no sense in organizing the deck chairs of a sinking ship—simplify and chuck them overboard.[32] He never stopped blogging at *Zen Habits*, but his focus changed, and the many posts on *mnmlist* from 2009 to 2011 correspond with an intense popular interest in minimalism.

In this same period, Colin Wright swapped a life of one-hundred-hour workweeks for a life with less than one hundred things; he blogged about it at *Exile Lifestyle* and published best-selling Kindle books on minimalism and travel.[33] Dave Bruno parlayed his blog, *The 100 Thing Challenge*, into a 2010 book about "how I got rid of almost everything, remade my life, and regained my soul."[34] This story of a crisis, of regaining one's soul, and of a commitment to revolution was not unusual. Rita Holt (a pseudonym) wrote an e-book on minimalism and how, after collapsing in tears, she broke from a lifestyle she hated. When she finally realized "it was now or never," she quit her job, committed to a minimalist revolution, and invited readers to follow her travels on Twitter.[35]

The Counting Nomad versus KonMari

In the past, if I thought about crafts, lifestyle, and household tips, Hints from Heloise came to mind. Yet life hacking has a masculine and high-tech sheen. So how do minimalist gurus compare to a more traditional source of household advice, to the feminine domesticity of Marie Kondo? In 2011, Kondo published a book describing her KonMari technique. She counseled millions of Japanese to discard whatever fails to spark joy.[36] The book was published in English in 2014, and despite Kondo's not speaking the language, she received more media attention than Millburn and Nicodemus. Obviously, the minimalists and Kondo share the idea of curating possessions. Also, they are both responses to a popular discontent with materialism and clutter, but the minimalists, unsurprisingly, are geekier. They show a fondness for counting, challenges, and travel.

A conspicuous facet of the minimalists' stories is the enumeration of possessions. Dave Bruno and *The 100 Thing Challenge* was the most visible example among many. Nick Winter, who wrote *The Motivation Hacker*, had ninety-nine things. Everett Bogue, the author of *The Art of Being Minimalist*, got down to fifty, before confessing he needed a few more items than that. Kelly Sutton, the blogger behind the *Cult of Less*, varied the formula: his goal was to condense his life into two boxes and two bags. The process of minimizing can make for a good story in itself. Tynan developed a protocol for what to keep, sell, toss, and give away; the last step made use of an ad on Craigslist announcing that everything in his house could be taken for free.[37]

All these men have lived in San Francisco and worked with computers, although minimalism isn't their exclusive province. Black minimalists such as Ylanda Acree are, according to the blog of the same name, building an intentional community for "simple living from a perspective that values our culture."[38] Courtney Carver's Project 333 challenged readers of her blog *Be More with Less* to "dress with 33 items or less for 3 months." In a post entitled "Women Can Be Minimalists Too," Carver highlights eight other women minimalists, including a pioneer in the tiny-house movement who has a list of ninety-seven things.[39] Minimalism isn't monolithic, but it is dominated by men and those who count their possessions.

Kondo doesn't care how many things you have, as long as they spark joy and are then neatly put away. Whereas minimalists approach possessions as a challenge to count and discard, Kondo approaches them with animistic care.

Objects are eager to serve and content with being bid farewell. In addition to her relationship to stuff being more relational, perhaps Kondo's appeal was that her story of exhaustion and insight was so dramatic. Kondo had been obsessed with organizing since childhood, which took a toll. One day, she "had a kind of nervous breakdown and fainted." Two hours later, "when I came to, I heard a mysterious voice, like some god of tidying telling me to look at my things more closely."[40] It told her to focus on the things to keep, rather than those things to throw away. The KonMari technique was born. Other differences between Kondo and other gurus include the recurrent gender imbalance: minimalists tend to be men, and Kondo's fans tend to be women. And many minimalists, unlike Kondo, are obsessed with travel.

Kevin Kelly labels himself a minimalist and began his globe-trotting decades before digital nomadism became a thing. Recall that Maneesh Sethi, inventor of the Pavlok wrist zapper, made a project of doing push-ups on exotic animals as he crossed the globe with only what he could fit in a backpack. Tim Ferriss traveled for eighteen months with next to nothing, though he made room for two books, Thoreau's *Walden* and Rolf Potts's *Vagabonding*. More recently, in 2017, he and Kelly traveled through Uzbekistan together. Leo Babauta regularly posts to *Zen Habits* about traveling lightly and how to maintain good habits and health while doing so. He also writes about traveling with a family, which is unusual but a welcome departure. Rita Holt asked the readers of her blog to follow her on Twitter as she began her international voyage of minimalist revolution. Colin Wright let the readers of *Exile Lifestyle* vote on which country he would live in for the next four months.

More so than any of these minimalists, Tynan exemplifies the "life nomadic," never settling anywhere for long and calling an RV his home base for almost a decade. In 2016, Tynan sold the RV but continued to live on cruise ships and at his other bases, including the island he and his friends bought in Nova Scotia. He writes that all of this is now normal for him, and he feels at home in Budapest, Las Vegas, New York, San Francisco, and Tokyo. Because most of his friends have a similar lifestyle, he is as likely to see them in these cities as their putative homes.

In short, the much-to-minimal story is one of liberation with ecstatic undertones. The traditional route, with its trapping of material success, prompts a crisis. Discontent and a breakdown are followed by insight. Throw off your career and possessions; write and travel the world as a missionary of minimalism.

The Dilemma of Stuff

Many life hackers told their much-to-minimal story during the 2009–2011 heyday, especially those who managed to become globe-trotting writers. But the minimalist tale eventually grew stale.

Among minimalist gurus, Graham Hill is not unusual. He is a tech-savvy entrepreneur who achieved success at an early age. His ventures included a web design consultancy in the 1990s and the popular *TreeHugger* blog in the naughts. He sold both of these for good money, and at one point had a 3,600-square-foot house in Seattle and a 1,900-square-foot loft in Manhattan, each of which he felt obliged to fill with stuff. Not surprisingly, his life was growing ever more complicated: "The things I consumed ended up consuming me. My circumstances are unusual (not everyone gets an internet windfall before turning 30), but my relationship with material things isn't." Hill's moment of insight came about when his girlfriend's visa expired. He returned with her to Barcelona, where they lived in a tiny flat "totally content and in love before we realized that nothing was holding us in Spain. We packed a few clothes, some toiletries and a couple of laptops and hit the road. We lived in Bangkok, Buenos Aires and Toronto with many stops in between." Along the way he rid himself of "all the inessential things I had collected" and began to "live a bigger, better, richer life with less."[41]

Hill shared his story in 2013, in the pages of the *New York Times* Sunday Review. He complemented his own experiences with damning statistics about American consumption, waste, and pollution. Hill concluded the piece by noting that he remained a serial entrepreneur and that his latest venture was designing small homes for those equally concerned about their freedom and environmental impact. I believe he expected kudos: Hill had been successful but stressed, and when he learned how to live a better life, he wanted to help others do the same. Yet Hill's timing, wealth, and tone led to criticism instead.

It isn't hard to see why people were getting tired of minimalism. Not everyone wants to live in an Apple store. Minimalism is a relatively sterile aesthetic and creativity sometimes requires messiness. Minimalists are extreme, and people's initial curiosity eventually turns to distaste. Also, the public lost patience with minimalists, especially the millionaires. Minimalists can be preachy, which is grating when the sermon is self-congratulatory. Rather than a high-minded philosophy, maybe minimalism is a personality defect or a delusion? Thomas sees digital minimalism as an attempt by the insecure to regain control, which only furthers "the fantasy of the techno-fix"; sadly, their "escape from stuff is, ironically, as tied to stuff as the world of stuff they are trying to leave behind."[42]

A wickedly funny satire of the minimalist personality is Alexei Sayle's short story "Barcelona Chairs"—it is prescient too, as it was written in 2001. The story is about rupert (with a lowercase "r"), an overly controlling archi-tect whose house is an "oasis of light and space." The house's metal chairs are striking but painful to sit on, the glass staircase is spectacular but ter-rifying to the children, and no household item can be seen or found. Still, this is better than clutter: "that was the thing about minimalism, it was demanding, and asked a lot of you, everything that was in the minimalist room was balanced on a hair trigger of harmony, every object was precisely where it was supposed to be and the slightest thing out of place threw the whole delicate equilibrium into utter chaos." One day rupert comes home to discover that one of his walls, which had been "clean and pristine and white as a sea mist," has a baffling word scrawled on it: "PATRICK." His efforts to have it cleaned, painted, and chiseled away only compound the disfigurement. He suffers a breakdown and drinks bleach, "reducing the untidy tangle of his insides to a minimalist shell."[43] Luckily, he is found by his family's Finnish au pair and survives. To recover, he and his family move to a quaint whitewashed farmhouse in southern Spain. rupert lets go, and he lets his hair grow. Yet over time, his personality reasserts itself. One day, he can take it no more and screams at his family about the mess. That night, his wife goes outside to the "white moonlit wall of the farmhouse" and writes in tiny letters: "PATRICK." If only Steve Jobs had read this, per-haps he could have avoided some of the anxiety and injury caused by the glass staircases and walls in Apple stores.

Beyond a dislike for pretense and prissiness, the simplest reason for mini-malist exhaustion was that it was a fad at the end of its hype cycle: Hill published his essay after the tide had turned. In 2011, Everett Bogue pulled his e-book, *The Art of Being Minimalist*, from distribution and replaced it with an essay at fuckminimalism.com. Simply, Bogue felt minimalism had done its job; it was time to move on. Rita Holt did so in 2012. When I asked her why her website had disappeared, she explained that minimalism had grown into a popularity contest, a race for clicks, shares, and e-book sales: "It just seemed like a facade, another pattern we all fell into, though shouting all the while we weren't like the rest of the herd. So I got out. Scrapped the website, all the posts, any links or interviews I may have put out there."[44]

Fads come and go, and individuals have different personalities and tastes. Even so, in self-help, individual behavior happens within a social context. Choices are informed by and affect others, be it opting for cosmetic surgery, boosting productivity, or decluttering. The important question, then, is: What assumptions underlie the self-help advice that is given?

Minimalism and Millionaires

For the well-meaning, there is a paradox inherent in shopping. If you choose the path of quality and sustainability at a higher price, are you acting the part of an entitled snob? A writer at *The Atlantic*'s CityLab suspects so after attending one of Hill's presentations for his new venture, LifeEdited. She writes, with a hint of covetous censure, that his slides featured "featherweight towels, colorful nesting bowls, easily stored hot plates... all fancy and sleek and very desirable."[45] An item that costs twice as much and lasts four times as long is a good deal, but it's not a deal everyone can afford.

Going the inexpensive route, in solidarity with the less fortunate, is not necessarily better. A writer at *The Nation* believes inexpensive products are made at the expense of the environment and workers. Although his *New York Times* piece is "a majestic display of guileless narcissism," Hill did not did not go far enough in scolding Americans for "how they actually spend too little on the goods that they do buy"[46]

These two takes are at odds, which is to be expected. When a fad loses its footing, everyone tries to take advantage of its fall. Even so, the story of minimalism does yield two insights into life hackers' relationship with stuff.

First, it's ironic but fitting that minimalism, which makes so much of the *Zen* label, followed the story of Buddhism's founder. In the origin tales of Buddhism, the parents of Prince Siddhārtha sheltered him from evidence of human suffering and gave him every luxury. But the prince was discontent. Early one morning, observing the disorder and ugliness after a late-night party, Siddhārtha decided he was done—it was now or never, as Holt writes about her own break. He sneaked away, leaving everything behind, and began his travels. He experimented with different lifestyles but gravitated toward asceticism, including fasting and forgoing sleep. After years of this, Siddhārtha collapsed by the roadside and was found by a girl and revived with a cup of rice milk. He concluded that extreme asceticism was no better than the extreme luxury his parents provided. He would later teach the middle way, a path between the extremes.

Many minimalists, too, concluded that extremes were not the way. They had escaped the enemy of too much stuff, only to fall prey to the near enemy of too little. Everett Bogue and Rita Holt abandoned the minimalist label altogether. Dave Bruno stopped keeping careful count. Colin Wright confessed extremes are easy for him and they sell books, but balance is the goal. Others counseled moderation: consumerism was not the answer, but neither was fetishizing minimalism. Even *Lifehacker*, in 2017, posted an entry about the trap of keeping up with the minimalist Joneses.[47] As a counterculture, minimalism had strayed far from the values of the *Whole Earth Catalog*: self-sufficiency had been displaced by convenience, value by luxury, and accessibility by exclusiveness. Minimalism needed a reform.

Greg McKeown, a Silicon Valley leadership guru, undertook a rebranding effort in 2014 with *Essentialism: The Disciplined Pursuit of Less*.

> The way of the Essentialist means living by design, not by default. Instead of making choices reactively, the Essentialist deliberately distinguishes the vital few from the trivial many, eliminates the nonessentials, and then removes obstacles so the essential things have clear, smooth passage. In other words, Essentialism is a disciplined, systematic approach for determining where our highest point of contribution lies, then making execution of those things almost effortless.[48]

"Minimalism" isn't mentioned in the book, but speaking of "the way" has a Zen feel, and McKeown does stress lifestyle design and systematization. This is still Silicon Valley self-help. Even so, it is a moderate approach that stresses apportioning focus toward life priorities, a common self-help recommendation.

In addition to the insight about moderation, a second is that we must take care in making assumptions. Charlie Lloyd, writing at Tumblr, captures this best. Although Lloyd works in a technical field, lately he's "been mostly on the lower end of middle class." In his backpack, which would never make *Lifehacker*, he carries a three-year-old laptop and, because the battery is dead, its power supply. His backpack has paper and pens and a cable to charge his old phone: "It has gum and sometimes a snack. Sunscreen and a water bottle in summer. A raincoat and gloves in winter. Maybe a book in case I get bored." Things would be different if he had more money: he would carry a MacBook Air and an iPad Mini; anything else could be bought as needed.

As with carrying, so with owning in general. Poor people don't have clutter because they're too dumb to see the virtue of living simply; they have it to reduce risk. ... If you buy food in bulk, you need a big fridge. If you can't afford to replace all the appliances in your house, you need several junk drawers. If you can't afford car repairs, you might need a half-gutted second car of a similar model up on blocks, where certain people will make fun of it and call you trailer trash.[49]

In short, rich people have the relationship between minimalism and wealth backward: "You can only have that kind of lightness *through* wealth." It is this relationship, and minimalism's bland demographics, that leads to the suspicion that minimalism is for well-off bachelors.

MacBook minimalism does require a certain amount of wealth, but we should be wary of overgeneralizing. Well-off people can be overtaken by stuff and can benefit from simplifying. Likewise, the poor are not immune to materialism, even if their desires remain unfulfilled or their stuff isn't as pricey. Having less is not necessarily a virtue, and having more is not necessarily a vice. The real problem is that self-help universalizes its advice, especially when the experiences of the successful and wealthy are presented as worthy and capable of emulation.

Soon after Hill's *New York Times* essay, Tynan posted a reflection, "The Less Fortunate," to his blog. He had just seen the documentary *Inocente*, the story of a homeless teenage girl who refuses to abandon her dreams, including marriage and a house. Tynan acknowledges that he was fortunate and that his lifestyle advice is at odds with Inocente's modest dreams: "Sometimes I rant about marriage and houses and how those are crappy goals. But you know what? That's for people like me who have been spoon-fed success from birth." Tynan has not faced the same issues of abuse and homelessness; the challenges Inocente faced, he feels, were "probably tougher than anything I can hope to do in my life."[50]

When bringing someone home to your RV, Tynan advises telling a story so that you are not confused with those who have no other choice. The stories that life hacking minimalists tell are of wealth: not necessarily about money, but about plentiful choice, about being able to pare down and travel the world—or even quit minimalism, as many have done, whenever they wish.

6 Hacking Health

In September 2008 a small group of enthusiasts met in the San Francisco home of Kevin Kelly, former executive editor of *Wired* and *Cool Tools* wrangler. Kelly had gathered about thirty people interested in health, enhancement, genetics, and life extension. The group included Gary Wolf, a colleague from *Wired*, and Kelly and Wolf had organized this get-together as the inaugural meeting of what they called the "Quantified Self" (QS). This was the movement's first Show & Tell for those interested in increasing "self knowledge through numbers"—the QS motto.

Kelly believes that QS can help answer questions both prosaic and transcendent. Through it, we might learn how to better manage our email or live to be a hundred years old. It might even answer the central question of the digital age: "What is a human?... Is human nature fixed? Sacred? Infinitely expandable?" Kelly is characteristically optimistic and tools-focused.

> We believe that the answers to these cosmic questions will be found in the personal. Real change will happen in individuals as they work through self-knowledge. Self-knowledge of one's body, mind and spirit. Many seek this self-knowledge and we embrace all paths to it. However the particular untrodden path we have chosen to explore here is a rational one: Unless something can be measured, it cannot be improved. So we are on a quest to collect as many personal tools that will assist us in quantifiable measurement of ourselves. We welcome tools that help us see and understand bodies and minds so that we can figure out what humans are here for.[1]

The idea that self-knowledge and improvement need measurement is a variation on the idea that "if you can't measure it, you can't manage it." This aphorism is often attributed to management consultant Peter Drucker, but his take was more nuanced. Although Drucker advocated measurement, he believed that a manager's relationships were primary and "cannot be measured or easily defined."[2] Even so, for some things, there is truth in the measure-manage aphorism. As we saw with productivity hacker Nick Winter in chapter 4, measurement facilitates personal goal setting, analysis, and accountability. But to stop there is naive.

There are also aphorisms about the limitations of measurement. Here is one often misattributed to Einstein: "not everything that can be counted counts, and not everything that counts can be counted." There is also the dilemma that measurement itself is distorting. Measuring one variable tends to prioritize it over others. (Winter's solution to this quandary was to double down on counting and set goals for his social and romantic activities.) Worse yet, measurement tends to be followed by manipulation and cheating in competitive contexts. This has been observed in many fields, by many scholars. An anthropologist, commenting on overzealous measurement in education, put it this way: "when a measure becomes a target it ceases to be a good measure."[3]

Kelly and Wolf, however, are unapologetic defenders of quantification. To announce QS more broadly, Wolf published two high-profile essays, accompanied by a TED talk. In the *New York Times Magazine*, Wolf declared that numbering had won the day: "We tolerate the pathologies of quantification— a dry, abstract, mechanical type of knowledge—because the results are so powerful. Numbering things allows tests, comparisons, experiments. Numbers make problems less resonant emotionally but more tractable intellectually. In science, in business and in the more reasonable sectors of government, numbers have won fair and square." The "last redoubt" of this victory was "the cozy confines of personal life": "sleep, exercise, sex, food, mood, location, alertness, productivity, even spiritual well-being."[4]

QS is the measurement-obsessed wing of life hacking, with a significant focus on health. Its proponents anticipate and work toward the pervasive measurement of people's so-called cozy confines. And unlike in traditional science, its answers will be "found in the personal," as Kelly suggests. For example, when hacking his motivation, Nick Winter did derive his tactics from science-based self-help. But he also personally tested their efficacy and tracked the results. Although his reporting of averages is more precise than necessary (e.g., "7.03/10 happiness"), he has evidence of what works for him.

The idea that we might find solutions to personal and cosmic concerns in measurement is a powerful belief among life hackers. It reveals an intriguing double vision, one that is both immediate—*self*-knowledge through *self*-tracking—and distant, given its aspirations toward the cosmic. Even so, this vision is not without distortion.

Data's Meaning

I've seen many QS Show & Tells over the years, in person and online, and I'm impressed by participants' candidness as they share their personal enthusiasms and difficulties. The most candid talk I've witnessed was by someone who tracked the genital, oral, digital, and anal microbiomes of himself and his wife before and after sex. Many people would, no doubt, prefer to keep these domains "cozy," as Wolf put it, especially if employers, insurers, or criminals can access the data. Yet he was pleased with his data and results. He had carefully swabbed everything before and after every session and discovered their biomes were more similar after sex.

Despite the novelty of his undertaking, his results weren't that surprising. What was the point of collecting all that data if only to awkwardly confirm the obvious? Not everything that can be counted counts.

My question about meaningful uses for self-tracking data is not unusual; it was raised at the first QS meeting by someone with a lot of data but no idea what to do with it. In a blog post written the day after, and in response to some "good-natured ridicule in the *Washington Post*," Gary Wolf explained that the group discussed how self-tracking data can spark new research questions, inform decisions, and be undertaken as art. Nonetheless, Wolf conceded "there's a compulsion, a curiosity, that seems to operate in advance of any particular use."[5] This is in keeping with the hacker ethos: experimentation and tracking is a matter of personality as much as anything else.

Beyond Wolf's reasons, my conversations with self-trackers reveal a practical motive. People use tracking and experimentation for nominal (therapeutic) health hacking, to manage symptoms and find remedies.[6] For example, Kay Stoner describes herself as a "data hoarder" and suffers from headaches. As a teen she kept journals, boxes of which are now in storage. And like most life hackers, she had an early affinity with computers. Her computer was nonjudgmental: "It didn't care who I was, as long as I followed the rules of syntax and realistic expectation." Tracking patterns and developing rules is also how she approached her headaches later in life. She developed an application for recording her symptoms and their context but eventually settled on a paper-based diary.

Chronic illness and pain is depressing. It feels as if one is helpless and that the suffering will never end. Having a record showed Stoner that she could do things to lessen her headaches and that they do eventually end: "if you've got objective data showing you that something [helpful] did happen before, and it might just be possible again, that can nip the depression and sense of helplessness in the bud." Having a record also allows her to clearly communicate with her doctors.

Life hackers, like anyone else, seek remedies for their ailments. Just as the author of *The Hacker's Diet*, in chapter 1, wanted to lose weight, Stoner wants to lessen her migraines. What makes these two hackers different from most people is their systematic approach to understanding and addressing their concerns. Additionally, for hacker-types, tracking itself can be reassuring. Sometimes Stoner's records of pain and failed remedies are dispiriting. At times she puts them aside. Yet ultimately, tracking and experimentation are the way she manages, finds hope, and communicates with others: "Data adds structure, meaning, and purpose to my life."[7]

The Transhuman Roots of Becoming Superhuman

As I kid, I loved the opening sequence of *The Six Million Dollar Man*, which begins with footage of an aeronautic catastrophe. Astronaut Steve Austin is barely alive, and over scenes of surgery and bionic schematics a voice declares: "We can rebuild him. We have the technology. We can make him better than he was. Better…stronger…faster." These three words are the title of the 2011 *New Yorker* profile of Tim Ferriss; two of them also appear in the title of the 2016 self-help book *Smarter Faster Better: The Secrets of Being Productive in Life and Business*.[8] A clip from a 1970s TV show, of using science and technology to enhance human performance, lingers as a way of describing an aspiration to be superhuman.

Two of Tynan's most popular titles are *Superhuman by Habit* and *Superhuman Social Skills*. Tim Ferriss's book *The 4-Hour Body* is, according to its subtitle, *An Uncommon Guide to Rapid Fat-Loss, Incredible Sex, and Becoming Superhuman*. The mantra of his TV show is that "you don't need to be superhuman to get superhuman results…you just need a better toolkit."[9] The bionic man's treatment was not only therapeutic: he was enhanced. Similarly, the goal of *optimal* hacking is to transcend the nominal.

Of course, the desire to rise above is not new. In Greek mythology, Icarus flew too close to the sun. In Abrahamic mythology, the people of Babel dared to build a tower that could reach heaven. Neither of these myths spoke to genuine possibilities. Rather, they warned of hubris, and Icarus and the people of Babel were scattered upon the earth. But with the advances of science in the twentieth century, some hoped that real transcendence was imminent.

In 1957 Julian Huxley, an evolutionary biologist, wrote *Transhumanism* in the belief that "the human species can, if it wishes, transcend itself—not just sporadically, an individual here in one way, an individual there in another way, but in its entirety, as humanity."[10] His mechanism for this transcendence was a progressive eugenics. Huxley was skeptical of the biological notion of race and cognizant of its abuses, so he proposed raising the living standard of the "poorest classes" via a "curative and remedial" program. Huxley knew that education and health care led to people having fewer children. Raising the living standard among the impoverished accomplished two things. Those who never had a chance to meet their potential would finally be able to do so. Those with little potential would live better lives and have fewer children, lessening their effect on the human stock.[11] This philosophy informed much of his work, including as the first Director-General of the United Nations Educational, Scientific and Cultural Organization (UNESCO).

In subsequent decades, personal technologies displaced population eugenics as the expected driver of change. In the 1980s, transhumanists looked to genetic engineering and nanotechnology. In the 1990s, computers and networks led to predictions of artificial intelligences and cyborgs; they also inspired the possibility of becoming posthuman. Mark O'Connell explains this far-fetched notion in his 2017 book *To Be a Machine: Adventures among Cyborgs, Utopians, Hackers, and the Futurists Solving the Modest Problem of Death*. Executives and investors at companies including Google, Microsoft, Facebook, and Tesla speak of a near future of machine intelligence. Some find this worrying. Tesla's Elon Musk routinely warns the public of an artificial intelligence apocalypse. Others eagerly anticipate the rise of machines smarter than us. Of these optimistic Silicon Valley entrepreneurs, O'Connell writes that "these men—they were men, after all, almost to a man—all spoke of a future in which humans would merge with machines."[12] For example, in 2012 Google hired a new engineering director, inventor and transhumanist Ray Kurzweil, to lead its efforts at machine learning. The following year, the company also launched a $750 million biotech company focused on antiaging. Kurzweil is famous for predicting in his 2005 book, *The Singularity Is Near*, that by around 2045 technology will advance so rapidly, as it learns to improve itself, that human life will become, literally, immaterial.[13] Pessimists like Musk fear we will be wiped out. Optimists like Kurzweil think we will merge with our creations and live forever. In any case, Google has both the synthetic and organic bases covered.

Beyond inspiration, the internet gave transhumanists a means to find one another, to cohere. In 1994 *Wired* published "Meet the Extropians," a profile of the latest transhuman advocates. Just as entropy is the universal tendency toward disorder, extropy is an opposing force, pushing us toward transcendence. Transhumanism sees the power of humanistic values, like creativity and reason, as expanding when coupled with technological advances. And extropianism is, in its most recent version, distilled into five principles: boundless expansion (of wisdom, effectiveness, life span), self-transformation (through reason and experimentation), dynamic optimism (rational and action based), intelligent technologies (so as to transcend our natural limits), and spontaneous order (arising from decentralized social coordination).[14]

It might seem like a reach to connect those trying to manage their inbox or migraines with extropians. Yet the latter's five principles encompass the hacker ethos. And Kevin Kelly believes QS *will* address cosmic questions. Elsewhere he writes that extropy is driving us toward the inevitable emergence of an information superorganism.[15] He's not as audacious as Kurzweil, but they are simpatico.

Not every life hacker is an extropian, but both movements are drawn from the same wellspring, the Californian Ideology. As a *New Republic* essay about "the hackers trying to solve the problem of death" put it: the pursuit of "extended youth, neurological enhancement, and physical prowess... carries with it a distinctly Californian air of self-improvement, of better living through technology."[16] This ideology intensifies a trend toward what scholars refer to as "healthism," wherein the struggle for well-being is privatized, categorizing health as an individual virtue and illness as a moral failing.[17] Much as productivity hacking can devolve into an oppressive regime of self-flagellation, health hacking can become an accusatory regime of vigor, with blame falling on those too sick to keep up. Not everyone has the resources of Kurzweil, who for a time employed an assistant to keep his hundreds of supplements straight.

The ultimate irony of the extropian view, of better living through technology, is that the optimal life is achieved only when it ceases to be living, in the biological sense. Until then, though, there are lots of other hacks for being better, stronger, faster—and even smarter.

"Butter Makes Me Smarter"

Back in 2008, among the small group of enthusiasts gathered in Kevin Kelly's studio, there were two men already famous for self-tracking and experimentation.

Tim Ferriss, author of the what was then the recent best seller *The 4-Hour Workweek*, was in attendance. As with the life hacking label, Ferriss does not often mention the Quantified Self, but he does identify as a self-experimenter and has become good friends with Kevin Kelly. Two years after that first QS meeting, Ferriss published *The 4-Hour Body*, a compendium of hacks for tracking and improving the body (e.g., losing fat, gaining muscle, improving sex, and perfecting sleep). With that book, Ferriss took the idea of self-tracking and experimentation mainstream.

Seth Roberts, a professor of psychology, was at the meeting too. Roberts, aged 54, was an expert on rat cognition who split his time between Tsinghua University in Beijing and UC Berkeley. Among enthusiasts, he was already a well-known self-experimenter.

The previous fifteen years of experimentation had taught Roberts a lot. It began with acne. A dermatologist told Roberts that diet had no effect, but Roberts found that also to be true of the antibiotic pills he was prescribed: "I did my best to count the number of new pimples each day. I varied the number of pills I took: Week 1 a certain number per day, Week 2 a different number, Week 3 the first number. The results implied that the pills had no effect. I told my dermatologist this result. 'Why did you do that?' he asked, truly puzzled and slightly irritated." Additionally, Roberts concluded that diet *was* a factor. In addition to benzoyl-peroxide cream, vitamin-B supplements helped, as did cutting out pizza and Diet Pepsi: "Taking all this together, I reduced my acne about 90%. Then, as predicted, it faded away."[18] This

early experience secured a distrust of mainstream medicine and a confidence in his own experimentation.

In the following years, Roberts learned that watching life-size talking
heads on TV in the morning improved his mood. Skipping breakfast and
standing more than eight hours a day improved his sleep. (He theorized
that our prehistoric ancestors spent a lot of time on their feet, ate no breakfast, and saw others' faces first thing in the morning.) Standing, plus early
morning light, also protected him from catching colds. Most significantly,
Roberts found that drinking unflavored sugar water led to significant and
long-lasting weight loss.

Roberts's theory was that foods that smell and taste good make the
body think it is a good time to pack on fat against future privation, so the body
increases appetite. Calories without much smell trick the body into thinking
it is in lean times, so it lessens hunger and the amount of fat to be held in
reserve. Roberts's unusual approach and novel theory were promoted by the
authors of *Freakonomics* in 2005. In 2006, he published *The Shangri-La Diet:
The No Hunger Eat Anything Weight Loss Plan.*[19] The title of the book refers
to a mythical utopia of easy weight loss. And the book sold well, especially
among hacker-types. Hundreds of people posted to the forums on his website with their own experiments, results, and theories. A popular topic was
nose clipping, an easy way of reducing smell and flavor by wearing a swimmer's nose clip while eating.

In the years after *The Shangri-La Diet*, Roberts continued his experiments,
discussing them on his blog, in forums, and in lectures. For example, he
found he could cut down his standing time by standing on a single leg, like a
crane, until exhausted. When his endurance at single-leg standing increased,
he started standing on one bent leg: "I could get exhausted in a reasonable
length of time (say, 8 minutes), even after many days of doing it."[20]

He continued to experiment with his diet as well. One day, he ate some
leftover pork belly—the stuff from which bacon is made—and slept well
and felt more energetic the next day. He set out to confirm this by tracking
his sleep quality relative to whether he ate or abstained from 250 grams of
pork fat a day. A few years later he concluded, "The main thing I learned
was that pork fat really helps. ... How curious we are so often told animal fat
is bad when an easy experiment shows it is good, at least for me."[21]

Just as standing eight hours a day was inconvenient, so was eating pork
belly. Roberts found a more accessible source of fat on a day he couldn't get

Figure 6.1
Seth Roberts on treadmill desk; found at CalorieLab.com.

pork. During lunch at a restaurant, he had two extra servings of butter: "A few hours after lunch, I felt a pleasant warmth in my head. Pork belly hadn't done that. Maybe butter was better for the brain than pork belly. I switched from pork belly to butter."[22] For years Roberts had also been tracking his daily brain function by having his computer time his response to simple challenges, such as adding numbers. After he began his butter diet (half a stick a day, about 60 grams), he noticed that his reaction time decreased, dropping from an average of 650 milliseconds per challenge to 620. His approach inspired others to test caffeine, soy, flaxseed oil, and fish oil.

Even if Roberts was getting a brain boost, he wondered if he was killing himself, as a cardiologist at one of his talks suggested. Roberts concluded the cardiologist didn't understand the evidence regarding the connection between animal fat and heart disease. Also, so-called experts had been "utterly wrong" about diets for years, so he remained skeptical of those who warned against saturated fat, and, more recently, sugar and processed foods. Roberts trusted his data more than experts, and he had a measure of his heart health.

> A few months before my butter discovery, I had gotten a "heart scan"—a tomographic x-ray of my circulatory system. These scans are summarized by an Agatston score, a measure of calcification. Your Agatston score is the best predictor of whether you will have a heart attack in the next few years. After a year of eating a half stick of butter every day, I got a second heart scan. Remarkably, my Agatston score had improved (= less calcification), which is rare. Apparently my risk of a heart attack had gone down.[23]

The sad irony is that this is the last paragraph of a posthumous publication. On April 28, 2014, two days after he died, "Seth Roberts' Final Column: Butter Makes Me Smarter" appeared in the *New York Observer*.

In May of that year, his mother posted to his blog with what she knew: he died from coronary artery disease and an enlarged heart. She had no recent cholesterol numbers, but what she did have showed no heart risks beyond a report of high mercury levels, a likely result of eating fish and living in Beijing. Dozens of friends and fans posted eulogies online. At the 2015 Quantified Self Conference in San Francisco, Richard Sprague spoke of how Roberts had inspired his own experiments with fish oil. Sprague showed a chart of his friend's final month of brain reaction time tests. On April 25, the day before he passed, Roberts's last score was the best it had ever been. Sprague then concluded with a question: Could it be that in trying to maximize reaction times, Roberts and other self-experimenters were only "trading one thing off for another?"[24] He did not know the answer, but he knew what Roberts would have said: "Keep measuring!"

Experts, Experience, and Uncertainty

Sitting in the audience, I felt sad at the passing of someone I knew of online and frustrated by the abrupt conclusion to Sprague's talk. Yes, Roberts would encourage others to keep measuring, *but why*? What does measuring and experimenting give you, especially if you might be harming yourself?

As Wolf notes, self-tracking can be compelling, compulsive even. For analytic types, this tracking and pattern seeking can leave them open to a powerful bias, which has its own allure. *Apophenia* is the human tendency to discern patterns in randomness, to perceive signal in the noise. It can manifest as the *clustering illusion*, when we forget that random data can be clumpy, and as *pareidolia*, when we hear voices in static or see faces in burnt toast. It also leads us toward spurious correlations. If you like finding patterns, the more data you have, the more you will find—regardless of how much signal is actually present. Promiscuous pattern detection is a strength and a weakness, and Roberts thought the balance should err on the side of discovery. Traditional science was too set on incremental improvements. He wanted unexpected correlations and novel theories.

Roberts's acne and butter experiments also arise from two motives discussed earlier: nominal (therapeutic) and optimal (enhancing) hacking. Curing an ailment, such as acne, is a nominal hack; maximizing your abilities, such as brain performance, is an optimal one.

There are also aspects of the digital age itself that make self-treatment appealing, the first of which is uncertainty about expertise. The sociologist Anthony Giddens, among others, believes that Enlightenment thinkers were naive to think humanity could replace magical thinking and arbitrary tradition with the certainty of reason. Reason did not result in a world of "greater and greater certainty, but in one of methodological doubt."[25] This is as it should be. Outside of formal logic, reasoning is never certain, only justifiable. Nonetheless, Giddens's point about naiveté stands, especially in the twenty-first century. The surplus of information online does not mean that everyone is better informed. Rather, it leads some to be naively skeptical and foolishly credulous. Those who still claim vaccines cause autism consider themselves informed and critical thinkers, but their confusion is leading to a recurrence of measles. Even those who want to follow a sensible consensus are confused when this week's health stories contradict last week's. Is coffee good or bad for us, already, and whom are we supposed to trust?

The QS vision stands astride two ways of knowing: there are the claims of *experts* and the insights of our own *experience*. Both of these words are related to *experiment*, and they all derive from the Latin root *experiri*, to try or test. Are we to trust the experiments of experts or our own experience?

On one hand, experts' health recommendations are based on the combination of plausible theories and significant and replicable findings. The latter are typically achieved via two methods. First, researchers look for correlations in large groups of people (e.g., is disease more common among smokers?). Second, they perform experiments (e.g., are those who complete a smoking cessation program healthier than those who are not?). In both cases, large *numbers* of subjects, say $N = 2000$, increase the reliability of the findings. These findings might then prompt or support a plausible theory (e.g., chemicals in smoke damage human tissue).

Large-N studies are the gold standard of science. When done well, they yield findings that are highly probable and applicable. More than that, having different groups of subjects permits us to correct for common cognitive illusions. A control group can reveal that a symptom soon resolves itself anyway. A placebo group can reveal that people improve even when given a sham treatment. An alternative group can reveal that the efficacy, cost, and side effects of an existing treatment remain superior to the new one. As we saw with the reproducibility crisis of chapter 4, a lot of popular health and self-help advice is based on research that falls short of this standard.

Self-experimenters, on the other hand, base their recommendations on their singular experience of one subject, of $N = 1$. They often track all manner of things and look for correlations. For example, Roberts routinely tracked his brain reaction time and noticed it improved when he ate a lot of butter. They also conduct experiments, as when Roberts subsequently varied the amounts of butter he ate to find the right dosage. Self-experimenters do test controls (no standing versus standing) and alternatives (pork fat versus butter). Yet they often do so in a haphazard way. With one person, it's hard to isolate the signal of an effect from the noise of daily life. How do you untangle how much you stood, how many faces you saw, and how much fat you consumed in a day? Also, since acne often does "fade away" as one gets older, a single subject can't easily distinguish between this normal fading effect and the effect of a treatment—and toying with the dosage of antibiotics is not a good idea, especially within the first week.

I don't recall any of Roberts's self-experiments using a placebo—many of his interventions, such as standing, are difficult to deceive *anyone* about, to say nothing of *yourself*. Roberts claimed that because most of his initial discoveries were accidental, they could not be the result of the placebo effect, but it is easy to see a random variation, seize upon it, and confirm it under the placebo effect. And as I read Roberts's sequence of claims about improving sleep (i.e., no breakfast, standing, eating fat, eating honey, taking vitamin D3, and orange light exposure) I couldn't help wondering how effective the previous remedy had been if he needed yet another?

This is not to disparage the role self-experimentation has played in science. There is a colorful history of researchers experimenting on themselves. Pierre Curie taped radium salts to his arm to demonstrate that radiation burns flesh. Pierre and Marie suggested that radiation could destroy cancer (without realizing it also causes it). This anecdote, and other successes, makes it seem as if self-experimentation is well worth it. And if the experimenter succeeds, it may be. Yet the history books are less likely to include the many stories of those who harmed themselves without any gain.

Single-subject studies do have some advantages. Traditional studies, diagnoses, and remedies are based on the notion of average persons, those at the center of a bell curve, rather than outliers.[26] Given that there are billions of people, each of whom has a unique genetic and environmental profile, we are all outliers in one way or another. Self-experimentation is tailored to the outlier self. Also, there is a lot of exciting work going on in the realm of citizen science. The participation of nonscientists in the collection and analysis of data according to safe and rigorous protocols is fantastic. Imagine big data studies, of millions of people, wearing trackers in daily life. (I think of these as big-N studies, $N = 1 \times 5,000,000$.) Doing this rigorously and ethically is challenging but worthwhile.

Health hackers also point out that traditional science and health care have significant problems. Roberts felt that health experts "routinely overstate benefits and understate costs of the treatment they are promoting." The diet recommendations of experts had been "utterly wrong" for years. Roberts wrote that he had been told animal fat is bad, but his pork belly experiment showed that "it is good, at least for me."[27] There is also the simple issue of trust. Is the medical industry really acting on your behalf? Do you even have access to affordable health care? In the United States some people are buying pet antibiotics on Amazon as a low-cost alternative for themselves.

Adding to these problems, the day-to-day experience of health care can be alienating. Kay Stoner finds it disconcerting to rely on those who barely know her.

> We're told that trained professionals are the only ones who are actually qualified to ensure our quality of life. To my mind, that fosters an artificial dependence on (and expectation of) something that's never going to happen—i.e., get everything you need from someone else who literally doesn't have the time to do a thorough job. If your doctor is only allowed to see you for 15 minutes at a time, and you only see them 4–5 times a year, they have all of an hour, each year, to get to know you and your health/life situation. It's unhelpful to all of us.[28]

It is easy to appreciate why people like Stoner turn to health hacking. There is a clear harm against which a benefit might be realized. Chronic ailments, including migraines, diabetes, and allergies, are distressing, and their sufferers seek whatever might help. Tracking and experimentation have proven themselves useful for these conditions, and working with a supportive professional is ideal. Stoner seems to have found this; Roberts did not. However, eating half a stick of butter to shave 30 milliseconds (5 percent) off an arbitrary test of acuity is another matter. There is an unlikely or slight benefit in exchange for uncertain but significant harm.

In addition to personal risk, which hackers do have the right to take, the larger concern is when self-experimenting signals an abandonment of rigor. For all of the problems traditional science and health care have, that doesn't mean alternatives are *necessarily* better. Steve Jobs's dalliance with acupuncture and supplements to treat cancer, over surgery, likely contributed to his early demise. Similarly, a lack of coherent diet advice from the establishment over the past few decades doesn't mean anything goes under the guise of self-tracking and experimentation. Unfortunately, being a bright hacker-type doesn't mean this insight is always taken to heart.

Supplements and Self-Help

In the history of self-help, there is a legacy of gurus who begin their careers selling supplements. In 2000, the same year he graduated from Princeton, Tim Ferriss began selling BrainQUICKEN, which claimed to be "the world's first neural accelerator":

> BrainQUICKEN is a lab-tested performance product scientifically engineered to quickly increase the speed of neural transmission and information processing (perceptual focus, memory storage, and recall), with a prolonged effect of 2–6 hours following each dosage.
>
> Active compounds in the patent-pending BrainQUICKEN complex are supported by clinical research and have been cited in over 4,050 scientific studies. Just 1 of the 18 active components alone has been demonstrated with computer-administered testing to safely increase short-term memory and reaction speed in excess of 35%.[29]

This supplement is what is referred to as a "nootropic," something that enhances cognitive sharpness and retention. Ferriss's supplement, which he sold online, was "guaranteed to produce results in 30 minutes or less, as proven by top students at Harvard, Princeton, Yale, Oxford, and Tokyo Universities."

This type of shady supplement claim is all too common in the United States. Despite BrainQUICKEN's having been lab-tested—whatever that means—there is no evidence of independent and controlled studies. Even if all the ingredients tested as safe, what of their interactions? And the patent-pending claim is just the latest iteration of quackery from the nineteenth century. Quackery is a term derived from *quacksalver*, a medieval "hawker of salve" whose greatest virtue was the loudness of his voice in a crowded market. Subsequent quacks claimed exclusives patents on their nostrums, hence *patent medicine*. I suspect Ferriss submitted a provisional patent application, which is perfunctory and temporary, and permits the filer to claim "patent pending."

Initial sales of BrainQUICKEN were slow, but Ferriss noticed that customers were also reporting physical benefits: "I was hearing from high-level NCAA athletes: 'I'm jumping higher!' 'My time off the blocks is faster!'" So he rebranded the product as BodyQuick and targeted athletes instead: "I thought people wanted to be smarter and they do. They just won't spend $50 on it."[30] As he writes in *The 4-Hour Workweek*, success followed—how much is a matter of speculation—and the stress of it all prompted him to flee overseas. There he learned to manage his business from afar and write a book about what he learned.

Ferriss is not the first supplement salesman to become a self-help guru. In fact, there's a lineage of supplement salesmen, from those on the road, to those on television, to those online.

In 1953, John Earl Shoaff was at a seminar on the "laws of success" in Long Beach, California. The talk was given by J. B. Jones, founder of a nutritional supplement company. Jones was a traveling supplements salesmen who also gave self-help talks. Shoaff was so inspired he joined Jones and followed his example of seminars and supplement sales. Shoaff would eventually found his own supplements company, and the pattern was repeated again when he was joined by Jim Rohn.

Rohn's 1985 book, *7 Strategies for Wealth & Happiness: Power Ideas from America's Foremost Business Philosopher*, is a compendium of wisdom passed on from Shoaff to Rohn. Rohn was hired by Shoaff after they met at a sales conference, and for the next five years, Rohn said, he "learned many of life's lessons from Mr. Shoaff. He treated me like a son, spending hours teaching me his personal philosophy."[31] Shoaff died relatively young, but Rohn had the torch well in hand and continued with supplements and seminars. In the 1970s, Rohn took Tony Robbins under his wing, and Robbins, at the age of seventeen, became a promoter of Rohn's seminars.

Robbins is likely the biggest self-help guru in the States—despite the subtitle of his biopic *Tony Robbins: I Am Not Your Guru* (2016). Instead of a traveling salesman, he is an infomercial star selling seminars over the airwaves. (He also sells supplements, of course.) When Robbins appeared on the *Tim Ferriss Show*, he and Ferriss discussed the profound influence of Jim Rohn. Ferriss, a collector of quotes, remarked that he was amazed at how many misattributed quotes originated with Rohn. And as a kid with insomnia, Ferriss watched lots of infomercials late at night. When Ferriss launched his early ventures while in college, he looked to them as his template. In addition to keeping a three-ring binder of persuasive ads, he'd call in to infomercials so as to deconstruct their sales scripts and tactics, which is evident in his Brain-QUICKEN marketing.[32] Ferriss continues Rohn's legacy by offering his supplements and self-help online.

Despite this tradition, Ferriss is an unrivaled pharmacological compendium. As one reviewer of *The 4-Hour Body* writes, "Mr. Ferriss talks up a witches' brew of juices, nuts, potions and drugs. Here's a typical burp from an early chapter: 'Overfat? Try timed protein and pre-meal lemon juice. Undermuscled? Try ginger and sauerkraut. Can't sleep? Try upping your saturated fat or using cold exposure.'"[33]

These kitchen interventions, like many supplements, are *mostly* harmless, but experimentation is not without its dangers. Ferriss once gave himself severe diarrhea by experimenting with megadoses of resveratrol. This compound is found in wine and may increase endurance and longevity—at least in rats. Ferriss wanted to impress the folks at a sports science lab with his endurance and took a bunch of tablets on his own without realizing they also contained a laxative. He was stricken with intense cramps and profuse sweating and remained on a toilet for forty-five minutes—an endurance record of a different sort.

Ferriss and others find supplements and self-help quotations compelling because they are tools: small, easily consumed boosts to body and brain—or so they believe.

It Works for Me

Hacker culture has been fostered by three San Francisco Bay Area publishers. We've already met Stewart Brand (of *Whole Earth* fame) and Kevin Kelly (*Wired*, *Cool Tools*, and QS). The third is publisher Tim O'Reilly, whose firm's technical books are beloved by programmers. Like Brand and Kelly, he is a convener, organizing conferences on tech-related topics. At these conferences, neologisms and movements emerge, including *Web 2.0* and *open source*. Recall that *life hacking* was first discussed at an O'Reilly conference, that O'Brien and Mann first wrote about it in a column for O'Reilly's *Make* magazine, and that they were supposed to publish a book for O'Reilly's Hack series.

When Tim O'Reilly joined Kevin Kelly on the *Cool Tools* podcast, he shared some of his favorite supplements: "They are kind of magical...they don't work for everybody." For colds, O'Reilly recommended a combination of Gan Mao Ling and black elderberry: "Some people find this to be quack medicine, but I think of my dad, who was a neurologist, talking about acupuncture and saying 'It doesn't make any sense, but if it works, it works.'" And Stewart Brand turned O'Reilly on to an antiaging and energy supplement: "Brand said you got to try this and I did and...I felt like it took 10 years off my life." O'Reilly especially appreciates that the supplement is touted by Bruce Ames, a famed Berkeley biochemist, who "says it doesn't work for him, but the science says it should work. I like that he acknowledges that it doesn't work for everybody."[34]

In both of O'Reilly's recommendations, he touches on the fundamentals of science, of plausible theories and rigorous results. However, his examples fall short of a high standard. Acupuncture's theory of energy meridians doesn't make any sense, and rigorous studies show no results. Scientific theory says the energy supplement Brand recommended should work, and the results are inconsistent, but it works for Brand and O'Reilly. Neither acupuncture nor the supplement are supported by solid theory *and* results, but they seem to work for some people and so they are "kind of magical."

Why do we find "kind of magical" and "works for me" thinking even among the rationally minded?[35] As already discussed, the Enlightenment, modernity, and the digital age can be characterized by *increasing* levels of uncertainty. People then look for ways to fill the void, especially in the face of personal suffering.

Beyond the penchant for experimentation, there is the inherent optimism of the hacker mind-set. With the right amount of understanding and cleverness, we should be able to hack the limitations of the human body. This belief isn't founded in the supernatural but by way of extrapolation. Some high-tech innovations scale at an exponential rate. So technologists like Ray Kurzweil take their supplements in hopes of reaching the moment when the advances of biotechnology outpace the declines of old age. Other Silicon Valley executives are attempting to forestall aging via eight-thousand-dollar blood transfusions from the young.

This belief in technology is not unfounded, and a first significant step toward an extraordinary future is already under way. An envisioned benefit of the Quantified Self is personalized medicine: tailoring interventions to patients' specific biology and history. For example, for decades we have known that about 25 percent of breast cancer patients have a gene that leads to excessive amounts of cellular growth receptors (HER2 proteins). These patients often receive a drug that targets this protein. With better gene sequencing and patient tracking, such customization could become commonplace. But we're not there yet.

Another explanation for this type of thinking is that, simply, it is human nature to trust one's lived experience, regardless of caveats about placebo effects and confounding variables. I am prone to this myself. At the onset of a cold, I start taking zinc lozenges. Research evidence for their efficacy is weak to none, and zinc can lessen your ability to taste. But I've seen colds dissipate after my lozenge regime and have never had long-term effects. It works for me. In turn, my spouse swears by her "hot toddies," a lemon, liquor, and honey drink. The merit of these two interventions is that they are long known, innocuous, and cheap.

Everyone is entitled to using his or her harmless pet remedies. But that which is novel, unlikely to be safe or effective, and a source of someone else's profit deserves scrutiny. The claim "if it works, it works" only works when the intervention is more effective and less costly (in money and risk) relative to sham treatments and proven alternatives.

Soylent, Choice, and Control

Rob Rhinehart applies the hacker ethos to every domain of his life. He's a minimalist and appreciates challenges. Rhinehart has run his home on a single 100-watt solar panel and once undertook the challenge of using no more than four liters of water a day. He calculates that instead of washing dirty clothing, it is more efficient and green to regularly donate it to charity and order custom clothing from China—a calculation reminiscent of Tynan throwing away pennies and nickels. And when it comes to eating, he believes he can engineer a nutritious meal replacement.

In a 2013 post entitled "How I Stopped Eating Food," the software engineer wrote of the benefits of his thirty-day experiment with an early version of Soylent, a powdered shake. Rhinehart studied textbooks and Food and Drug Administration (FDA) publications and ordered constituent nutrients online. As he blogged about it, others commented and made suggestions. He offered free batches of his mix to those who would send him blood work: "Bonus points for getting a psych evaluation before and after. The brain is an organ."[36]

Rhinehart's own results were extraordinary. He reported that he had healthier skin, whiter teeth, and thicker hair, and his dandruff was gone. He felt like the Six Million Dollar Man: his physique had improved, his stamina had increased, and his mental performance was sharper than ever. His awareness was elevated, and he found music more enjoyable. Rhinehart marveled, "I notice beauty and art around me that I never did before." In terms of his "quantified diet," his cravings and tastes finally matched his needs; he had "full visibility and control" over what was going in to his body."[37]

I was aware of Soylent from Rhinehart's blog from early on but was skeptical *because* of all of these purported benefits. He sounded like a high-tech quacksalver with a less-than-palatable elixir. Throughout much of its history, from version 1.0 in early 2014 through version 1.7 in late 2016, Soylent users complained of gastric distress and flatulence. ("Version 2.0" is the ready-to-drink version launched in 2015.)

As the product matured, Rhinehart discontinued the health claims and shifted focus. In 2015, he declared that Soylent was "perhaps the most ecologically efficient food ever created."[38] Elixir was out, and efficient food was in. If it didn't improve health, it would at least provide convenient nutrition for a low cost. Yet early in 2017, his blog was replaced by an enigmatic quote from Ralph Waldo Emerson: "Undoubtedly we have no questions to ask which are unanswerable." That is, anything we might ask has an answer, if we have sufficient perseverance. I suspect he took down his website at the behest of Soylent's investors and lawyers. Apparently, taking down his website was not enough. Later in 2017, Rhinehart stepped down as Soylent's CEO—taking instead the title of Executive Chairman. Soylent enthusiasts feared investors wanted Soylent as a high-end niche product rather than a universal solution to nutrition.

In any case, and independent of work on this book, I know a number of folks who have used meal replacements for breakfast or lunch. And as with the dominance of quantification, the privileging of experience over expertise, and the allure of high-tech gadgets, their reasons for consuming Soylent speak to their personality and the character of the digital age.

—

I met Ron A. at a park where our dogs played together. From our brief conversations, I knew he was a software engineer, and he knew that I had written a book about Wikipedia. We were fellow geeks. By the way he dressed, I also suspected he would be a good source for this book. Ron often wore a colored T-shirt with the day of the week printed on it. At midweek he wore a green "Wednesday" T-shirt; on the next day he wore a "Thursday" T-shirt in navy blue. When I interviewed him, he said the shirts were part of an effort to "make a 'uniform' of simple repeatable things to wear in order to reduce daily routine cognitive load."[39] Ron Googled such clothing to see whether it existed, and, indeed, shirts of this type could be had at the site Minimalist Tees—now defunct. Many other geeks and designers have done something similar, including Steve Jobs with his blue jeans and black turtlenecks.

A complement to the uncertainty of the digital age is our extraordinary amount of choice: we are invited to rate, like, click, and swipe every facet of life. Although this sounds wonderful, paradoxically, choice can be anxiety provoking as we waste time deciding what to choose and then second-guessing ourselves.[40] Some look to celebrities for direction. Thousands believe that if something is sold on Gwyneth Paltrow's goop.com it must work, including "Wearable Stickers that Promote Healing (Really!)" Although hackers appreciate choice and complexity in specific domains, they seek to simplify everywhere else. Gear lists and minimalism are two such approaches to simplifying their relationship to stuff: prioritize what is valuable and discard everything else. As minimalism is to stuff, meal substitutes are to nutrition.

Soylent allows Ron to simplify: to save on time (shopping, cooking, and cleaning), money (it is an inexpensive source of nutrients), and waste (it can keep for weeks). He consumes it for lunch, except when he goes out with coworkers.

I asked Ron what prompted him to try Soylent, and he explained it was related to his interest in bitcoin, the online crypto-currency. Ron followed Rhinehart's early experiments and noted that "as a fellow software engineer," he related to Rhinehart's approach to nutrition. When Rhinehart announced he would accept bitcoins in the crowdfunding of a salable product, Ron pitched in.

Lee Hutchinson, senior editor at *Ars Technica*, writes that Soylent divides people into those who are repulsed by the idea and those "desperate to receive their orders." The latter turn to Soylent because they are "geek types" for whom cooking is a "fuzzy" analog process, which prompts anxiety. (Baking, in contrast, is thought to be more deterministic.) Also, it helps people with unhealthy relationships to food.

> Soylent is food methadone. It's not quite the magic food pill from science fiction, but it does have a lot of that pill's qualities. It's satiating without being delicious; eating it won't provide the endorphin rush that overeaters experience when gorging; and it's easy to prepare. It's a thing you can replace snacks or some meals with (or even all meals, if you want), without having to fight urges. Or, to put it another way—when you're used to eating chicken nuggets and hot dogs exclusively, the effort that might go into either making a healthy salad or going to a restaurant and ordering one might seem overwhelming next to just eating some more nuggets or just ordering the hot dog. Soylent, then, can be just a thing that fuels your body without triggering anxiety or more depression about eating the wrong thing.[41]

It seems paradoxical that some Soylent users are delving into the minutiae of nutrition and blood work, whereas others choose Soylent for its simplicity. The very idea of choosing simplicity seems paradoxical. But for hackers, not so much.

As we've already seen, hackers are happy to invest time and energy up front if they end up with a system to use in the future. As Tynan wrote about the benefits of automation: "I love one-time investments that pay off over the very long term. The reason I call my books *Superhuman* is because you can often achieve results that look superhuman just by setting up lots of easy systems. . . . And you get to keep those benefits for a long time with little or no maintenance."[42]

Also, life hackers appreciate abstraction and modularity, which they use to master complex systems. Imagine that in a software application I need to sort a list of names. Without caring about how it works, I can pass my names to the sort() function, and it returns a sorted list. In this way, sorting is modularized: I don't need to know the details. Should I need to get into the details and implement my own version, I can, but otherwise I defer to sort(). When Rhinehart wrote that he had "full visibility and control," this meant that he and other enthusiasts could engineer the Soylent formula, but most users need not bother. Because the process is transparent, they can join the conversation should they need to, but once they've done their initial investigations, they can save themselves the cognitive load of preparing a meal.

In short, hackers are used to working with complex systems and many choices, but they set good defaults at the start so they can focus on what most interests them. As Colin Wright wrote about minimalism: "It's cutting out the things you don't care about—that you don't need—so you can invest more of yourself in the stuff you're passionate about."[43] As it was with software and stuff, so it is now with food.

Wanting to Believe

Like Kevin Kelly and Gary Wolf, Chris Anderson is another prominent *Wired* alumnus, having served as editor-in-chief from 2001 to 2012. Anderson began tracking early on, shortly after Kelly's first meeting, with lots of questions in mind. In April 2016 he tweeted that "after many years of self-tracking everything (activity, work, sleep)," he had decided it was "~pointless. No non-obvious lessons or incentives :(."[44] In response to his tweet, some folks defended the practice: they learned which food caused weight gain, they enjoyed plotting their data, and supposedly someone had self-diagnosed a disease missed by professionals. A few were keeping at it in the hopes that better analytics in the future might yield insights. Others agreed with Anderson and shared their disappointment or their frustration with unreliable devices and data. Stewart Brand replied: "Being lazier than Chris, I only lasted a few months self-tracking. Not all mirrors are windows."[45] Self-tracking proved to be a near enemy of self-knowledge. When Anderson was asked why he had persisted for so long, he tersely responded: "Wanted to believe."

This chapter has been about QS's vision, which is directed inward, toward "self knowledge through numbers." Kelly and others believe any resulting insights might also address big questions of the distant horizon: What is human? Are we necessarily biological and mortal? Both the prosaic and cosmic questions are compelling. First, who doesn't want to sleep better, stay fit, and be rid of all the embarrassing and painful nuisances of the body, especially as it ages? Self-tracking and experimentation can be useful, when done with care. However, despite Kelly's suggestion that answers "will be found in the personal," the personal is not a panacea: "it's working for me" may, in fact, not be. Second, anyone who grew up with bionic heroes will find the idea of cyborgs and machine intelligences intriguing. Some believe this to be a worthwhile aspiration, and it gives them hope in the face of an uncertain future. However, this vision of immediate benefits and distant possibilities is not always clear sighted.

We've seen that the digital age's abundance of information and choice can be overwhelming. We are uncertain about whose advice to follow, whom to trust. Hackers like Roberts, naturally, choose to take it upon themselves, to trust their own systems and formulations of how to live well, often for good reasons, but not always with good results. Hackers tend to be an optimistic lot; they want to believe, if for no other reason than to have a sense of control and meaning. As I noted earlier, Kevin Kelly's pinned tweet is that "over the long term, the future is decided by optimists."[46] Transhumanists, extropians, hackers, and optimizing optimists aren't simply predicting the future, they are working to make it. With the help of experiments, systems, and supplements, they strive to be superhuman: stronger and smarter—even if only by 30 milliseconds. Yet those running toward the future, with their gaze fixed on the distant horizon, can also easily miss the approaching edge.

7 Hacking Relationships

In 2005 a little-known subculture was placed in the spotlight by Neil Strauss's best seller *The Game: Penetrating the Secret Society of Pickup Artists*. The book's central character is an aspiring illusionist who goes by the stage name Mystery. For years Mystery had been a prolific contributor to online seduction forums. There, pickup artists (PUAs) discuss their theories about seduction and post field reports of their real-world sorties. *The Game* portrays the inception and unraveling of Project Hollywood, a group of PUAs living in Dean Martin's former Los Angeles mansion. Tynan, digital nomad and self-help superhuman, was a participant in the project, and he writes that the latter half of the book portrayed "Mystery and I teaching workshops, me stealing his girlfriend (twice), Courtney Love moving in, my second attempt at going polyphasic, and a bunch of other great stories."[1] The book was a sensation because its stories of masculine hijinks and dissolution can be read as tabloid, character study, how-to manual, *and* cultural indictment. It has something for everyone.

Many of the men portrayed in *The Game* capitalized on the book's popular reception—even if much of that attention was critical. Those running seduction seminars and workshops expanded their businesses. Tynan followed with *Make Her Chase You: The Guide to Attracting Girls Who Are "Out of Your League" Even If You're Not Rich or Handsome*. Mystery wrote *The Mystery Method: How to Get Beautiful Women into Bed*, which was followed by a VH1 reality show.[2]

Mystery describes his method for seduction as an "algorithm for getting women." The only math most of his readers care about are the digits "of the girl in the tight sweater," but an algorithm is key to a solid game, and he claims, "I invented that algorithm."[3]

Life hackers use systems and algorithms in every domain of life. Recall Paul Buchheit's belief that "our entire reality is systems of systems" and that "wherever there are systems, there is the potential for hacking." As evidence, Buchheit cites Tim Ferriss's kickboxing, Seth Roberts's health hacking, and *The Game*.[4] Even within computer hacking, *social engineering* is a potent security exploit. Hackers use impersonation and guile to convince targets to reveal their passwords. If computer security can be hacked with social engineering, why not social interaction itself?

The idea that everything is a system calls to mind the expression about everything looking like a nail to someone with a hammer. This aphorism has a handful of variations, including Abraham Maslow's 1966 musing: "I suppose it is tempting, if the only tool you have is a hammer, to treat everything as if it were a nail."[5] Thinking about life hacking in light of this has two virtues. First, it highlights the power of metaphor: in life hacking, systems can be understood as games and hacking as a tool. Second, Maslow's Hammer implies a critique: that possessing a tool can distort one's vision and lead to the tool's being misused. Hacking is a powerful tool, and for those that believe reality is "systems of systems, all the way down," everything appears amendable to its force. But as we will see, overreliance on a tool can lead to heartache.

"Why I Will Never Have a Girlfriend"

You can't understand relationship hacking without appreciating something about geek identity. To be a geek is to be outside the mainstream, often ensconced in a subculture. Geeks are not, stereotypically, known for their social skills; rather, their defining traits are intelligence and their enthusiasm for computers, games, and comics. Geek identity, then, is characterized by feelings of insecurity and superiority relative to the mainstream, often simultaneously.[6]

This juxtaposition is seen in a 1999 classic of internet lore, "Why I Will Never Have a Girlfriend." In it, Tristan Miller, a computational linguist, presented "a proof, using simple statistical calculus, of why it is impossible to find a girlfriend." He dismissed the possibility that there was "some inherent problem with me." It wasn't awkwardness or a lack of fashion sense; rather, it was a matter of numbers: there aren't that many suitable women. Miller began his calculation with the requirement that a woman must be two standard deviations above the norm for beauty; she must also be intelligent, but she doesn't have to be as intelligent as she is beautiful. After further winnowing by age, availability, and reciprocal attraction, Miller was left with thousands of possible women across the globe. But these gems were lost in the population at large; if he went on a blind date with a new woman every week, it would take over three thousand weeks before he dated one of these women: "we can safely say that I will be quite dead before I find the proverbial girl of my dreams."[7] Miller wrote this, tongue-in-cheek, almost twenty years ago, and it shows how insecurity about having no girlfriend can be masked with the pretense of superior mathematical reasoning.

Today, on the bitter fringes of online culture, men speak of being "incels" (involuntary celibates). In time, they might take the red pill (a reference from *The Matrix*), awaken, and join the other MGTOW (men going their own way). The *Rational Male*, also the title of a blog, is trapped in a system in which his desires are either ignored or exploited by the likes of gold diggers.

Pickup artists, though, have not yet lost hope. They believe that the AFC (average frustrated chump) can be transformed into an alpha male. (Masculinist culture is laden with pop-culture references, jargon, and abbreviations.) The PUA uses his reasoning to discern the patterns of seduction and to learn the algorithm by which his desires can be fulfilled rather than exploited.

Scholars of this subculture believe that these feelings of insecurity are potent. Matt Thomas argues that pickup and life hacking attract the same sort of "white male geek" and that a "post-industrial 'crisis of masculinity'" underlies both. Pickup artists cope by hacking seduction: "They have reversed engineered it and reduced it to a series of steps, scripts, and procedures that any man—theoretically—can follow and be successful." "Is it any surprise," he asks, "that Tim Ferriss and Neil Strauss are friends? Or that one of the episodes of 'The Tim Ferriss Experiment' is about him learning how to pick up women? Or that in that episode Ferriss consults with [computer] hacker Samy Kamkar?"[8]

Complementing the geek's insecurity is a sense of rational superiority, sometimes manifesting as braggadocio. Upon discovering pickup culture, one famous computer hacker wrote: "I'm what PUAs call a 'natural,' a man who figured out much of game on his own and consequently cuts a wide sexual swathe when he cares to." Fortunately, other hackers "don't have to be helpless chum in the dating-game shark pool. We have some advantages; with a little understanding of human ethology we can learn how to use them effectively."[9]

Learning how to deploy their geeky advantages is what Mystery offers his readers.

> I was a geek, too. The truth is, generally speaking, geeks are intelligent individuals who simply haven't yet applied that intelligence to social scenarios. ... When you look at all other human beings as beautiful, elegant biological machines embedded with sophisticated behavioral systems designed to align with others to maximize their chances for survival and replication, the task of understanding humanity and your place in it becomes surmountable. ... With me as your friend and guide, you'll start uploading Venusian arts programming into your behavioral system and then practice and internalize it so you won't have to think about picking up.[10]

In short, the successful pickup artist is a reformed geek, one who has reprogrammed his behavior to hack that of others: insecurity gives way to superiority. The self-help sell is that the average frustrated chump will be frustrated no more, with the right tools in hand.

The Origins of Pickup

Mystery's claim that he invented the algorithm for seduction is disingenuous. He did, however, make significant contributions to its latest iteration. As a performer, he brought flare (known as "peacocking") and new routines for establishing rapport with strangers. He excels at eyeliner and feather boas, at parlor tricks and mind reading. But modern pickup culture can be traced back at least fifty years.

There were two things about the 1970s that gave rise to pickup culture: the sexual revolution and the computer as a metaphor for the mind. The sexual revolution meant that people could more easily engage in sexual trysts. Eric Weber's 1970 book *How to Pick Up Girls* spoke to the man who could have sex outside of marriage but didn't know how to make it happen. Weber assured his readers that "normal, healthy young chicks like sex" and they "will be glad to have sex with you if you only ask them." For example, peace rallies are great places to pick up "fantastic broads," "even if you're [privately] for war."[11]

Weber's book is deeply creepy and written from the perspective of male entitlement and female objectification. Weber infamously begins the book with a scenario of seeing a woman walking down the street: "You've just got to see more of her long legs. Her fine rounded breasts. Her high, firm behind. For an instant you even consider rape."[12] This dark legacy persists in pickup today. In language, women are objectified and quantified by way of a 1–10 "Hot Babe" scale. In practice, one pickup guru who endorsed psychological abuse and physical coercion was banned from traveling and teaching seminars in some countries. Pickup manuals have also been banned from the Kickstarter crowdfunding site because of similar concerns. This is self-serving and other-harming ideology, sold as pickup tips and relationship advice. Beyond the harm done to its targets, it warps the attitudes and character of those who read it.

In addition to increased sexual opportunities, popular culture in the 1970s reflected the growing power of computing. Although computer matchmaking can be traced back to Harvard undergrads in 1965, computing's contribution to pickup in this period was by way of metaphor. Much of the theory behind pickup is an extension of neuro-linguistic programming (NLP), which began in the 1970s as an attempt to identify the techniques of successful therapists. NLP was cast in the mold of ascendant technology: language was a way of programming the neural machine. It claimed to be the "art and science of excellence" and promised that the communication skills of "top people" could be learned by anyone.[13] Much of NLP understands the self and communication as maps or models, shaped by stepwise processes.

NLP has since been discounted as legitimate psychotherapy; one scholarly review characterizes it as "cargo cult psychology."[14] Nonetheless, it has been influential among self-help gurus, including Tony Robbins. Scott Adams, creator of Dilbert and self-help author, readily acknowledges NLP's influence. In an interview with Ferriss, Adams traces his interest in persuasion and hypnosis back to these roots and recommends that listeners think of their lives as a system. He begins his book *How to Fail at Almost Everything and Still Win Big* by explaining, "Your mind isn't magic. It's a moist computer you can program."[15]

Even though NLP was intended as a means of self-improvement, it was most tightly embraced by those wishing to seduce others. Ross Jeffries, a proponent of "speed seduction," incorporated NLP and hypnosis into pickup in the 1980s. With the help of a computer hacker, Jeffries also took his approach online, founding the Usenet group alt.seduction.fast in the 1990s. Many pickup gurus, including Mystery, got their start there. Jeffries continues to be active in the scene today—and a little resentful of the attention the latest generation of gurus has received.

The overlap between NLP and pickup is seen in their shared concepts, including *accessing cues, anchoring, mirroring,* and *reframing.* For example, accessing cues are eye movements that reveal internal mental states. Mirroring builds rapport or reinforces behavior by mimicking others' subtle behaviors. Jeffries's uses these notions, and the suggestive power of metaphors and homophones, throughout his writing. In a 2011 blog post, he wrote of a hypnotic-like interaction with a German woman, his friend's assistant. When Jeffries spoke a little of his high school German, she complimented him on his pronunciation. He responded: "I find languages have a certain feeling and a CERTAIN SHAPE IN YOUR MOUTH. When it's right you can FEEL IT IN YOUR MOUTH."

> She thought about it a moment and said. "That's very true. I speak a little French and it feels much different in my mouth."
>
> I said, "That's right. French is very soft. But German is VERY HARD IN YOUR MOUTH." (This time I leaned on it a bit and put more of a sexual tone to it.)
>
> Her pupils dilated for a moment, she took in a deep breath, and visibly reddened. As she did I gently nodded my head "yes" and she mirrored it back, nodding gently in return without being aware of it.[16]

Because he had a girlfriend, Jeffries practiced "hook 'em, catch and release," but he encouraged his readers to try to use the same techniques in their conversations with women. Practice makes perfect even if—at that moment—you aren't able to follow through.

Jeffries's story is a weird combination of crassness and pseudoscience. Language is powerful, but it's not magic. Conceiving of the brain as a computer and a relationship as a system has both advantages and limitations. The idea that we can change ourselves and our surroundings is a useful one, but it can be taken too far. I doubt dropping "new direction" into a conversation is going to make women more receptive to a "nude erection," as Jeffries suggests. I suspect the German woman was simply being polite to her boss's friend.

In this way, seduction hacking is like some of the claims of health hacking: marginal science is overextended to questionable applications via anecdotes and testimonials. Nonetheless, for the lonely and systematic thinker, the allure of behavioral patterns and systems is obvious.

Optimal: Two Bisexual HB10s

People are desperate to reduce life's complexity, and this is not limited to men or hackers. Whereas Jeffries released *How to Get the Women You Desire into Bed* in 1992, Ellen Fein and Sherrie Schneider published *The Rules:*

Time-Tested Secrets for Capturing the Heart of Mr. Right in 1996.[17] In the latter book, readers were encouraged to become "rules girls" by following thirty-five precepts for attracting and keeping a husband—the books' gender stereotypes complement one another nicely. Despite Fein's marriage's falling apart during the release of *The Rules*, she and Schneider followed with other rules-based relationship books. Fein, of course, blamed her divorce on *not* following her own rules.

Even if rules-based approaches to relationships are not unique to men or the new millennium, they are more potent in the twenty-first century. The excesses of rating others and of treating others (and yourself) as rules-based "wet machines" is facilitated by the ease of quantification and optimization. In the 1970s, the metaphor of programming was enough to shape how people interacted with one another. Today, actual programs shape our interactions—as we like, swipe, and rate others on our smartphones.[18]

In the search for human connection, bedding an HB10 (a 10 on the "Hot Babe" scale) and capturing a successful man become goals that are optimized toward ill-fated ends. If there is a moral to *The Game*, this is it. The drama of Strauss's book is the alpha male's crash after his elation at no longer being a chump. Strauss succeeds as the PUA known as "Style," but in doing so realizes that "all the techniques that are so effective in beginning a relationship violate every principle necessary to maintaining one."[19] Seduction can be the near enemy of connection. Additionally, even the goal of getting laid or finding a girlfriend, he found, had been displaced by the need to maintain his status among his male peers. Strauss later declares himself a sex addict and checks himself in for treatment—the topic of his next book. Mystery ends up in a psychiatric hospital as his failed pursuit of having two bisexual girlfriends—both 10s, ideally one Asian and one blond—knocks him askew. The danger of optimizing is that it is easy to fixate on that which is tempting, quantifiable, or easy at the expense of other goals and values.

Skilled programmers are actually sensitive to this danger. Although people naively use terms like *programming* and *optimization*, junior programmers are warned that "premature optimization is the root of all evil." When coding, it is easy to fall into the trap of optimizing something without appreciating whether it is causing an actual performance bottleneck. It's like perfectly dicing your onion with a well-honed blade without ensuring you have all the recipe's ingredients first.

Those who design optimizing algorithms especially appreciate this point—they speak of local optima that fall short of a global optimum. Imagine you are blindfolded but wish to find a tall hill within a specified region. A naive search algorithm is to take steps only forward or up; you will likely find a hill, but probably not a tall one. So designers intentionally introduce fuzziness into their algorithms and allow them to wander a bit, even if it means sometimes going downhill before reaching a higher peak. Naive optimization often yields suboptimal results, and optimal results often require some flexibility—a point I'll return to at the end of this chapter.

An experienced and skilled life hacker might be able to design a well-balanced and globally optimal system. This is what Nick Winter attempted when hacking his productivity by also tracking health and social goals. But such a system is unlikely for anyone other than the dedicated hacker who is willing to quantify and optimize *everything*. Otherwise, the danger of optimal hacking is to naively optimize on finding an HB10 or a successful husband. For many, such goals are not easily achieved, and when reached, are found to be shallow and unsatisfying.

To put this in terms of Maslow's Hammer: if you have an optimized hammer, it will serve brilliantly for pounding a screw into drywall. The problem is that when you stand back to enjoy the picture you just hung, the screw is not likely to hold.

Nominal: The Challenge of Being Likable

Not everyone wants to optimize toward a harem or wealthy husband, but many still lack the skills and confidence for more modest aspirations. To this end, hackers take on challenges as a step toward even the nominal goal of not being alone.

Challenges are a favorite tool of the life hacker. For example, surviving a cold shower lends a sense of efficacy independent of, but transferable to, other life goals. Similarly, the shy and hesitant can undertake rejection therapy. In pickup, approach anxiety is countered by repetition. A student will approach a dozen women in an evening, with the possibility of receiving as many rejections. In the process they learn, become less fearful, and possibly succeed. This is not limited to pickup. One life hacker sells decks of cards with challenges, which can be used alone or as part of a game with others. The "Entrepreneur Edition" includes "30 unique suggestion cards designed to expand your comfort zone and your wallet." For example, "Ask for one month free from a service provider."[20]

Unlike a lot of pickup books, Tynan's are not focused on manipulation. *Make Her Chase You* and *Superhuman Social Skills* are thoughtful—and systematic—suggestions on how to be a likable person. His goal is to teach the reader "how to share the best parts of you in an honest and authentic way."

> In this book, I will be unabashedly analytical, examining and quantifying aspects of social skills that are usually not spoken about. We'll talk about power dynamics, our value as friends, opportunity cost, and efficient use of time. Whether or not we acknowledge these, and other, factors, they underpin our social interactions and play an enormous role in the quality of relationships in our lives. Some find these topics unpalatable, or even offensive, but it's hard to make a better sausage if you don't take a look at what's going inside the factory.[21]

Even if this approach is analytical, Tynan's aspiration is humane. How can we reconcile Tynan's mission with the unpalatable PUA tactic of *negging*?

In *The Game* Strauss defines *negging* as an accidental-seeming insult or backhanded compliment: "The purpose of a neg is to lower a woman's self-esteem while actively displaying a lack of interest in her—by telling her she has lipstick on her teeth, for example, or offering a piece of gum after she speaks."[22] This was the sort of negging critiqued by Randall Munroe in his webcomic XKCD, popular among geeks. In a 2012 strip, a man attempts to neg a woman in a restaurant (figure 7.1). He notes her fruit plate and says, "You look like you're on a diet. That's great!" She turns the tables and blisters the PUA (life hacker) with disdain, telling him that his epiphanies about productivity, creativity, and connection are hopeless because his mediocrity is inherent.[23]

As a fan of XKCD, Tynan felt obliged to respond. He conceded that there are plenty of assholes, within pickup and without, male and female: "Bad people exist." Yet the point of a neg, contra Strauss, is not to undermine a woman's confidence. It is, instead, a way of showing you're not intimidated, that you're willing to relate to someone in a joking and teasing way, as you would among friends. Tynan finds the woman's response in the comic harsh but appropriate "given that she was just approached by a random stranger and tactlessly insulted." Even so, he finds the comic to be cynical and hypocritical because it implies mediocre men should be left to suffer—and inflict themselves on others—without any hope of improvement: "When a guy is faced with the harsh truth he has to improve himself to have a better dating life, he can either ignore that and dismiss pickup

Figure 7.1
Randall Munroe, "Pickup Artist," XKCD, 2012, https://xkcd.com/1027/.

wholesale, or he can begin down the difficult road of learning social skills, understanding women, and becoming the kind of guy that girls want to be with. That's what pickup is."[24]

That's what pickup is, as long as it avoids the excesses of optimization. *Make Her Chase You* provides interpersonal tools for the man seeking to be attractive, even if "not rich or handsome." As the catchphrase from the home improvement parody *The Red Green Show* states: "If the women don't find you handsome, they should at least find you handy." In this case, *handy* means good with the tools of self-presentation and interaction. Tynan seeks to teach the unskilled how to use these tools, increasing utility and safety for all. However, when they are weaponized and used as a means of maximizing the quantity and optimizing the "hotness" of the women seduced, pickup deserves the criticism it receives.

Data and Dating

Amy Webb, a "quantitative futurist," was saddened and disappointed by the breakup of her last relationship. Sadness is expected when someone who was once close becomes part of the past, but her disappointment was related to the future. She had just turned thirty, and the prospect of starting over imperiled her plans for a family. In a popular TED talk, "How I Hacked Online Dating," Webb spoke of a calculus similar to that behind Miller's explanation of why he had no girlfriend. In Webb's estimation, there were only thirty-five men of a similar age, "Jew...ish," not interested in sports, living in Philadelphia, and whom she would find attractive. If she wanted to find such a man, she could no longer rely upon happenstance. She would have to go online.[25]

But if online dating improved Webb's chances of finding Mr. Right, it also increased her exposure to the Mr. Wrongs. After a series of bad dates, including one who abandoned her with an exorbitant dinner bill, she realized she needed a filter.

Webb's philosophy is that of a hacker. When faced with a problem, she says, "I'm going to use some data, run it through a system, and get to a solution." She devised a rating scheme of differently weighted traits, divided into two tiers, and set a minimum threshold. Among first-tier traits, being cigarette and drug free was worth ninety-one points. On the second tier, a height between 5'10" and 6'2" was worth fifty. She would no longer waste her time on anyone with a total below seven-hundred points. Problem solved—except it wasn't. She might have cracked the code for finding a Jewish Prince Charming, but he never messaged her back.

Webb's calculations hadn't taken into consideration that she was competing with other women. Her profile of frumpy photos and text pasted from her resume wasn't working. So she created fake profiles of ten men she would like to marry and analyzed the attributes of the popular women contacting these fake accounts. She found that her competitors' profiles were short and nonspecific and used optimistic language. They had nice photos, which showed a bit of cleavage or shoulder. When she applied these insights to her own profile, she became the most popular person on the site.

Webb is not the only one to have hacked online dating, been the subject of popular attention, and followed with a book. Two years after he was profiled in *Wired*, Christopher McKinlay published *Optimal Cupid: Mastering the Hidden Logic of OkCupid*.[26] OkCupid matches people based on user-created questions and answers. Like Webb, McKinlay used fake profiles to collect answers to common questions from thousands of women. He used these data to identify and target clusters of women he found appealing and tailor his approach, without being deceitful, so he would be similarly appealing.

Although Webb and McKinlay both created fake profiles, Webb to assess competitors and McKinlay to target candidates, their approaches differ in a significant way. McKinlay gave little thought to winnowing the chaff. He did rank his candidates, but he also went on *eighty-eight dates* before finding someone he would begin a relationship with. In the end, he considered the endeavor a success, but it sounds exhausting.

If only there were a way to delegate some of this work, which is what Tim Ferriss naturally did. Whereas others made use of spreadsheets and code, he used outsourcing. As a way to get attention for *The 4-Hour Workweek*, he delegated the finding and scheduling of dates to competing teams throughout the world, including India, Jamaica, Canada, and the Philippines. He gave each team a one-page spec sheet with goals, guidelines, and links to women he found attractive. His teams were able to schedule twenty café dates into three days, all within half a mile of his home: "It worked extremely well. Perhaps a 70% hit rate," which far exceeded his efforts at bars and parties.[27] And it cost him only $350, including the $150 bonus he established for the team that set up the most good dates.

Online dating exemplifies the systematization of life, even for those who do not share the hacker ethos. Thanks to digital technology and its creators, we have an extraordinary amount of choice, which we manage via swipes and likes, providing a stream of data to algorithmic matchmakers. Given that hackers built these online dating systems, it makes sense that other hackers are well suited to exploiting them.

Such exploits, of course, are not without their perils, especially when it comes to the high-frequency dating of McKinlay and Ferriss. Ferriss felt bad about mistakenly giving the cold shoulder to a woman with whom he was supposed to be having a date because one of his outsourcers had neglected to put her in his calendar: "She walked right up to me, I was writing on my laptop, and started chatting like an old friend. I had absolutely no idea what was going on."[28] I imagine she felt the same, but worse. Another hacker, Sebastian Stadil, went on 150 dates in four months—topping even McKinlay. This led to some blunders, including with "a girl who had spent the entire first date telling me a very sad story about her being an orphan. On our second date, I asked her how her parents were doing. That was an awkward moment. If you're reading this, I apologize."[29]

Even so, most every hacker concluded his or her approach was a success. Ferriss, Webb, and McKinley all thought so—but they were also selling books. Stadil is the exception. He writes, "I still believe technology can hack love, though that belief is likely irrational." Why? He confesses that "having more matches increased my odds of finding someone interesting, but it also became an addiction. The possibility of meeting that many people made me want to meet every one of them, to make sure I wouldn't miss the One."[30] Stadil's insight is about the paradox of choice in the digital age: with many options, it is easy to look to the horizon and imagine greener fields.

The hacking mind-set, especially an optimizing one, is especially susceptible to this pathology of the digital age. Much like the productivity hackers who obsessively hone their tools without ever getting on to the task, the dating hacker, if not careful, is liable to never move on to the task of building a relationship.

Yootling and Marriage

The life hacker is, above all else, a rational *individual* seeking *self*-help, even when it comes to relationships. We have already seen criticisms of this and of millionaire minimalists and philosopher bachelors. But not all life hackers are millionaires or bachelors. We encountered Heidi Waterhouse's "life-hacking for the rest of us," including those with kids. Dave Bruno had to distinguish between family and personal items as part of his *100 Things*

Challenge. Similarly, in 2012 Nick Winter had been inspired by Tynan to only have ninety-nine things, but he later acquired a wife and two kids. He does not include their stuff in his annual list. When I asked Winter how his new family affected his minimalism, he responded that his intention is to restrain his personal appetite, which isn't a problem with baby stuff: "If I were loading up on baby toys, then I'd have to modify the rule." He concedes he no longer has the benefits of being able to move in an hour, backpack for months at a time, or live in a tiny home, but he still appreciates having only a few high-quality things of his own.[31]

What happens when we move beyond stuff, toward marriage, children, and chores? In the course of his productivity hacking, Winter made use of the application Beeminder. To balance his work productivity, he gave himself social goals, such as romantic dates and platonic outings. Recall from chapter 4 that with Beeminder, if you fail to meet your goal, you forfeit your pledge to its creators, Bethany Soule and Daniel Reeves. This couple, with graduate degrees in machine learning and computational game theory, also use monetary exchange to manage their marriage.

Soule and Reeves's unusual approach to their relationship has been featured on *NBC News*, and Soule is forthright about how it works on their blog. At the center of their system are the values of egalitarianism (everyone's happiness is equally important), autonomy (everyone has their own values and can make their own choices), and fairness (equal contributors to group effort should benefit equally). The last is so important they named their daughter "Faire"—at eight years of age, she was said to be the youngest Beeminder user, tracking things like sugar consumption and screen time.[32] Their son, Cantor, is named after a nineteenth-century mathematician.

In short, Soule and Reeves keep individual financial accounts and bid on things like putting the kids to bed, taking out the trash, and planning a trip. In a process similar to rock-paper-scissors, Soule and Reeves each hold their hands behind their back and simultaneously reveal a dollar amount they would pay the other to do the task—they call this "yootling." The person with the higher number pays the loser's bid. If Soule flashed a four and Reeves a two, Soule would then pay Reeves two dollars to take out the garbage. From an economic point of view, this is an efficient allocation. Soule least wanted to do it since she was willing to pay four dollars, and she happily pays the two dollars at which Reeves was happy to do it. (They have additional rules to simplify the record keeping, such as randomly recording only 10 percent of their yootles.) Reeves sees this as a distillation of bartering and turn-taking. For Soule, "it ends up feeling a lot more amicable than feeling each other out and making compromises, and trying to guess between what a person is saying and what they actually mean and navigating all that kind of stuff."[33]

Even so, it's not difficult to foresee where things might get difficult. Their children might be hurt to learn their parents bid on who tucks them in at night. However, given they are being brought up this way—Faire's name was determined by an auction between her parents worth several thousand dollars—I don't imagine the kids would be surprised. There is also the matter of producing children in the first place. Soule and Reeves don't yootle in the bedroom, but most everything else, from the value of giving birth to that of staying at home with the kids, needs to be reckoned, which is nontrivial.

If this sounds cold and miserly, Soule explains that it is possible to be kind and generous using the system: "We do nice things for each other all the time, and frequently use yootling to make sure it's socially efficient to do so." For example, Reeves doesn't *have to* accompany Soule to a *Buffy the Vampire Slayer* sing-along, but he might kindly yootle for it: "He magnanimously decides to treat his joining me as a 50/50 joint decision. If I have greater value for him coming than he has for not coming, then I'll pay him to come. But if it's the other way around, he will pay me to let him off the hook."[34]

As geeky as this sounds, Reeves and Soule appreciate it as such. Even so, they are not alone; similar approaches have appeared in the mainstream. The authors of *Spousonomics: Using Economics to Master Love, Marriage and Dirty Dishes* recommends using concepts like division of labor and supply and demand to minimize conflicts and maximize the benefits of marriage.[35] Whereas the Beeminder couple keeps economics out of the bedroom, *Spousonomics* begins with the case of an unenthusiastic woman considering the costs and benefits of sex with her horny husband.

Mismatched libidos are something that Ferriss thinks about too. He is fond of a story about a married couple and how they manage their different needs. Every quarter, the wife gives her husband a report card covering four categories: lover, husband, provider, and father. In each category, she rates him on a ten-point scale, and the husband can have a low score in one as long as he keeps the average up. Hence, if the husband succeeds at work, increasing his provider score, he can also have a dalliance, lessening his husband score. As long as the husband keeps his total score above the wife's minimum threshold, it's okay. Ferriss finds this "very appealing, maybe as I like measuring things as a way of course-correcting and keeping things in check."[36]

If clear expectations and communication are necessary to good relationships, all of this sounds exemplary. Except as you can imagine, critics find such quantified relationships troubling—with a side of cringe when it comes to sex. The question, then, is why the discomfort?

"You Are Doing It Wrong"

When Soule and Reeves's story of an exchange-based relationship was published, it attracted a few responses from far-flung corners of the internet. Luke Zaleski, a writer at *GQ*, finds the game-theoretic bidding of "these two imbeciles" to be misguided: "folks like the Pay-for-Play couple in Oregon, YOU ARE DOING IT WRONG."[37]

In their defense, Soule and Reeve appreciate that their approach is unusual. It is geeky, but their app and blog has a small following among the like-minded. For such folks, yootling can feel more comfortable than figuring out the meaning behind others' words. Perhaps Soule and Reeves are deficient in the interpersonal skills necessary for "navigating all that kind of stuff," but it is what it is, and they are who they are. They are geeks sharing what works for them—rather than gurus *prescribing* their approach as best. Also, Zaleski doesn't say much about how to "do it right" beyond alluding to sacrifice and selflessness. Reeves and Soule are not opposed to such virtues, they simply strive to make their allocation fair. For example, they explicitly recognize the value of giving birth and spending time with their kids; at least such things are not taken for granted. This approach would not work for most people, myself included, but I can't claim they are "doing it wrong."

Elsewhere on the web, Sarah Gould, a blogger at *Catholic Insight*, thinks yootling sounds mercenary. Shouldn't love and help be given freely within a family? She also believes yootling ignores "God and the higher realities of life": "Might this elevation of fairness to god-like status contribute to an inability to deal with the unfairness of life?"[38] In her view, we ought to recognize that life is unfair but that God's grace is freely given.

Gould's critique is bound to a particular religion, which not everyone shares, and "higher realities" are invoked but never explained. She concedes that people need to find what works best for them and that yootling seems to work for this pair of nerds. Yet for her, reducing love to "weights and measures" would extinguish genuine gratitude and make a farce of love and a false god of fairness and money.

Even secular critics make arguments about the transcendence of human behavior and life's unfairness. In her 2000 book *Cyberselfish: A Critical Romp through the Terribly Libertarian Culture of High-Tech*, Paulina Borsook wrote about this a few years before life hacking's emergence.

> With cause, many programmers are *proud* of the rule-based bounded universe they create; so if simple propositional logic were all that were operating in human affairs, then human affairs might very well be fixable through simple rules. But game theory, powerful as it is, can't explain all of human behavior. ... In addition, dealing in rule-based universes can put you in a continual state of exasperation verging on rage at how messy and imperfect humans and their societies are.[39]

However, Soule and Reeves do recognize the importance of love, selflessness, and generosity. For them, yootling is a clear and playful way of expressing these things. And just because human behavior is complex, it doesn't mean there is a ghost in the gap between what we can explain and what we cannot. Yootling need not extinguish the deeper bonds that form from years of exchange.

Borsook, like Gould, questions how hackers face life's difficulties, including "messy and imperfect" people. I share this question—it's the topic of the next chapter—and it is reminiscent of an episode of *Seinfeld*. In "The Deal," Jerry and Elaine discover that even with clever rules (e.g., sleeping over is optional and no phone call the next day), they cannot have casual sex and remain friends. Feelings can be hurt and jealousies stirred even within the perfect system.

Although humans are messy and imperfect, Gould and Borsook sound defeatist. If you have nails popping up from the decking of your flooring, why not hammer them down? You might miss one and later stub your toe, but that does not damn your earlier efforts. Life hackers do tend to be less accepting of imperfection than is typical, but this is both a strength and a weakness. They optimistically seek improvements, which leads to inventiveness *and* credulity. There are lessons to be learned from those hacking relationships, but complaints that they are too weird and ungodly do not suffice.

The most concerning thing about relationship hacking emerges when quantified and transactional approaches are dehumanizing and exploitative—which they have a tendency to be. For example, in outsourcing, there can easily be an imbalance of power, in which choice is more a reflection of necessity than preference, in which the other is objectified via market imperatives, in which deceit and opaqueness obscure the context and consequence of exchange. We see elements of this among unsavory PUAs and industrial-scale dating, but less so among mutually consenting geeks.

The Right Tools for the Job

Like any tool, some metaphors are more appropriate to their contexts than others. As I argue in chapter 1, calling life hacking a "cult" is hyperbolic, but referring to professional lifestyle advisors as "gurus" is a decent fit. What about relationships as rules-based games? Some things are more game-like than others, and some people are more likely to enjoy playing, but the metaphor is apt. We can discern rules (some explicit, some implicit), and there are elements of luck and skill. What's more, life is increasingly game-like, given the proliferation of rating and gamification on our devices. Yet there are also assumptions about whether the game is competitive or cooperative and what counts as victory. As Strauss and Fein found, becoming adept at seducing a woman or capturing a man is not necessarily a win. Their notion of games and rules assume rigid stereotypes and zero-sum competition. Fein and Schneider's Rule #5 is to never call a man and rarely return his calls, keeping him uncertain and insecure. A PUA playing the game might neg a woman to the same end. An alternative is to conceive of relationships as a cooperative and jointly beneficial undertaking. For example, Soule and Reeves conduct aspects of their relationship in transactional terms, but their intention is to respect each other's "utility functions" rather than exploit them.

Maslow famously used the hammer metaphor to communicate the danger of overusing a tool, observing, as noted earlier in the chapter, that we tend to treat everything as a nail when a hammer is in our hand. A stronger version of Maslow's intuition is that we not only *treat* everything as a nail, we *see* it as such. What, then, are some of the limitations of seeing relationships as systems to be hacked with rule sets and spreadsheets?

Consider the case of Valerie Aurora, who in 2015 returned to the dispiriting task of online dating. This time, she hoped she might make the experience palatable, fun even, by hacking dating. Inspired by Amy Webb, she developed a spreadsheet for ranking candidates on the basis of two top-level categories: "dealbreakers" and "extra credit."[40] Aurora also included five attributes of interpersonal chemistry: ease/closeness, fun, safety, mutual respect, and affection/passion.

However, a weakness of the spreadsheet approach is the assumption that an excellent match is out there and waiting to be rated and ranked. An alternative assumption is that people invest and grow in their relationship, that a good match is not found but made. Aurora eventually came to this insight with respect to her spreadsheet and dealbreakers.

> My original intention for making this tool was to make me more aware of and responsive to my "dealbreakers"—things that meant a relationship wasn't possible. But while making and using this tool, I discovered that my own ideas about what was a "dealbreaker" were frequently wrong. I am now in a happy relationship with someone who had six of what I labeled "dealbreakers" when we met. And if he hadn't been interested in working those issues out with me, we would not be dating today. But he was, and working together we managed to resolve all six of them to our mutual satisfaction. Talking to my friends, I found that this was a pretty common experience.[41]

To hold too tightly to the spreadsheet's dealbreakers would've been to hold too tightly to a tool not fit for the task.

Among computer programmers, there can be a similar overreliance on behavioral rule sets. Programmers often rely on what they call "patterns" of successful structures and best practices. Antipatterns, in turn, are to be avoided. The problem is that programmers can get stuck using the patterns, tools, and practices with which they are most familiar and proficient; they refer to this as the Golden Hammer antipattern—yes, overusing patterns is an antipattern.

This can be seen in the case of David Finch, a former semiconductor engineer, who chose a journal of best practices as his relationship tool. In his "quest to be a better husband" he compiled a list of best practices, which he later published as a memoir. These rules included things like taking his wife's perspective, going with the flow, and having fun. He made great use of these practices until they started getting in the way; at that point he realized "the final best practice: don't make everything a best practice."[42] Sometimes a favorite tool needs to be put aside.

We might put a tool away for a number of reasons. Maybe the job is done, as with Finch's best practices. Maybe the tool is inappropriate or dangerous, as Strauss realized about pickup and meaningful relationships. Maybe it doesn't work, as we might infer from Fein's divorce. Maybe it needs to be used less rigidly, as with Aurora's spreadsheet of dealbreakers. When it comes to relationships, the game really is to build and maintain something together, for which there is no single tool.

8 Hacking Meaning

Dale Davidson was adrift. He had graduated college and been accepted into Navy SEAL training, just as he had been working toward. Yet several months in, he dropped out for reasons he's still unsure of. It would have made sense if he had another option in mind, but he didn't: "I was thrust back into 'civilian life' and felt aimless." It was as if he had set his sights on a big wave, paddled out to catch it, but then let it pass underneath. He was afloat with no sense of what to do next. Then he came across Tim Ferriss's *4-Hour Workweek* (4HWW) and envisioned making easy money while working remotely from an exotic beach—an alternative title for Ferriss's book was *Broadband and White Sand*.

Earlier we learned how Maneesh Sethi, like Davidson, had been inspired by Ferriss. Sethi set out to live the 4HWW lifestyle. Sethi managed to create an absentee business (writing content to attract Google AdSense money), travel the world (doing push-ups on animals), quadruple his productivity (by paying someone to slap him), and invent the Pavlok wrist zapper. Davidson's efforts, though, did not work out.

> After I dropped out of Navy SEAL training in 2010, I spent a few years trying to become a "digital nomad" by moving overseas to Egypt to teach English and start an online business. Though I enjoyed the adventure, my business did not take off and overall, I wasn't any happier. I tried to double down on all the Lifehacker and Tim Ferriss tips by trying to test new business ideas out and becoming super productive, but something was still missing. I felt stuck, like I was spinning my wheels.[1]

In 2014, Davidson tried something different. He turned away from Ferriss and *Lifehacker* and began an experiment, an "ancient wisdom project." He hadn't abandoned the hacker approach, just the source of his inspiration.

Davidson would focus on eight different spiritual traditions that had survived for more than five hundred years: "Ancient wisdom is robust; lifestyle design blogs are fragile." His challenge was to adopt a practice from an ancient tradition every thirty days in the hope of cultivating a virtue.

> I learned from Stoicism that to maintain our tranquility, we need to cultivate a certain level of detachment from things outside your control. I learned from Catholicism that to add meaning to our lives, we should focus less on what we want and focus more on the servings. Epicureanism taught me that we are bad at enjoying ourselves, and that true pleasure comes primarily from avoiding things that bother us.[2]

Clearly, life hackers are looking for more than tips on how to tie their shoes. Even if their approach is unusual, they seek what most people want: comfort, health, and connection. Often, life hackers first pursue near enemies: fierce efficiency, optimal fitness, and tidy interactions. They go about this in their characteristic way, as rational individuals fond of systems and experimentation, to varying degrees of success. Because of their fondness for self-measurement and management, they have been called control freaks. Yet like Davidson, some will realize that much of life is outside of their control, that even as they pursue a good life, they will confront disappointment and loss. In one of Ferriss's books, he equates living the good life with VIP treatment at restaurants and bars.[3] But there is another notion of the good life, that of a meaningful life despite its disappointments. To riff on the Serenity Prayer, life hackers seek the cleverness to hack what can be hacked and the Wisdom 2.0 to know and accept what cannot.

When it comes to hacking meaning, to making sense of disappointment and loss, life hackers often translate principles and practices from ancient traditions. Davidson's experiment was unusually eclectic; life hacking, more generally, pulls from two sources. From Stoicism, life hackers adopt a way of coping with loss and a lack of control. From Buddhism, they borrow the aesthetics of Zen and the practice of mindfulness. Translation, however, is always accompanied by drift. Some things are exaggerated, others elided. When Stoicism is understood as a "personal operating system" and mindfulness as a "performance enhancing tool," what is lost in translation? To answer this, we must understand something of the source text, its appeal, and the mindset of its translators.

The Ancient Stoics

Some life hackers tend toward extremes. For example, we saw digital minimalists quit their jobs, pare down to a hundred things, and move to a new country every few months. For some, in time, this lifestyle became its own sort of fetter. The minimalists had escaped the enemy of too much stuff, only to fall prey to the near enemy of too little. Consequently, many abandoned the minimalist label and stopped keeping as careful a count of their stuff. They embraced moderation.

This appreciation of moderation is shared with the ancient Stoics. As a life philosophy, Stoicism is a set of principles and techniques for blunting life's hardships and enhancing its joys. The ancient Stoics took a middle path between the competing schools of the sensual Hedonists and ascetic Cynics. Seneca the Younger, Roman statesman and author, cautioned that "philosophy calls for simple living, not for doing penance, and the simple way of life need not be a crude one."[4] The simple life is one in which you can appreciate what you have and not despair over what you don't. But achieving such equanimity is not easy.

In the previous chapter, we saw criticism of a couple who strive for fairness in their marriage by bidding on chores. Critics worry that the couple is unrealistic, given that people are imperfect and life is unfair. Although disappointment is inevitable, this position is defeatist if taken to imply we shouldn't bother. Such efforts are worthwhile, even as they are frustrated. The challenge is to remain engaged with life, nonetheless. Whereas some turn to supernatural beliefs—or belief in the power of supplements, cryogenics, and sentient machines—Stoics seek equanimity by way of two practices. They prepare for inevitable loss, appreciating what they have in the present. And they acknowledge they have little control over the external world, turning inward to shape their own disposition.

Ancient Stoics did not shy from recognizing discomfort and loss. In *Letters from a Stoic*, Seneca warned: "Winter brings in the cold, and we have to shiver; summer brings back the heat and we have to swelter....These are conditions of our existence which we cannot change." Even so, we can experiment with hardship to see if it is as bad as we fear. Seneca suggested setting aside days "during which you shall be content with the scantiest and cheapest fare, with coarse and rough dress, saying to yourself the while: 'Is this the condition that I feared?'"[5] In other words, "Is that it? That wasn't

so bad." Stoics also run experiments in their minds via negative visualization known as *premeditatio malorum*. The Stoic who asks "Could this disaster befall me?" will never cry "How could this happen to me?" The point
is not incessant worry, but occasional contemplation. This allows Stoics to
prepare for all eventualities, take the sting out of upsets and, more important, be grateful for what they have. There's little sense in ruminating about
a past that is done or pining for a future that may never come. By experimenting with discomfort, Stoics steel themselves against misfortune and
become more appreciative of the present.

In addition to exaggerated fears of loss, we also imagine we have far more
control over life than we do. We are sorely disappointed when our most fer-
vent hopes and best-laid plans fail us. Stoics attempt to focus on what can
be controlled, on reasoning and disposition. As Epictetus, a Roman slave for
much of his life, wrote: "External things are not within my power; choice is
within my power. Where am I to seek the good and the bad? Within myself, in
that which is my own."[6] Marcus Aurelius, a Roman emperor, often reminded
himself not to let others annoy him: "Do unsavory armpits and bad breath
make you angry? What good will it do you? Given the mouth and armpits the
man has got, that condition is bound to produce those odors."[7] Perhaps
the man could be reasoned with and given hygiene tips, but beyond that, it's
not something you can change, even if you're the emperor, so why get upset?
On the flip side, Cato the Younger thought it foolish to worry about what
others thought of his appearance, so he was purposefully unfashionable, so
as to elevate his choice over the arbitrary judgment of others.

Given Stoicism's fondness for experimentation and reliance on reason,
life hackers' fondness for Stoicism should not be surprising.

Stoicism's Translators

Stoicism has of late been experiencing a renaissance of a sort. In addition
to appearing on *Lifehacker*, *Boing Boing*, and *Study Hacks*, it is discussed in
the pages of *The New Yorker*, *The Atlantic*, *The New York Times*, *The Wall Street
Journal*, and even *Sports Illustrated*. This is in part because of the willingness
of two academic philosophers to return to the field of practical philosophy.
William Irvine, author of *A Guide to the Good Life: The Ancient Art of Stoic Joy*,
believes that although practical philosophy is no longer taught in school, the
need to make sense of life remains.[8] In addressing this need, Irvine is joined

by fellow philosopher Massimo Pigliucci, author of *How to Be a Stoic: Using Ancient Philosophy to Live a Modern Life*.[9] Pigliucci is responsible for a number of highly placed opinion pieces extolling Stoicism.

In addition to these two philosophers, two life hacking gurus have greatly contributed to Stoicism's popularity: Tim Ferriss and Ryan Holiday. Near the end of his interviews with guests on *The Tim Ferriss Show*, Ferriss asks a bunch of questions as part of his rapid-fire Q&A—these are also the basis of his 2017 book *Tribe of Mentors: Short Life Advice from the Best in the World*.[10] For example, what book have you given to others the most and why? It's a good question. Giving a book is a profound communication: I hope this will be meaningful to you and help you better understand me. When Ferriss answers this question himself, he estimates he's given away over a thousand copies of Seneca's *Letters*. Believing that busy folks prefer audio books, Ferriss also published an audio version in 2016, *The Tao of Seneca*, segments of which he includes on his podcast.[11] The importance of Stoicism for Ferriss is even seen in the fine print of his online content, which is owned by Seneca and Marcus, LLC. Through his blog, podcast, and audiobook, Ferriss has expanded Stoicism's reach, especially in Silicon Valley.

Like Ferriss, Ryan Holiday is more showman than engineer, and they both excel at hacking systems of attention and success. Like Tony Robbins, Holiday began his self-help career as an apprentice to an existing guru, Robert Greene, author of *The 48 Laws of Power*.[12] (Robbins was seventeen when he went to work for Jim Rohn; Holiday dropped out of college at age nineteen to work with Greene.) From there, Holiday went on to promote authors, brands, and musicians using tactics that courted controversy, including risqué American Apparel ads and various media stunts: he purchased billboards on behalf of a client, surreptitiously vandalized them, and then publicized the vandalism to attract attention. Holiday quickly turned his work—and notoriety—into a career as an author. He began with business best sellers: *Trust Me, I'm Lying: Confessions of a Media Manipulator,* in 2012, followed by *Growth Hacker Marketing* the following year.[13] *Growth hacking* is used to describe self-help for start-ups, which has been described as "traditional marketing's aggressive, automated, and masculinely-coded baby brother."[14]

Soon thereafter, with Ferriss's help, Holiday pivoted from growth hacking to meaning hacking. The two men connected back in 2007 over their common appreciation of Seneca. In 2009, Ferriss invited Holiday to write a long guest post entitled "Stoicism 101: A Practical Guide for Entrepreneurs."

Interest from book publishers followed. Five years later, Holiday published his first book of practical philosophy using the hero format: telling the story of an accomplished subject and extracting a life lesson connected to some bit of insight. He had the titles of his subsequent 2014 and 2016 books, *The Obstacle Is the Way* and *Ego Is the Enemy*, tattooed on his left and right forearms, respectively, to remind him of the aphorisms' importance. Holiday was also one of the first guests on Ferriss's podcast, and Ferriss published the audio version of *The Obstacle Is the Way*, which he also excerpted on his podcast. In 2016, Holiday distilled all of this into a book of quotations for each day of the year.[15]

Some find Holiday's pivot vexing. In major newspapers, Holiday's media manipulation and hacking has been described as deceitful, disturbing, and chilling. An unflattering *New York Times* article accused Holiday of using these wiles to sell "Stoicism as a life hack": "He is like a snake-oil salesman who swears he has abandoned snake oil, but not the highly effective sales tactics."[16]

These two prolific promoters, then, are our translators: porting source material for an audience of ambitious type-A personalities—as Ferriss often describes himself and his audience. You might already guess how this will color the source materials' translation.

The Stoic Life Hacker

Even absent Stoicism's renaissance and its promotion by Ferriss and Holiday, you can see parallels between it and the hacker ethos. Tynan, the former professional gambler and pickup artist, demonstrates this in a post about "Emotional Minimalism."

> In the same way I strive to need almost no possessions, I also want my emotional needs to be minimal. What does that look like? I think a simple test is to think of how long you could remain in solitary confinement and be okay. I think I could last there indefinitely and, in fact, there's some appeal to the idea. ...
>
> Meditation is good training for this. So is just cold-turkey removing your favorite stimulating activities and dealing with whatever arises in your mind. ...
>
> Once you achieve some level of emotional minimalism (mental minimalism really sounds like a euphemism for stupidity), you find a different sort of satisfaction from it than you get from more stimulating times. You'll appreciate both for what they do for you. For me, spending a week at home eating the same food every day, drinking tea, and doing work, is a great week. I feel energized and satisfied with the progress I make.[17]

Such an attitude is also helpful in his poker playing, in which emotional upset is anathema to sound game play. For example, Tynan did well in the 2015 World Series of Poker and tells of making it to the final twenty players. Sitting to his left was a stronger player, with three times as many chips, but the guy had a "bad beat," "went on tilt," and blew through his money. Even if others have better technical skills, Tynan believes he has better "emotional mastery, nothing is going to affect me."[18] In any case, in the excerpted post we see an appreciation of simple pleasures, a desire for equanimity, and a willingness to consider deprivation. Tynan is acting the Stoic though he never mentions the word; he later told me he had no philosophy in mind when he wrote about his ideal disposition, "but I suspect most of my original ideas aren't as original as I think they are."[19] Beyond Tynan, it is not difficult to find other examples of Stoicism's intersection with the life hacker ethos of rationality, systematization, experimentation, and individualism.

For the Stoics, reason was the defining characteristic of being human and a necessary tool in pursuit of the good life. Although they spoke of gods, they did so without supernatural supplication. Zeus was not asked to intervene; rather, the Stoics felt obliged to be the reasonable beings Zeus created them to be. Because the life hacker ethos aligns with the rational style, Stoicism's focus on reason is appealing. And for those who are religious, Stoicism is not necessarily incompatible with their beliefs. In *A Guide to the Good Life*, Irvine writes that Stoicism complements Christianity nicely and that there are also parallels with Buddhism. In fact, his own interest in Stoicism began as part of a project about human desire, which led him to Buddhism. He wondered if this research would result in his becoming a Buddhist, but he "came to realize that Stoicism was better suited to [his] analytical nature."[20]

For the analytically minded, Stoicism can be understood as a system of principles and rules. Ferriss typically describes the philosophy as a personal operating system for making better decisions in a high-stress environment. When Ferriss invited Holiday, then twenty-one years old and working at American Apparel, to write "Stoicism 101" for entrepreneurs, Ferriss prefaced the piece by referring to the philosophy as "a simple and immensely practical set of rules for better results with less effort."[21] Long before life hacking emerged, the French philosopher Michel Foucault also noted the Stoics' fondness for formulating rules of conduct. Foucault included such rules among his *technologies of the self*, which enable people to transform themselves "in order to attain a certain state of happiness, purity, wisdom, perfection, or immortality."[22] In this regard, Foucault's technologies of the self anticipated life hackers and their fondness for Stoicism.

Those rules are validated and optimized, of course, by way of experimentation. We've seen life hackers challenge themselves to work maniacally, to live minimally, to do push-ups, and to talk to strangers. Other Stoic-like challenges includes taking cold showers, which is central to a number of life hacking regimes.[23] Ferriss and some friends conducted a multiweek no-complaining experiment, and it doesn't get much more Stoic than that. Ferriss's "No Booze, No Masturbating" thirty-day challenge was unusually candid and entrepreneurial: more than six thousand people signed up for the challenge at coach.me, a site in which Ferriss is an investor. Following Seneca, Ferriss has also undertaken one-week practicing-poverty experiments. And following Cato, Ferriss once wore ugly "party pants" and grew a "creepy porn mustache" "so as to inoculate myself to superficial attachment to what others think."[24]

Finally, Stoicism is suited to an individualistic and competitive digital age, one of get-rich dreams and fail-fast realities. Just as it was "popular with the educated elite of the Greco-Roman Empire," Holiday writes that Stoicism is perfect for the entrepreneur of today: "it's built for action, not endless debate."[25] Ferriss notes that Stoicism is being adopted by "thought leaders in Silicon Valley" and players in the NFL "because the principles make them better competitors."[26]

It's striking that, like minimalism's, Stoicism's target audience is so skewed toward the elite. In response, Epictetus's status as a slave—*Epíktētos* means *acquired* in Greek—is called upon as evidence that anyone can benefit. But even here, it is coupled with a rags-to-riches story. Before he was freed, Epictetus was an educated slave who served at court; his own master was a wealthy freedman. What of a loincloth-to-nothing story? In *A Guide to the Good Life*, Irvine argues that a man with only a loincloth can still be happy that he at least has that. If the man were to lose his loincloth, he could *still* be content in his good health: "It is hard to imagine a person who could not somehow be worse off."[27] This is true, but it appears that this sort of imagining is reserved for clever folks with much more to lose than a loincloth—similar to entrepreneur Paul Graham's belief that he'd still be happy as the lowest rung in a super-rich society.

Minimalism and Stoicism can be of use to anyone, but empirically, they are most appealing to those who believe in the merit of hustle and who have much to lose.

Mindfulness and Its Translators

In the popular imagination, Zen is associated with the beauty of a bonsai tree, the elegance of a brush stroke, and the ceremony of drinking tea. Similarly, when programmers discuss the essence of an elegant technology, they speak of its zen. "The Zen of Python" (the Python of the title being a programming language) famously begins:

> Beautiful is better than ugly.
> Explicit is better than implicit.
> Simple is better than complex.
> Complex is better than complicated.[28]

Life hackers, too, have a fondness for this type of aesthetic. They read *Zen Habits* on their Macbooks. They practice material (and emotional) minimalism and thrive under daily routines. Some even engage with Asian culture directly. Ferriss majored in East Asian studies at Princeton and speaks Japanese and Mandarin. Tynan met with his Japanese tutor at Samovar, a San Francisco tea lounge—where you can buy "Tynan's Traveling Tea Set" for $69.

For the most part, this affinity is distant from deeper spiritual beliefs or practices. Even though Buddhism has principles similar to those of Stoicism (e.g., both stress equanimity in the face of impermanence), Stoicism is more accessible to Western life hackers. Buddhist teachings, or *sutras*, reflect their origins as an oral tradition with many redundancies and enumerations. Stoics wrote in Latin, making for easier translation into English and other Western languages. Buddhism is deeply embedded in Asian cultures in which myth, veneration, and chanting are common. Stoicism requires nothing so alien or, possibly, superstitious. Nonetheless, beyond aesthetics, there is another element of Zen that life hackers are fond of: meditation. Just as with Stoicism, our understanding of this practice is influenced by what is selected and how it is translated.

There are many types of Buddhist meditation to choose from. In mantra meditation you repeat a phrase as the object of meditation. With koan meditation you ponder a statement while awaiting insight. During Tibetan Tonglen meditation you visualize the transformation of suffering into compassion and healing. Metta (loving-kindness) meditation is similar, involving visualization of well-being and ease for yourself, a loved one, a neutral acquaintance, a difficult person, and all living beings. (You work your way up in an empathy spiral.) In mindfulness meditation, you pay attention to the present moment. Following your breath while sitting is popular, but mindfulness can also be applied to walking or drinking tea—anything really.

Out of all this source material, it is mindfulness that has received the greatest attention among techies and life hackers. Its translators include secular researchers, engineers, and app designers.

Mindfulness's current success is due, in large part, to the efforts of Jon Kabat-Zinn. In the 1970s, as a young doctor, Kabat-Zinn studied Buddhism and believed that meditation could be useful to a wider audience. While at the University of Massachusetts Medical School, he developed the Mindfulness-Based Stress Reduction (MBSR) program to help patients manage pain. In the following decades, research by Kabat-Zinn and others demonstrated the therapeutic benefits of secular meditation. The MBSR program went mainstream with the publication of Kabat-Zinn's 1991 book, *Full Catastrophe Living: Using the Wisdom of Your Body and Mind to Face Stress, Pain, and Illness.*[29]

Not surprisingly, meditation and life hacking intersected in California. In the mid-1800s, the San Francisco Bay Area served as a new home of Buddhist immigrants from China, Japan, and Korea. A century later, this immigrant culture intersected with the American counterculture. In 1959 Shunryū Suzuki arrived in San Francisco to serve as the priest of its Soto Zen temple. He quickly gained a following among Americans, and his Zen Center became a hub for Zen's popularization in the 1960s. The area continues to serve as a locus for many Buddhist traditions in the United States. It is also home to entrepreneurs from Silicon Valley, researchers from nearby universities, and engineers at Google.

One such engineer is Chade-Meng Tan, who was born in Singapore, studied computer engineering at UC Santa Barbara, and thereafter joined Google in 2000 (as employee number 107). Though Tan was hired to work on search products, Googlers can offer extracurricular classes to one another, and Tan did so in 2007 with "Search Inside Yourself" (SIY). This course, inspired by Kabat-Zinn's MBSR, was popular and influential at Google. Because of this, Tan was able to dedicate himself to SIY and became known as Google's "Jolly Good Fellow." In 2012, he was able to spin out the SIY program as its own nonprofit institute.

That same year, Tan published *Search Inside Yourself: The Unexpected Path to Achieving Success, Happiness (and World Peace).* The book presents mindfulness for tech-types—one of the better books on the topic. Tan focuses on MBSR practices as a way of developing emotional intelligence (EI), including self-awareness, self-regulation, motivation, empathy, and social skills. He think engineers generally lack these attributes, so he gives advice on building trust, offering skillful praise, restoring relationships, and living according to one's values. He believes there are unexpected benefits in having an engineer teach this topic: he can do so from a skeptical and scientific point of view. Also, he says, "my engineer-oriented brain helped me translate teachings from the language of contemplative traditions into language that compulsively pragmatic people like me can process." For example, "where traditional contemplatives would talk about 'deeper awareness of emotion,' I would say 'perceiving the process of emotion at a higher resolution.'"[30] In Tan's translation, "higher resolution" can stand in for "deeper awareness."

While Tan looks the part of a Buddhist and is often photographed sitting cross-legged and wearing a shirt with a mandarin collar, Bill Duane looks more Harley-Davidson. He is another longtime engineer who happened to attend a Google Tech Talk by a Stanford neuroscientist. It was an eye-opening experience. Duane realized that the mind could be beneficially hacked using scientifically sound practices. When he took Tan's SIY course, he was hooked. In 2013, with Tan turning his focus to his institute, Duane transitioned into being Google's "Superintendent of Well Being." Duane teaches Google's "Neural Self Hacking" course with the intention of reaching "his people." Instead of selling "hippie bullshit" to those in yoga pants, he says, "I wanted to speak to the grumpy engineer who may be an atheist, may be a rationalist."[31]

In 2015, Tan's book was followed by a similar effort by Michael Taft, *The Mindful Geek: Mindfulness Meditation for Secular Skeptics*. Taft also teaches meditation at Google and works with Tan's SIY institute and with Wisdom Labs, a corporate wellness consultancy. He caters to his audience by referencing geeky staples, including *Blade Runner*, *Dune*, and *Star Trek*. Taft speaks of meditation as a technology, explaining that it fits the definition of a "practical application of knowledge."[32] He even includes a flowchart of meditation as an algorithm (figure 8.1)—though this seems like overkill.

Tan, Duane, and Taft are three of the most prominent mindfulness gurus now circulating in the high-tech world. They distill the zen of Zen and translate what remains into terms suitable for geeks. What they choose to translate

The Meditation Algorithm

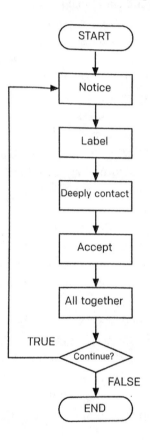

Figure 8.1

From Michael Taft, *The Mindful Geek: Mindfulness Meditation for Secular Skeptics* (Kensington, CA: Cephalopod Rex Publishing, 2015), 11.

(secular mindfulness) and their audience (entrepreneurs and engineers) influences the result, as we will soon see. But before that, let's consider the hype that surrounds what is being translated in the first place.

Apps, Gadgets, and Woo

Meditation gurus and wellness consultants are now commonplace in the corporate tech scene—so much so that this is parodied in the HBO series *Silicon Valley*. Gavin Belson, the CEO of a large social media company, has a South Asian spiritual advisor on call. When faced with a crisis of conscience, Belson summons Denpok from afar.

> **BELSON:** Denpok, I know you were in Aspen, thank you for coming. Please, have a seat.
>
> **DENPOK:** I'm not sitting this summer.
>
> **GAVIN:** Of course: incredible![33]

Denpok's practice is reminiscent of the health claims we saw about standing all day in chapter 6, now applied to spirituality. Of course, not everyone is wealthy enough to have a personal guru, but guidance can be had via personal gadgets, accompanied by similarly dubious claims.

The larger meditation market is estimated to be worth a billion-plus dollars, so the Android and iPhone stores are full of Zen wallpapers and meditation guides and timers. Some of these apps are promoted by life hacking gurus and make problematic claims similar to those seen in previous chapters.

The market leader among meditation apps is Headspace, born of a meeting between Andy Puddicombe, a former Buddhist monk running a meditation clinic in London, and Rich Pierson, a stressed-out advertising executive. In 2010, the two launched the app with the hope of making meditation accessible to millions, and they succeeded. In 2017, *Forbes* reported the app had been downloaded eleven million times and had more than four hundred thousand paying subscribers, bringing in about $50 million in annual revenue.[34] The company runs advertising campaigns, sponsors podcasters (including Ferriss), and is widely covered in the press.

Despite this success, and like Denpok's summer of no sitting, meditation apps are mostly hype. The efficacy of meditation itself is increasingly challenged because its effects might not be universal or unique. Meditation might not be universally applicable because it can actually be an anxiety-provoking experience for some. And its positive effects don't appear to be specific: meditation is one of many techniques for promoting relaxation and limiting ruminations. It can be effective, but it is not a panacea. Researchers find that mindfulness apps, in turn, are poorly designed and that their purported benefits could easily be the result of a "digital placebo effect."[35] In response to such criticism, Headspace's Pierson claims that the company has ongoing research underway, and, in any case, "We are just trying to put stuff out there that will help people." He adds, "I don't think Western science has a monopoly on the human condition"[36] The Western science complaint is a trite canard. The placebo effect, for instance, is not a Western phenomenon.

I've found only a single controlled study on the effectiveness of a meditation app. In "Putting the 'App' in Happiness," researchers randomly placed subjects in one of two groups, both of which used an app for ten minutes a day.[37] Those in the experimental group ($N = 57$) used Headspace; those in the control group ($N = 64$) used a note-taking app to journal their daily activities. Subjects were surveyed, before and after, with questions about their subjective feelings of well-being. The researchers found no statistically significant differences in satisfaction with life, flourishing, or negative emotions. (Social scientists have a bevy of distinct but related concepts.) They did find statistically significant medium-sized effects on positive emotions and small effects in reducing depressive symptoms. Yet these notions of medium and small effect sizes are specific to the research context. Practically, after using Headspace, the mean score for reports of positive emotions rose 8 percent. The mean for those in the control group dropped 5 percent. However, this 8 percent lift is the strongest finding, out of many measurements, in which the control group varied by 5 percent anyway.

This study, which was a short-term intervention, indicates that Headspace *might* be a useful way of facilitating some of the benefits of meditation, but these findings need to be rigorously replicated. There are also many questions to ask. How do meditation apps compare to human-facilitated meditation? Are meditation apps more useful to newcomers or experienced meditators? Because apps are more convenient, are users more or less likely to stick with the practice? What are the consequences of using a smartphone, a source of distractions and notifications, as a mindfulness facilitator?

There is a lot of hype for little evidence. Fortunately, there are few harms beyond wasted time or a few dollars spent on an app, but as one critic suggests, taking a long walk could be just as good, if not better.[38]

———

Life hackers, of course, like to take things further. Beyond the seeming passivity of meditation, what if we could more directly manipulate the mind? This possibility inspires the Consciousness Hacking movement, started in 2013.

One approach to consciousness alteration is pharmacological, using psychedelics to enhance performance, address mood disorders, and deepen spirituality. As a supplements enthusiast, Tim Ferriss, not surprisingly, is an advocate. Although he has discussed microdosing LSD—and contributed to its uptake in Silicon Valley—he focuses his advocacy on psilocybin, a mushroom-derived psychedelic. On the research side, he led a crowdsourced campaign to fund work at Johns Hopkins University on psilocybin's usefulness for treating depression. On the questionable side, Ferriss promotes Four Sigmatic mushroom-infused coffee, a podcast sponsor.

Another technique for consciousness hacking is transcranial stimulation, using electric impulses or magnetic fields to affect the mind. Instead of the mind being trained to relax, as in biofeedback, the brain is stimulated directly. On the research side, the field has the same, or worse, problem of replicability as psychology as a whole.[39] On the consumer side, device makers use the same evasions as their peers in the supplements industry. They reference the uneven research with suggestions of improved mood, accelerated performance, pain reduction, and improved sleep but offer little to no evidence for their specific devices. Instead, testimonials extol immediate and amazing results. So as to not run afoul of the FDA, device makers then disclaim any medical use in small print: they do not claim to "treat, diagnose, assist, cure, or prevent any medical condition." This is the typical *woo dance sidestep*—*woo* is a skeptic's term for pseudoscientific claims.

In the end, what differentiates consciousness hacking from things like homeopathy and crystal healing is that the latter are certain nonsense. As we saw with health hacking, claims ought to have plausible theory about how an intervention works and rigorous evidence that it does so. Homeopathy and crystals are classic woo—what Google's Bill Duane would call "hippie bullshit." They have no intelligible mechanism for how they could work, and there is rigorous evidence that they do not. As yet, psychedelics and transcranial stimulation have potential to benefit and harm us—especially those dosing and zapping their brains on their own—but we have only tentative theories for how they might work and uneven evidence that they do.

Look Outside Yourself

Silicon Valley is notoriously competitive, and this is what precipitated Gavin Belson's crisis of conscience in HBO's *Silicon Valley*.

DENPOK: What's weighing on you Gavin?

BELSON: Jared Dunn quit today to join Pied Piper. I hate Richard Hendrix, that little Pied Piper prick. Is that wrong?

DENPOK: In the hands of a lesser person perhaps.... In the hands of the enlightened, hate can be a tool for great change.

BELSON: You're right once again![40]

Denpok's observation about hate is probably right, but Denpok is a con man, and Belson is not yet enlightened. Critics of the mindfulness hype are similarly concerned not only that it is being used to sell snake oil, but about how selfish it has become.

When Tim Ferriss speaks of meditation, he speaks of it as a tool for success: it "helps [him] be more effective, not just more efficient."[41] Meditation allows him to focus and prioritize. Even so, he has worried that it might also cause him to lose his edge. In a conversation with Tara Brach, a Buddhist psychologist and teacher of meditation, Ferriss asked, "How do I manage energies like anger or aggression, when those have served me well?" Ferriss is competitive and ambitious, and the expression "second place is the first-place loser" easily comes to his mind. So does the anecdote of a wealthy tech entrepreneur dashing the pieces off a chessboard after losing: "Show me a good loser, and I'll show you a fucking loser." He conceded this has caused him suffering, but isn't this what drives Silicon Valley success? In turn, Brach skillfully redirected Ferriss, asking him what he would choose to be known for by the end of his life. Ferriss responded, "Creating learners that are better than I am. If I can do that, I can create a benevolent army of tens of thousands, maybe hundreds of thousands, maybe millions of world-class teachers that self-replicates." Ferriss still spoke in terms of comparison and domination (i.e., an army of better), but Brach suggested that his goal is a collaborative undertaking, not a competitive one.[42]

Ferriss's candidness about his struggle is commendable. It reveals that his strength (ambition) can also be a source of suffering (anger). He, like anyone else, is finding a path toward his understanding of a good life; in time, this might even broaden from a focus on personal success toward one of greater compassion.[43] As a guru, however, the example he sets, the path he advocates, and his vision of a good life deserves scrutiny, especially when mindfulness is translated as a tool for individual effectiveness and corporate wellness.

Ferriss's instrumental approach to meditation is not unique. Its appeal to individuals can be seen in a high-profile ad campaign for Headspace that featured ordinary athletes next to pithy testimonials. In one, a woman curls a dumbbell: "I meditate to crush it." Others meditate to "stay present," "not freak out," "get [basketball] buckets," "have the edge," and "not compete with myself." These are all competitive, even the last, as competing with yourself gets in the way of competing against others. There is also the corporate sell. In a *Wired* piece about how mindfulness was the new rage in Silicon Valley, Chade-Meng Tan, founder of Search Inside Yourself, spoke of the consequent benefits of greater emotional intelligence: "Everybody knows EI is good for their career.... And every company knows that if their people have EI, they're gonna make a shitload of money."[44] Tan's intentions go beyond "shitloads of money," but his audience of Silicon Valley techies has colored his translation of the Buddhist source.

In Buddhism, compassion for oneself is interconnected with that for others. Tonglen and Metta meditation, which work to transform suffering, are a realization of the principles of interdependence and nonself. When I looked for discussion of these types of meditation on Headspace's forums, I found only a few postings, including two people asking for guided Metta meditations. In the third, a user asks about their absence: "Whilst I see separateness from religion and religious concepts as a valid point, I don't see love as a specifically Buddhist or religious concept and I wonder what others think."[45] None of these lonely posts received a response.

Even typical hacker-types have noticed this paucity. Alex Payne is a software developer and investor who has been practicing meditation on and off for more than a decade. He would not begrudge anyone his or her own meditation practice, whatever its form, but reading about it in the corporate world makes him uneasy. The problem, he writes, is that mindfulness has become wrapped up in the idea of the Quantified Self, making it "socially acceptable amongst the self-serious." He continues that "mindfulness is so much more than a performance enhancing tool.... If that's what you're searching for, you're better off with caffeine; there's better data on it, anyway." Otherwise, mindfulness should raise questions about the social context: Why do we feel the need to be more effective, and who benefits?[46]

Questions about the larger context came to the fore at the 2014 Wisdom 2.0 conference. The Wisdom 2.0 series of conferences, begun in 2010, brings together technologists and top gurus. If there is such a thing as a meaning hacker conference, this is it. It is usually held in San Francisco, a city struggling with the increasing cost of living brought about by wealthy technologists. At the 2014 conference, during the session "3 Steps to Build Corporate Mindfulness the Google Way," protesters jumped on stage and unfurled an "Eviction Free San Francisco" banner. The panel members were Chade-Meng Tan ("Jolly Good Fellow"), Bill Duane ("Superintendent of Well Being"), and Karen May (VP of "People Development"). The protesters were four affordable-housing advocates. Once on stage, they chanted, "Wisdom means stopping displacement! Wisdom means stopping surveillance! San Francisco is not for sale!"[47] After a few minutes, they were ushered off stage, and Duane asked the audience to "use this as a moment of practice": "check in with your body and see what's happening with what it's like to be around conflict and people with heartfelt ideas that may be different than what we're thinking." The panelists and audience then sat quietly. This was a skillful response, perhaps the only one that could have reasonably followed. And the protesters had made their point, which was soon taken up by others.

Ron Purser and David Forbes are professors who study the movement of meditation into secular contexts. Even before the Wisdom 2.0 conference, they worried about "McMindfulness," the "atomized and highly privatized version of mindfulness" being adopted by corporations. Mindfulness is appealing to businesses because it is "a trendy method for subduing employee unrest, promoting a tacit acceptance of the status quo, and as an instrumental tool for keeping attention focused on institutional goals." For Purser and Forbes, this bears a close resemblance to the human relations and sensitivity training of the 1950s and 1960s, during which corporations exploited counseling techniques, such as active listening, to mollify employees: "These methods came to be referred to as 'cow psychology,' because contented and docile cows give more milk."[48] The same is now being done with mindfulness.

Purser and Forbes followed the conference protest with the claim that the mindfulness community had been seduced by Google and the Wisdom 2.0 crowd. The idea of kinder and gentler capitalists is appealing, "but mindfulness has escaped its moral moorings." Buddhists differentiate between wrong and right mindfulness, in which the latter is characterized by wholesome intentions, including "well-being for others as well as oneself."[49] Purser and Forbes believed the Googlers' response to the protest revealed a head-in-the-sand type of spirituality: "their form of corporate mindfulness is at best a privatized spirituality, narrowly conceived as a practice for searching only inside your self, encouraging a 'spiritually correct' form of passivity, quietism and dissociation from societal malaise."[50]

It's difficult to lay the blame for the expensiveness of San Francisco at the feet of the individual panelists, but the broader critique of McMindfulness is spot on. If we are lucky, we might soon see this incident parodied in an episode of *Silicon Valley*.

Lost in Translation

Something is always lost in translation. Today's definitions of the words *cynic*, *stoic*, and *epicurean* would be unrecognizable to their ancient proponents. Dedicated readers of Seneca and Marcus Aurelius—myself included—have multiple translations of the same Latin texts because they vary in meaning and meter. Alongside Stoicism, Buddhism is the other source most often translated by meaning hackers. Most of their focus is on aesthetics and meditation, but there are Buddhist sentiments that seem to align with the hacker ethos. A popular aphorism attributed to the Buddha is to "believe nothing, no matter who said it, not even if I said it, if it doesn't fit in with your own reason and common sense." This is a suitable credo for the self-reliant individual fond of reason and experimentation. Yet when the Buddhist monk Ṭhānissaro Bhikkhu sees variations of this sentiment in popular culture, he believes its meaning has been "lost in quotation."

One way that we translate is by metaphor. We've seen Stoicism likened to a personal operating system and mindfulness to a performance-enhancing tool. In keeping with this, "Headspace frames the user's experience of their brain as if it was a computer, and the mobile phone is a recalibration tool used to update and improve it," as one scholar of these apps notes.[51] We've also seen aspects of life represented as a flowchart, from calories consumed and expended, to work, to meditation. Taft's "meditation algorithm" chart is especially gratuitous, as there are no forking decisions, only linear steps. Nonetheless, Taft believes calling the steps an algorithm, represented as a flowchart, makes meditation more accessible to techies. Similarly, Headspace's framing might make meditation accessible to smartphone users, though putting gadgets aside altogether could be the wise thing to do.

Another way we translate is to highlight and elide, often unintentionally. The Buddhist aphorism about being skeptical and self-reliant is taken from the Buddhist sutra known as the "Charter of Free Inquiry." It is attractive to many because of its seeming regard for self-reliance. But Ṭhānissaro notes that the original teaching includes a skepticism in regard to external *and* internal authorities.[52] Yes, you should not exclusively rely upon external rumors, legends, traditions, scripture, or status. You should also not rely exclusively on your internal reasoning—but this warning is dropped in translation. Although reason, self-reliance, and experimentation appeal to the life hacker, the Buddha's recommendation was to *combine* these things with the support of community and teachers.

Dale Davidson's thirty-day experiments of engaging with different traditions highlight some things and miss others. When he experimented with the eight traditions, he attended church, synagogue, mosque, and a yoga class. For Buddhism, "all I did was sit on the floor for 10–20 minutes every day and try to pay attention to my breath." Epicureanism, Stoicism, and Taoism were similarly lone undertakings. Davidson is admirably cognizant of these differences and the limits of DIY religion, but he nonetheless pursued an asocial translation of Buddhism.[53]

The danger of the individualistic and instrumental pursuit of wisdom is that "you can easily side with your greed, aversion, or delusion, setting your standards too low," as Ṭhānissaro warns. To counter this tendency, practitioners need those who can challenge and guide them. And just as the apprentice carpenter learns to better appreciate his mentor's skills as his own increases, so it is with wisdom. Finding wise teachers is a skill itself, one that grows with practice. Yet this is usually forgotten in the cut-and-paste Buddhism found in the West: "In particular, the idea of apprenticeship—so central in mastering the habits of the dhamma [teachings] as a skill—is almost totally lacking. Dhamma principles are reduced to vague generalities, and the techniques for testing them are stripped to a bare, assembly-line minimum."[54] Most ancient philosophies, Stoicism included, were apprenticeship based. In Western philosophy, the Socrates-Plato-Aristotle lineage is well known. The transmission of Zen from master to student can be traced back to the sixth century, perhaps further.

Davidson shows that life hackers have many principles and techniques from which to craft their life philosophies. As in every domain of life, they like to tinker and experiment on the path to a meaningful life. The individualistic and instrumental translation of Stoicism and Buddhism into Wisdom 2.0 has its strengths, especially for hacker types. Yet as the Zen saying goes: the finger pointing to the moon is not the moon itself. Wisdom 2.0 can be a near enemy of wisdom if it serves only to justify, without challenge, the corresponding weaknesses inherent in the hacker ethos.

On a good day, Tim Ferriss's morning includes making the bed, meditating, hanging by his feet (which helps with back pain), drinking tea, and journaling: "If I can hit at least three of these items, then I've won the morning. And, as the saying goes, 'If you win the morning, you win the day.'"[1] This is good advice. It's too easy to fritter away the morning, which then taints the whole of the day.

At the start of this book, I claimed that life hacking reveals something about life in the twenty-first century. Mark Rittman's eleven hours spent on an automated Wi-Fi kettle is evidence that even mundane features of life are increasingly taken as systems to be hacked. We can infer something similar from Ferriss's morning regime. His morning ritual, arrived at by way of experimentation, is a system for bootstrapping a successful day. Yet just as an automated kettle's promise of usefulness can turn to frustration, the idea that the morning requires a checklist can turn to irritation.

Shem Magnezi is a software engineer at WeWork, a company that provides shared workspaces for freelancers, entrepreneurs, and other members of the creative class. Although he loves to code and works at a company that caters to start-ups, Magnezi wrote a post entitled "Fuck You Startup World." In the piece, he criticizes the self-improving attitudes espoused by life hacking gurus. Magnezi rails against entrepreneur wannabes and workaholics ("You're not Elon Musk"), extreme eaters (junk-food bingers and Soylent-drinking optimizers), and intellectual pretenders (those who go on about their favorite book of the week). Most importantly, "Fuck you productivity freaks": "You try to make me feel bad because I woke up 'only' at 6AM. Shit, you woke up at 4:30, meditated for 30 minutes, reviewed your quarterly and yearly 'goals' for another 30 minutes, and slurped on a delicious

Soylent shake while checking daily retention trends."[2] Magnezi then goes on to flip off other fads. He scorns the pretense of cool and flexible workplaces, irrelevant job interview challenges, ridiculous jargon, engineering hype, and even the shallow adulation of *Mr. Robot* and *Silicon Valley*: "But more than all, start-up world, fuck you for making me one of you."

If the start-up world made Magnezi into a life-optimizing freak, he is complicit. WeWork is a unicorn—the rare start-up valued at more than a billion dollars—and is aggressively expanding into other domains of life such as housing, fitness, and child care. Such is the reciprocal relationship between the hacker and his or her world, which is increasingly everyone else's. Even if you disagree that life is "systems of systems, all the way down," as former Googler Paul Buchheit suggests, the ascent of the hacker means it is increasingly becoming so.

Beyond the increased scope and pressure of life's systematization is the absurdity of its excesses. In a parody in *McSweeney's*, Holly Theisen-Jones writes of a morning routine that would certainly win the day.

> I rise blissfully at 4:30 am, thanks to my Tibetan singing bowl alarm clock. After 20 minutes of alternate nostril breathing, I start my day with a three-minute cold shower. This I follow with twenty minutes of stream-of-consciousness journaling, then another twenty minutes of gratitude journaling.
>
> For breakfast, I always enjoy a half liter of organic, fair-trade, bulletproof coffee (I use a ghee, coconut oil, and yak butter blend instead of MCT oil), which keeps me in ketosis until I break my intermittent fast. By the way, if you haven't tried it, nothing does the trick like intermittent fasting for maintaining less than 17% body fat. (For my full fasting protocol, see my e-book.)[3]

Theisen-Jones's fictitious morning is followed by additional screwball concoctions for lunch and dinner, references to high-end gadgets including a Vitamix blender and Dyson vacuum cleaner, efficient emailing, software development of a language learning app, Eastern spirituality, exercise with kettle bell swings, decluttering, regimented social interactions, and unsubtle self-promotion of e-books and personal coaching. The thirteen-hundred-word parody is aptly entitled "My Fully Optimized Life Allows Me Ample Time to Optimize Yours." The piece reveals the many ways in which life is treated as a system to be optimized. It also, importantly, reveals who this self-help is intended for.

Beyond self-help that targets men or women, the genre rarely limits its audience intentionally. The promise of self-help is that if you cannot yet afford a Vitamix blender, you will soon be able to, if you follow its advice. Yet many people, like the product pickers in Amazon warehouses, can only look upon the emblems of such a lifestyle as they pass by. Additionally, they must suffice with being a part of a system, something that is to be optimized rather than someone who is optimizing. Amazon's proposed wrist device, which buzzes workers when they reach for the wrong item, is evidence of this—until the workers are replaced by automation altogether.

Life hacking is self-help for the creative class. Those fortunate enough to escape the regimentation of others must adopt a regime of their own, perhaps donning the Pavlok wrist device, which will zap them when they get distracted. For those with some autonomy, there's much to be said in favor of the hacker ethos. Self-reliance, a rational and systematizing mind-set, and a willingness to take risks and experiment befit a world of high-tech distractions and opportunities. The ethos is optimistic and optimizing—both words share the same Latin root. Life hacking geeks embrace this because it fits their personality and circumstance, and it can yield positive results. Gurus can even make a career of selling it as a path toward success.

Yet even within the creative class, life hacking is not an absolute positive. For the individual, optimism is susceptible to credulousness and optimization to excess. And that which first appears as a virtue can instead be a near enemy. Efficiency is not always effective, minimalism can be grasping, and healthism pathological. Romantic conquest is not the same as human connection, and Wisdom 2.0 is not always wise.

Beyond the individual, when the system being hacked involves others, the ethics of life hacking span a spectrum of gray. Though life hacking purports to reveal the gap between commonly understood rules and what is actually possible, its own vision tends to be impaired. In our final life hacker exemplar, we can see excesses of the hacker mind-set, and more importantly, shortsightedness when it comes to others.

"I Choose Me"

James Altucher, tech entrepreneur and writer, had promised his daughter that they could go to a teen fashion show. Yet his friend's offer to put them on the guest list had gone astray. Altucher didn't get upset, but he didn't leave: "I find when you act confused but polite then people want to help. There was a line behind me. I wasn't fighting or angry. So there was no

reason for anyone to get angry at me. They just wanted to end the confusion."[4] So the attendant quietly handed them standing-only passes.

Once inside, Altucher approached an organizer and said, "I write for the
Wall Street Journal and I thought we would get great seats." She ran off to
check but returned to tell him they had already seated someone from there—
not surprising, given that Altucher was a blogger for the website rather than
a reporter for the paper. Altucher was again, politely, bounced to the back.
There, he and his daughter made friends with the folks around them, including the ushers. When the lights dimmed, an usher waved his daughter to an
empty seat near the front. Mission accomplished.

After the show, Altucher and his daughter went to play ping-pong, but
the venue had been rented out for a corporate event. Nonetheless, they saw
an empty table with paddles and a ball and played for an hour. When a staff
member finally noticed, they were asked to leave. Altucher offered to pay for
the time, but that wasn't necessary. He had, again, gotten what he wanted.

Altucher is an interesting character. He attended top-notch computer science programs, but he scraped by as an undergraduate and was kicked out
of a PhD program. He's traded hedge funds and founded more than a dozen
companies. Most failed, but some investments have been huge wins. He loves
games, including chess and Go. For a maniacal period his all-consuming passion was poker, during which he would take a helicopter to Atlantic City for
nonstop weekend binges. He is a minimalist, as he wrote in a post on *Boing
Boing*: "I have one bag of clothes, one backpack with a computer, iPad, and
phone. I have zero other possessions." This lifestyle was the focus of a *New
York Times* profile a few months later.[5] He is a prolific blogger, author, and
podcaster on the topics of investing and broader self-help. He has taken the
title of his 2013 book, *Choose Yourself: Be Happy, Make Millions, Live the Dream*,
as his self-help slogan. For example, Altucher's main newsletter promises to
teach you how to "choose yourself." Readers need only enter their email
address and click "I CHOOSE ME." This is a stepping-stone on the path to his
other newsletters, which cost hundreds to thousands of dollars.

Altucher's most recent enthusiasms are digital currencies, like bitcoin,
and stand-up comedy. He's even combined the two: in one performance he
notes that the bitcoin he used to pay for lap dances at his bachelor party
is now worth $17 million. That's kind of funny. He also characterizes his
teenage daughters as not very bright and incapable of understanding digital
currencies. That just seems mean. In 2018, he became a focus of derision

himself when news sites began reporting on "The Man behind Those 'Bit-coin Genius' Ads All Over the Internet." Altucher was using these tacky ads to promote his "crypto trader" newsletter and drive interest to a service in which he had invested: "I guarantee you'll see how to make 10 times your money in the next 12 months."[6] If you lose all your money following his expensive advice, you'll get an extra year's worth for free. Such digital currency ads have since been banned by Google and Facebook.

Altucher might even be the source of Ferriss's anecdote, from the last chapter, about the merits of being a sore loser. (Ferriss was a guest, guest-host, and advertiser on *Question of the Day*, Alutcher and Stephen Dubner's joint podcast.) Altucher has written about dashing chess pieces to the floor in two blog posts: "How Being a Sore Loser Can Make You Rich (or Crazy)" and "Life Is like a Game. Here's How You Master Any Game." His stories about gate crashing are from the post "How to Break All the Rules and Get Everything You Want."[7]

The idea that life is a zero-sum game, with rules to be bent or broken in order to get what you want, is the most hawkish expression of life hacking. It isn't essential to the ethos, but it follows naturally as a technique for quick fixes, especially among gurus, given it is an easy sell. Of course, this idea isn't unique to Altucher. Sethi "hacks the system" by doing the opposite of what everyone else does, such as doing push-ups on exotic animals. Ferriss promises to "make the impossible possible by bending the rules," as in the case of his dubious kickboxing championship.[8] The question, then, remains: What happens to others when you "break all the rules to get everything you want"?

Bending the Rules

Altucher's story of gate crashing highlights that the hacker ethos is tightly coupled with individualism, which is inherent in American self-help and the Californian Ideology. In Stoic terms, the individual is responsible for and can achieve a good life by way of his or her own rational disposition and behavior. This attitude begets the strengths of self-reliance, engagement with the world, and experimentation toward improvement. It is well suited to a world where systems, and the potential for hacking, are everywhere. Altucher's intelligence and affinity for systems thinking has made him wealthy and famous. His advice is now sought after and appreciated by many thousands of readers and listeners.

For the individual, the flip side of these attributes is excess bordering on obsession and maladaptive behavior. For example, most people want a good (nominal) night's sleep. The optimizing hacker, opting for the Uberman sleep cycle, might achieve great efficiency, but at the expense of mental stability and social compatibility. Similarly, in periods of his life, Altucher has lost millions, been broke, friendless, and despondent. He once binged on poker for a year straight and confesses that on the day his first daughter was born, he escaped the hospital as soon as he could to return to the table. As Altucher puts it, his approach "can make you rich (or crazy)."

When it comes to others, Altucher draws a lesson from his adventure with his daughter: don't steal, murder, or break the laws, "but most other rules can be bent. If you act like the river, you ultimately flow past all the rocks along the way."[9] Yet some of those rocks, no doubt, are people who are stuck in place.

What separates most bendable rules from nonbendable ones? Altucher does not say, but I can imagine a simple principle and a more complex assessment. Rule bending is okay when no one is harmed. For example, being friendly led to his daughter's getting a seat at the fashion show: no harm. Being friendly is also a universal imperative, in the sense that I discussed in chapter 1. The more friendly people there are, the better. However, I imagine Altucher was a minor irritant to the fashion show staff, those behind him in line, or anyone waiting to play ping-pong. If everyone acted similarly, the world would be a little worse off. This is unlike, for example, the case of disability hackers sharing tips for holding and manipulating household items. These hacks are beneficial and remain so no matter how many people use them.

At worst, life hacking gurus hawking enhancement supplements, as Ferriss did, and crypto-currency get-rich schemes, as Altucher does, are perpetrating scams. They are claiming to have found a gap between conventional thought and the actual rules underlying biological and economic systems. Ferriss's BrainQUICKEN boosted "neural transmission and information processing," and Altucher "cracked 'the crypto code.'"[10] This doesn't mean gurus are necessarily insincere. Ferriss's fondness for supplements, at least, seems more self-servingly credulous than knowingly deceitful. He likely believes in the advice he gives, or at least thinks of it as providing options for others to experiment with. Nor does this mean gurus never offer good advice; after all, the broken clock is correct twice a day. And even flat-out bogus advice can give people a sense of hope or inspiration. The question is, How much does the advice cost, and are there better alternatives?

At best, life hacking entrepreneurs miss that their advice is rooted in their own experiences, which are not universal. Perhaps Ferriss's morning routine grates on others because he assumes that others have similar circumstances and will have similar results. Those who are awakened by screaming kids might roll their eyes at the fantasy of such a morning. Those who replicate the regime without similar results might feel disappointed. And those who can't manage the necessary discipline might grow resentful.

Similarly, people's varied circumstances mean that not everyone has the same freedom to bend the rules and get away with it. Research suggests entrepreneurship is associated with "smart and illicit" tendencies early in life. This is advantageous for young white men whose rule breaking, such as skipping school and gambling, does not impair their future as it does others'. Additionally, these rule breakers are more likely to have the financial, social, and cultural resources to launch entrepreneurial ventures and recover from them when they fail.[11] Mark Zuckerberg's flouting of convention by dropping out of college or wearing a hoodie is read differently than a black kid's doing the same. So for one critic, Altucher's story isn't about being nice and bending rules, it is about life hacking as entitlement and privilege. She suggests Altucher's tips work only if you preface them with "if you are a white male." And even then, "oftentimes, when you take (or ask for!) things that do not belong to you, women are giving you the side-eye and exchanging glances with each other."[12] Altucher broke the rules and got everything he wanted, but he was also oblivious to those around him.

The Blinkered Path

The Californian Ideology has found a new home at South by Southwest (SXSW) in Austin, Texas. Fifteen years ago, this label was affixed to the Bay Area hackers, writers, and entrepreneurs who blended their countercultural sensibilities, technological determinism, and libertarian individualism into a "hybrid orthodoxy" of the digital age.[13] At SXSW you can find a similar mix of people abiding by that orthodoxy. At the conference there are sessions dedicated to self, bio, and health hacking. You can find Tim Ferriss talking about the future of psychedelics and James Altucher talking about how to outthink the future. In fact, Ferriss is a regular at SXSW and uses his first book's success at the 2007 event as a case study in optimized self-promotion. Ten years later, he moved to Austin, finding it to be friendlier than San Francisco and less overrun with start-up mania and political correctness.

In 2018, I saw something from SXSW that epitomized the challenges of our moment and the life hacker's response. In fact, the metaphor I had settled upon for this book had become a reality. Panasonic's exhibition, Future Life Factory, included the design concept WEAR SPACE: human blinkers equipped with noise-canceling headphones. Just as horses are fitted with blinkers to block out the periphery and focus their attention, WEAR SPACE does the same for people. The thing looks like a pair of behind-the-head earmuffs reaching for the nose. It's an adjustable cubicle for the head.

In Panasonic's stilted description of the gadget, they note that workers in open offices and digital nomads in cafés are prone to distraction: "today's workers who are required to demonstrate high levels of performance are demanding personalised spaces." WEAR SPACE meets this need and "create[s] visual and psychological boundaries instantly." Additionally, the device comes in handy "in daily life, such as learning a new language, building up focus, or working at home when a spouse is playing with the children."[14] I don't imagine this will ever be a real product, though its designers' sincerity is remarkable. There's no hint of irony or recognition that in donning this contraption, you'll prompt those around you to think you've slipped your "psychological boundaries." Nonetheless, Panasonic's device speaks to challenges of the digital age.

We live in an economy that prizes quick and quantifiable results, a culture that values self-reliance, a period of increasing measurement and uncertainty, and an environment of abundant distraction and choice. Despite transhumanist dreams of silicone-based immortality, we continue to face uncertainty and loss.

In this environment, the creative class, like anyone else, seeks to live a good life. They can work remotely, outsource chores, and track and experiment with every aspect of life. Rather than being a cog in a system, life hackers seek to hack it. And they go about this in a particular way, as rational individuals fond of systems and experimentation. Fortunately for them, our world is increasingly suited to this approach; at times, it demands it. Hackers' successes in designing digital systems are applied to the broader expanse of life. The same technique for testing whether a blue or a red web banner brings more clicks can be applied to productivity, nutrition, fitness, and dating—with attendant limitations. Life hacking is the collective manifestation of personality, of an ethos, in a reciprocating relationship with a world of systems.

Even if you do not share this ethos, the geeks and gurus I discuss in this book reveal a challenge we all face. The path to a good life—to being "healthy, wealthy, and wise"—is a complicated one. Even straight paths headed toward beacons on the horizon can mislead. Indeed, near enemies sit at the end of the best-paved roads. You wish to be content? Try accumulating all the toys, then getting rid of all but ninety-nine. You wish to be well? Try coconut oil in your coffee. You wish to be wise? Meditate.

Another reason for resentment about morning regimes for winning the day is that the suggestions keep piling up. The profitable paradox at the heart of self-help is that it never suffices. As self-help critic Steve Salerno notes in *Sham: How the Self-Help Movement Made America Helpless*, the best indicator of whether someone will buy a self-help book on a given topic is whether they have bought a similar one in the preceding eighteen months.[15]

In the face of the self-help deluge, a potential insight is that *the path is the way*. There is no destination, per se, only how you traverse the path. Of course, this insight is corrupted if you then race about the maze acquiring additional systems and gadgets to add to your regime—many of which will be fads and snake oil. However, unlike Salerno, we ought not dismiss all of self-help (and life hacking) as a sham. There are clever techniques to be discovered and shared, as well as useful frames for making sense of life. More substantively, we need regular reminders. Take the distinction between efficiency and effectiveness; this has been a key lesson of productivity self-help for decades now. Every handful of years we need such lessons bundled up and couched in the vocabulary, enthusiasms, and worries of the current moment.

Life hacking can have utility, with occasional deleterious side effects. And a hack can be useful to a point, after which it has diminishing or negative returns. Clever tricks and lifestyle design work well for some people. They are even enjoyable to those who like to run the maze, yet few life hackers stop to ask about the inequities built into the maze's design.

Life hacking is a tool, like a set of blinkers that restrict vision. In an age of ubiquitous distraction, blocking the periphery is helpful. In an age of economic turbulence, staying focused on a better future is valuable. Even so, the resulting tunnel vision leaves much overlooked, especially among those bent on optimizing. Individual hackers can fail to appreciate that they are in danger of stepping off the edge. For those around them, there is the risk of being bumped aside or trod underfoot. And even those who once embraced blinkers realize that they can chafe, especially when you have to don them first thing in the morning.

Notes

1 Introduction

1. Mark Rittman, "3 Hrs Later and Still No Tea. Mandatory Recalibration Caused Wifi Base-Station Reset, Now Port-Scanning Network to Find Where Kettle Is Now," Twitter, October 11, 2016, https://twitter.com/markrittman/status/785763443185942529; Bonnie Malkin, "English Man Spends 11 Hours Trying to Make Cup of Tea with Wi-Fi Kettle," *The Guardian*, October 11, 2016, https://www.theguardian.com/technology/2016/oct/12/english-man-spends-11-hours-trying-to-make-cup-of-tea-with-wi-fi-kettle.

2. Whitson Gordon, "How to Return Nearly Anything without a Receipt," *Lifehacker* (blog), October 26, 2011, https://lifehacker.com/5853626/how-to-return-nearly-anything-without-a-receipt.

3. My characterization of the hacker "ethos" is different but compatible with that of others, including Steven Levy, *Hackers: Heroes of the Computer Revolution*, 25th anniv. ed. (1984; repr., London: Penguin, 2010); Eric Steven Raymond, "How to Become a Hacker," catb, 2001, http://www.catb.org/esr/faqs/hacker-howto.html; Douglas Thomas, *Hacker Culture* (Minneapolis: University of Minnesota Press, 2002); Tad Suiter, "Why 'Hacking?,'" in *Hacking the Academy: New Approaches to Scholarship and Teaching from Digital Humanities*, ed. Daniel J. Cohen and Tom Scheinfeldt (Ann Arbor: University of Michigan Press, 2013), 6–10, https://doi.org/10.3998/dh.12172434.0001.001; Kyle Eschenroeder, "The Pitfalls of Life Hacking Culture," *The Art of Manliness* (blog), April 13, 2015, https://www.artofmanliness.com/articles/stop-hacking-your-life/; Matt Thomas, "Life Hacking: A Critical History, 2004–2014" (PhD diss., University of Iowa, 2015).

4. Robert Andrews, "GTD: A New Cult for the Info Age," *Wired*, July 12, 2005, https://www.wired.com/culture/lifestyle/news/2005/07/68103.

5. Danny O'Brien, "Life Hacks: Tech Secrets of Overprolific Alpha Geeks," O'Reilly Emerging Technology Conference, February 11, 2004, http://conferences.oreillynet.com/cs/et2004/view/e_sess/4802.

6. Tim Ferriss, *The 4-Hour Workweek: Escape 9–5, Live Anywhere and Join the New Rich* (2007; repr., New York: Crown, 2009), 15.

7. The commonalities of minimalism and pickup are identified in Thomas, "Life Hacking," chaps. 2, 4.

8. Richard Florida, *The Rise of the Creative Class*, 10th anniv. ed. (New York: Basic, 2012), 8–11.

9. Joe Berlinger, *Tony Robbins: I Am Not Your Guru* (RadicalMedia, 2016), https://www.imdb.com/title/tt5151716/.

10. The dangers of commercialization are something the Quantified Self community wrestles with. See the "quantrepreneurs" of the "tracking industrial complex" in Whitney Erin Boesel, "Return of the Quantrepreneurs," *Cyborgology* (blog), September 26, 2013, https://thesocietypages.org/cyborgology/2013/09/26/return-of-the -quantrepreneurs/; see also "soft resistance" in Dawn Nafus and Jamie Sherman, "This One Does Not Go Up to 11: The Quantified Self Movement as an Alternative Big Data Practice," *International Journal of Communication*, no. 8 (2014), http://ijoc .org/index.php/ijoc/article/viewFile/2170/1157.

11. Laura Vanderkam, "The Paperback Quest for Joy," *City Journal*, 2012, https://www.city-journal.org/2012/22_4_self-help-books.html.

12. Steven Starker, *Oracle at the Supermarket: The American Preoccupation with Self-Help Books* (New Brunswick, NJ: Transaction, 2002), 38.

13. Rebecca Mead, "Better, Faster, Stronger," *New Yorker*, September 5, 2011, https://www.newyorker.com/magazine/2011/09/05/better-faster-stronger.

14. William B. Irvine, *A Guide to the Good Life: The Ancient Art of Stoic Joy* (Oxford: Oxford University Press, 2009), 226.

15. Starker, *Oracle at the Supermarket*, 170, 7–8.

16. Boris Kachka, "The Power of Positive Publishing: How Self-Help Publishing Ate America," *New York*, January 6, 2013, http://nymag.com/health/self-help/2013/self -help-book-publishing/.

17. Dave Bruno, *The 100 Thing Challenge: How I Got Rid of Almost Everything, Remade My Life, and Regained My Soul* (New York: Harper, 2010); Joshua Fields Millburn and Ryan Nicodemus, *Everything That Remains: A Memoir by the Minimalists* (Missoula, MT: Asymmetrical, 2014).

18. Steve Salerno, *Sham: How the Self-Help Movement Made America Helpless* (New York: Crown, 2005).

19. Paul Buchheit, "Applied Philosophy, a.k.a. 'Hacking,'" October 13, 2009, http://paulbuchheit.blogspot.com/2009/10/applied-philosophy-aka-hacking.html; on Buchheit and life hacking, see Thomas, "Life Hacking," 44.

20. Starker, *Oracle at the Supermarket*, 2.

21. Buchheit, "Applied Philosophy."

22. Whitson Gordon, "Welcome to Lifehacker's Sixth Annual Evil Week," *Life-hacker* (blog), October 26, 2015, https://lifehacker.com/welcome-to-lifehackers-sixth-annual-evil-week-1738276927.

23. Ramy Inocencio, "U.S. Programmer Outsources Own Job to China, Surfs Cat Videos," CNN.com, January 17, 2013, https://edition.cnn.com/2013/01/17/business/us-outsource-job-china.

24. Margaret Olivia Little, "Cosmetic Surgery, Suspect Norms, and the Ethics of Complicity," in *Enhancing Human Traits: Ethical and Social Implications*, ed. Erik Parens (Washington, DC: Georgetown University Press, 1998), 162–176; Carl Elliott, *Better Than Well: American Medicine Meets the American Dream* (New York: Norton, 2003), 190–196.

25. Sara M. Watson, "Toward a Constructive Technology Criticism," *Columbia Journalism Review*, October 4, 2016, 3, 69, https://www.cjr.org/tow_center_reports/constructive_technology_criticism.php.

26. Elliott, *Better Than Well*, 190–196; Gina Neff and Dawn Nafus, *Self-Tracking* (Cambridge, MA: MIT Press, 2016), 39.

27. John Walker, "Introduction," in *The Hacker's Diet*, 2005, http://www.fourmilab.ch/hackdiet/e4/introduction.html.

2   The Life Hackers

1. Boris Kachka, "The Power of Positive Publishing: How Self-Help Publishing Ate America," *New York*, January 6, 2013, http://nymag.com/health/self-help/2013/self-help-book-publishing/.

2. Matt Thomas, "Life Hacking: A Critical History, 2004–2014" (PhD diss., University of Iowa, 2015), 81.

3. Danny O'Brien, "Life Hacks: Tech Secrets of Overprolific Alpha Geeks," O'Reilly Emerging Technology Conference 2004, February 11, 2004, http://conferences.oreillynet.com/cs/et2004/view/e_sess/4802.

4. Gina Trapani and Danny O'Brien, "Interview: Father of 'Life Hacks' Danny O'Brien," *Lifehacker* (blog), March 17, 2005, https://lifehacker.com/036370/interview-father-of-life-hacks-danny-obrien.

5. Steven Levy, *Hackers: Heroes of the Computer Revolution*, 25th anniv. ed. (1984; repr., London: Penguin, 2010), 8.

6. Peter R. Samson, "This Is the First TMRC Dictionary, Which I Wrote in June, 1959," gricer.com, June 26, 1959, http://www.gricer.com/tmrc/dictionary1959.html.

7. "Authorpreneurship," *Economist*, February 14, 2015, https://www.economist.com/news/business/21643124-succeed-these-days-authors-must-be-more-businesslike-ever-authorpreneurship; the characterization of digital minimalists as authorpreneurs was first made by Thomas, "Life Hacking," 94.

8. Cory Doctorow, "Download Makers for Free," *Craphound* (blog), October 1, 2009, https://craphound.com/makers/download/; Cory Doctorow, *Down and Out in the Magic Kingdom* (New York: Tor, 2003), https://craphound.com/down/Cory_Doctorow_-_Down_and_Out_in_the_Magic_Kingdom.pdf.

9. Merlin Mann, "Independent Writer, Speaker, and Broadcaster," March 8, 2016, http://www.merlinmann.com/; Merlin Mann, "Merlin's Bio," 2015, https://web.archive.org/web/20170316005949/www.merlinmann.com/bio/.

10. Cory Doctorow and Danny O'Brien, "Life Hacks: Tech Secrets of Overprolific Alpha Geeks," *Craphound* (blog), February 11, 2004, https://www.craphound.com/lifehacksetcon04.txt; Merlin Mann, "Getting Started with 'Getting Things Done,'" *43 Folders* (blog), September 8, 2004, http://www.43folders.com/2004/09/08/getting-started-with-getting-things-done.

11. David Allen, *Getting Things Done: The Art of Stress-Free Productivity* (New York: Penguin, 2001), 85–86, 3; David Allen, quoted in Robert Andrews, "A New Cult for the Info Age," *Wired*, July 12, 2005, https://www.wired.com/culture/lifestyle/news/2005/07/68103.

12. David McCandless, "Technology: Fitter, Happier, More Productive: Thanks to David Allen's Cult Time-Management Credo," *The Guardian*, October 20, 2005, https://www.theguardian.com/technology/2005/oct/20/guardianweeklytechnologysection; Mann, "Getting Started with 'Getting Things Done.'"

13. Merlin Mann, "Four Years," *43 Folders* (blog), September 8, 2008, http://www.43folders.com/2008/09/08/four-years.

14. Danny O'Brien and Joey Daoud, "Interview with Danny O'Brien," in *You 2.0— A Documentary on Life Hacking*, ed. Joey Daoud (Coffee and Celluloid Productions, 2010), https://web.archive.org/web/20171224145027/http:/www.lifehackingmovie.com/; Danny O'Brien, "Danny O'Brien," Electronic Frontier Foundation, April 8, 2014, https://www.eff.org/about/staff/danny-obrien-0.

15. Merlin Mann, "43 Folders: Time, Attention, and Creative Work," *43 Folders* (blog), September 10, 2008, http://www.43folders.com/2008/09/10/time-attention-creative-work; Merlin Mann, "Better," September 3, 2008, http://www.merlinmann.com/better/.

16. Merlin Mann and Joey Daoud, "Interview with Merlin Mann," in *You 2.0—A Documentary on Life Hacking*, ed. Joey Daoud (Coffee and Celluloid Productions, 2010), https://web.archive.org/web/20171224145027/http:/www.lifehackingmovie.com/.

17. Gina Trapani, "So Long, and Thanks for All the Fish," *Lifehacker* (blog), January 16, 2009, https://lifehacker.com/5132674/so-long-and-thanks-for-all-the-fish; Gina Trapani, email to author, November 17, 2017.

18. Gina Trapani, *Lifehacker: 88 Tech Tricks to Turbocharge Your Day* (Chichester, UK: Wiley, 2006); Gina Trapani, *Upgrade Your Life: The Lifehacker Guide to Working Smarter, Faster, Better* (Hoboken, NJ: Wiley Technology, 2008); Adam Pash and Gina Trapani, *Life Hacker*, 3rd ed. (Indianapolis: Wiley, 2011), xxiii.

19. Gina Trapani and Joey Daoud, "Interview with Gina Trapani," in *You 2.0—A Documentary on Life Hacking*, ed. Joey Daoud (Coffee and Celluloid Productions, 2010), https://web.archive.org/web/20171224145027/http:/www.lifehackingmovie.com/.

20. There is not yet consensus as to whether systematic and intuitive styles are two poles of a single dimension or whether a person can be both highly systematic and intuitive. Christopher Allinson and John Hayes, *The Cognitive Style Index: Technical Manual and User Guide* (London: Pearson Education, 2012), 2.

21. Lilach Sagiv et al., "Not All Great Minds Think Alike: Systematic and Intuitive Cognitive Styles," *Journal of Personality* 82, no. 5 (October 21, 2013): 414, https://doi .org/10.1111/jopy.12071; Sarah Moore, Donncha O'Maidin, and Annette McElligott, "Cognitive Styles among Computer Systems Students: Preliminary Findings," *Journal of Computing in Higher Education* 14, no. 2 (Spring 2002): 54, https://doi.org/10.1007/ BF02940938; Michael Bachmann, "The Risk Propensity and Rationality of Computer Hackers," *International Journal of Cyber Criminology* 4 (2010): 652, http://www .cybercrimejournal.com/michaelbacchmaan2010ijcc.pdf.

22. Brian Christian and Tom Griffiths, *Algorithms to Live By: The Computer Science of Human Decisions* (New York: Holt, 2016), 5.

23. Steve Silberman, "The Geek Syndrome," *Wired*, August 30, 1993, https://www.wired .com/2001/12/aspergers/; Simon Baron-Cohen, *The Essential Difference: The Truth about the Male and Female Brain* (New York: Basic, 2003); Simon Baron-Cohen, "The Hyper-systemizing, Assortative Mating Theory of Autism," *Progress in Neuro-Psychopharmacology and Biological Psychiatry* 30, no. 5 (July 2006), https://doi.org/10.1016/j.pnpbp.2006 .01.010; for a critique of Baron-Cohen, see Cordelia Fine, *Delusions of Gender: How Our Minds, Society, and Neurosexism Create Difference* (New York: Norton, 2010).

24. Steve Silberman, *NeuroTribes: The Legacy of Autism and the Future of Neurodiversity* (New York: Avery, 2016).

25. Trapani and Daoud, "Interview with Gina Trapani."

26. Tim Ferriss, "Bio," *4-Hour Workweek* (blog), March 16, 2016, https://fourhour workweek.com/about/.

27. Jerry Guo, "Tim Ferriss's Latest Book Wows," *Newsweek*, January 4, 2011, http:// www.newsweek.com/4-hour-body-tim-ferrisss-latest-book-wows-66817.

28. Stephanie Rosenbloom, "Tim Ferriss, the 4-Hour Guru," *New York Times*, March 25, 2011, https://www.nytimes.com/2011/03/27/fashion/27Ferris.html; emphasis added.

29. Tim Ferriss, *The 4-Hour Workweek: Escape 9–5, Live Anywhere, and Join the New Rich* (2007; repr., New York: Crown, 2009), 128.

30. M. J. Kim in Rebecca Mead, "Better, Faster, Stronger," *New Yorker*, September 5, 2011, https://www.newyorker.com/magazine/2011/09/05/better-faster-stronger.

31. Tynan, "My Friends and I Bought an Island," *Tynan* (blog), September 16, 2013, http://tynan.com/island; Adrian Chen, "Tech Geeks Celebrate after Famous Pickup Artist Buys a Private Island," *Gawker* (blog), September 17, 2013, http://gawker.com/tech-geeks-celebrate-after-famous-pickup-artist-buys-a-1333855628.

32. Tynan, "7 Goals for 2006," *Tynan* (blog), January 2, 2006, http://tynan.com/goals-for-2006.

33. Neil Strauss, *The Game: Penetrating the Secret Society of Pickup Artists* (New York: ReganBooks, 2005).

34. Tynan, *The Tiniest Mansion: How to Live in Luxury on the Side of the Road* (Seattle, WA: Amazon Digital Services, 2012); Tynan, "About," *Tynan* (blog), September 8, 2013, http://tynan.com/about.

35. Tynan, *Superhuman Social Skills: A Guide to Being Likeable, Winning Friends, and Building Your Social Circle* (Seattle, WA: Amazon Digital Services, 2015), Kindle.

36. Tynan and Maneesh Sethi, "How Tynan Became a Pickup Artist, Made Earrings Out of Human Bone, and Lives in an RV," *Hack the System* (blog), April 11, 2012, 00:19:00.

37. Tynan, "If It's Too Good to Be True …," *Tynan* (blog), August 4, 2008, http://tynan.com/if-its-too-good-to-be-true.

38. Tynan, "The Benefit of Automating Everything," *Tynan* (blog), April 7, 2017, http://tynan.com/automateit.

3   Hacking Time

1. Stephen J. Dubner and Tim Ferriss, "How to Be Tim Ferriss," *Freakonomics*, May 18, 2016, http://freakonomics.com/podcast/tim-ferriss/.

2. Tim Ferriss, quoted in Sanjiv Bhattacharya, "Timothy Ferriss: The Time Management Master," *Telegraph*, December 2, 2013, https://www.telegraph.co.uk/culture/9791532/Timothy-Ferriss-the-time-management-master.html.

3. Penelope Trunk, "5 Time Management Tricks I Learned from Years of Hating Tim Ferriss," *Penelope Trunk Careers* (blog), January 8, 2009, http://blog.penelopetrunk.com/2009/01/08/5-time-management-tricks-i-learned-from-years-of-hating-tim-ferriss/.

4. David Z. Morris, "Tim Ferriss and the Ideology of Achievement," *Minds Like Knives* (blog), January 24, 2011, http://mindslikeknives.blogspot.com/2011/01/against -greatness-tim-ferriss-and.html; for life hackers' fondness for Franklin, see Matt Thomas, "Life Hacking: A Critical History, 2004–2014" (PhD diss., University of Iowa, 2015), 31–32.

5. E. P. Thompson, "Time, Work-Discipline and Industrial Capitalism," libcom.org, 2008, 8, 2, https://libcom.org/library/time-work-discipline-industrial-capitalism-e-p -thompson; also see Tracey Potts, "Life Hacking and Everyday Rhythm," in *Geographies of Rhythm: Nature, Place, Mobilities and Bodies*, ed. Tim Edensor (Burlington, VT: Agate, 2010); Judy Wajcman, *Pressed for Time: The Acceleration of Life in Digital Capitalism* (Chicago: University of Chicago Press, 2014), 40–41.

6. Frank B. Gilbreth Jr. and Ernestine Gilbreth Carey, *Cheaper by the Dozen* (New York: Perennial Classics, 2002); Frank B. Gilbreth Jr. and Ernestine Gilbreth Carey, *Belles on Their Toes* (New York: HarperCollins, 2003).

7. Nikil Saval, "The Secret History of Life-Hacking," *Pacific Standard*, April 22, 2014, https://psmag.com/business-economics/the-secret-history-of-life-hacking-self -optimization-78748.

8. Charles Duhigg, *Smarter Faster Better: The Secrets of Being Productive in Life and Business* (New York: Random House, 2016), Kindle.

9. Phoebe Moore and Andrew Robinson, "The Quantified Self: What Counts in the Neoliberal Workplace," *New Media & Society* 18, no. 11: 2774–2792, https://doi.org/ 10.1177/1461444815604328; Melissa Gregg, "Getting Things Done: Productivity, Self-Management, and the Order of Things," in *Networked Affect*, ed. Ken Hillis, Susanna Paasonen, and Michael Petit (Cambridge, MA: MIT Press, 2015), 187–202; Laurie Penny, "Life-Hacks of the Poor and Aimless," *The Baffler*, July 8, 2016, http:// thebaffler.com/latest/laurie-penny-self-care.

10. Tim Ferriss and Kevin Rose, "Kevin Rose and Tim Ferriss Discuss Angel Investing and Naming Companies," *4-Hour Work Week* (blog), March 31, 2009, https:// fourhourworkweek.com/2009/03/31/kevin-rose-and-tim-ferriss-discuss-naming -companies-angel-investing/.

11. Tim Ferriss, *The 4-Hour Workweek: Escape 9–5, Live Anywhere, and Join the New Rich* (New York: Crown, 2007), 67–68, 73.

12. Stephen Covey, *The 7 Habits of Highly Effective People: Restoring the Character Ethic* (New York: Simon & Schuster, 1989), 161.

13. Richard Koch, *The 80/20 Principle: The Secret of Achieving More with Less* (1999; repr., New York: Doubleday, 2008).

14. Alan Lakein, *How to Get Control of Your Time and Your Life* (New York: Wyden, 1973), 2.

15. Lakein, *How to Get Control of Your Time and Your Life*, 6–7.

16. Lakein, *How to Get Control of Your Time and Your Life*, chap. 21.

17. Stephen Covey, *The 7 Habits of Highly Effective People: Powerful Lessons in Personal Change* (New York: Simon & Schuster, 2013), 180.

18. David Allen, *Getting Things Done: The Art of Stress-Free Productivity* (New York: Penguin Books, 2001), 17.

19. Roy F. Baumeister and John Tierney, *Willpower: Rediscovering the Greatest Human Strength* (New York: Penguin, 2011), 80–82.

20. Nathan Ensmenger, *Personal Kanban: Mapping Work, Navigating Life* (Seattle, WA: Modus Cooperandi, 2011), 22.

21. Alex Cavoulacos, "Why You Never Finish Your To-Do Lists at Work (and How to Change That)," The Muse, August 4, 2015, https://www.themuse.com/advice/why -you-never-finish-your-todo-lists-at-work-and-how-to-change-that.

22. Nancy Kress, *Beggars in Spain* (New York: HarperCollins, 2009), Kindle.

23. Tim Ferriss, *The 4-Hour Body: An Uncommon Guide to Rapid Fat-Loss, Incredible Sex, and Becoming Superhuman* (New York: Crown Archetype, 2010), chap. 7.

24. Jonathan Crary, *24/7: Late Capitalism and the Ends of Sleep* (New York: Verso, 2013), 9, 17, https://twenty-four-seven.wikispaces.com/file/view/Late-Capitalism-and -the-Ends-of-Sleep-Jonathan-Crary.pdf; see also Evgeny Morozov, "Lifehacking Is Just Another Way to Make Us Work More," *Slate*, July 29, 2013, http://www.slate.com/ articles/technology/future_tense/2013/07/lifehacking_is_just_another_way_to_make _us_work_more.html.

25. Maneesh Sethi, "Maneesh Sethi—4HWW Success as a Digital Nomad," YouTube, December 26, 2009, https://youtu.be/1merER1zVFg.

26. Tim Ferriss, "Cold Remedy: 18 Real-World Lifestyle Design Case Studies (Now It's Your Turn)," *4-Hour Workweek* (blog), December 31, 2009, https://fourhourwork week.com/2009/12/31/cold-remedy-15-real-world-lifestyle-design-case-studies-now -its-your-turn/; Maneesh Sethi, "Maneesh Does Pushups," Tumblr, 2009, http:// maneeshdoespushups.tumblr.com/.

27. Steve Haruch, "Why Corporate Executives Talk About 'Opening Their Kimonos,'" NPR, November 2, 2014, https://www.npr.org/sections/codeswitch/2014/11/02/ 360479744/why-corporate-executives-talk-about-opening-their-kimonos.

28. Maneesh Sethi, "4HWW Submission—ManesshSethi.com," YouTube, May 1, 2011, https://youtu.be/8Gn9gH4T2hU; Maneesh Sethi, "The Sex Scandal Tech- nique: How to Achieve Any Goal, Instantly (and Party with Tim Ferriss)," *Scott H. Young* (blog), February 2012, https://www.scotthyoung.com/blog/2012/02/06/sex -scandal-technique/.

29. Ramit Sethi, *I Will Teach You to Be Rich* (New York: Workman, 2009).

30. Maneesh Sethi, "About," *Hack the System* (blog), December 13, 2012, http://hackthesystem.com/about/.

31. Maneesh Sethi and Trevor Cates, "Break Bad Habits with Maneesh Sethi," *The Spa Dr. Secrets to Smart, Sexy, Strong* (blog), December 2, 2014, http://drtrevorcates.com/break-bad-habits-maneesh-sethi/; Maneesh Sethi, "Pavlok Breaks Bad Habits," Indiegogo, November 30, 2014, https://www.indiegogo.com/projects/pavlok-breaks-bad-habits#/; Maneesh Sethi, "Why Is Pavlok Better Than a Rubber Band?," *Pavlok* (blog), August 8, 2016, https://pavlok.com/blog/why-is-pavlok-better-than-a-rubber-band/.

32. Sethi, "The Sex Scandal Technique."

33. Micki McGee, *Self-Help, Inc.: Makeover Culture in American Life* (Oxford: Oxford University Press, 2005), 173; Jana Costas and Christopher Grey, "Outsourcing Your Life: Exploitation and Exploration in 'The 4-Hour Workweek,'" in *Managing "Human Resources" by Exploiting and Exploring People's Potentials*, ed. Mikael Holmqvist and André Spicer (Bingley, UK: Emerald Group), 223, https://doi.org/10.1108/s0733-558x(2013)0000037012; Melissa Gregg, *Work's Intimacy* (Malden, MA: Polity, 2011), 170.

34. Tim Ferriss, quoted in Rebecca Mead, "Better, Faster, Stronger," *New Yorker*, September 5, 2011, https://www.newyorker.com/magazine/2011/09/05/better-faster-stronger.

35. Sarah Grey, "Between a Boss and a Hard Place: Why More Women Are Freelancing," *Bitch*, August 2, 2016, https://www.bitchmedia.org/article/between-boss-and-hard-place-why-more-women-are-freelancing; Brooke Erin Duffy, "We're Not All Entrepreneurs," *Points: Data & Society* (blog), November 17, 2016, https://points.datasociety.net/were-not-all-entrepreneurs-pew-data-reveals-yawning-gaps-in-platform-economy-c53decf864b0; Siddharth Suri and Mary L. Gray, "Spike in Online Gig Work," Points, November 17, 2016, https://points.datasociety.net/spike-in-online-gig-work-c2e316016620.

36. Peter Thiel, "Two Years. $100,000. Some Ideas Just Can't Wait," The Thiel Fellowship, 2010, http://thielfellowship.org/; for Silicon Valley's narrow vision and blindness, see "Boys of Mountain View," in Nicholas Carr, *Utopia Is Creepy and Other Provocations* (New York: Norton, 2016), 279–285; for life hacking's being "blind to larger structures," see Thomas, "Life Hacking," 94, 145; for critiques of Silicon Valley personalities, see Noam Cohen, *The Know-It-Alls: The Rise of Silicon Valley as a Political Powerhouse and Social Wrecking Ball* (New York: New Press, 2017).

37. Heidi Waterhouse, "Life-Hacking and Personal Time Management for the Rest of Us," YouTube, March 8, 2015, 13:13, https://youtu.be/gKAQtnbQ1-U.

38. McGee, *Self-Help, Inc.*, 17, 12, 173; Gregg, "Getting Things Done," 187–189; Moore and Robinson, "The Quantified Self," 4.

39. Alice Marwick, *Status Update: Celebrity, Publicity, and Branding in the Social Media Age* (New Haven, CT: Yale University Press, 2013), 180–183.

40. Steven Levy, *Hackers: Heroes of the Computer Revolution* (1984; repr., London: Penguin, 2001); Pekka Himanen, *The Hacker Ethic and the Spirit of the Information Age* (New York: Random House, 2001); E. Gabriella Coleman, *Coding Freedom: The Ethics and Aesthetics of Hacking* (Princeton, NJ: Princeton University Press, 2013), https://gabriel lacoleman.org/Coleman-Coding-Freedom.pdf.

41. Tim Ferriss, "Mail Your Child to Sri Lanka or Hire Indian Pimps: Extreme Personal Outsourcing," *4-Hour Workweek* (blog), July 24, 2007, https://fourhourwork week.com/2007/07/24/mail-your-child-to-sri-lanka-or-hire-indian-pimps-extreme -personal-outsourcing/.

42. Kress, *Beggars in Spain*, loc. 462 of 6855, Kindle.

43. Kress, *Beggars in Spain*, loc. 1002 of 6855, Kindle.

44. Kress, *Beggars in Spain*, loc. 3789 of 6855, Kindle; Ursula K. Le Guin, *The Dispossessed: An Ambiguous Utopia* (New York: Harper & Row, 1974).

45. Joseph Reagle, "'Free as in Sexist?': Free Culture and the Gender Gap," *First Monday* 18, no. 1 (January 2013), http://reagle.org/joseph/2012/fas/free-as-in-sexist.html.

46. Paul Graham, *Hackers & Painters: Big Ideas from the Computer Age* (Cambridge, MA: O'Reilly, 2010), 118–120; Paul Graham, "Economic Inequality," PaulGraham .com, January 6, 2016, http://www.paulgraham.com/ineq.html.

47. Shigehiro Oishi, Selin Kesebir, and Ed Diener, "Income Inequality and Happiness," *Psychological Science* 22, no. 9 (August 12, 2011): 1095–1100, http://www.factor happiness.at/downloads/quellen/S13_Oishi.pdf.

48. Graham, *Hackers & Painters*, 50.

4   Hacking Motivation

1. Nick Winter, *The Motivation Hacker* (self-published, 2013), 3–6, Kindle, http:// www.nickwinter.net/the-motivation-hacker.

2. Piers Steel, *The Procrastination Equation: How to Stop Putting Things Off and Start Getting Stuff Done* (New York: Harper, 2011); lukeprog, "How to Beat Procrastination," *LessWrong* (blog), February 5, 2011, https://lesswrong.com/lw/3w3/how_to _beat_procrastination/.

3. Nick Winter, interview with author, July 7, 2015.

4. Thomas C. Schelling, "Egonomics, or the Art of Self-Management," *American Economic Review* 68, no. 2 (May 1978): 290.

5. Stephen Covey, The 7 Habits of Highly Effective People: Powerful Lessons in Personal Change (New York: Simon & Schuster, 2013), 159.

6. Roy F. Baumeister and John Tierney, *Willpower: Rediscovering the Greatest Human Strength* (New York: Penguin, 2011), 51.

7. Charles Duhigg, *The Power of Habit: Why We Do What We Do in Life and Business* (New York: Random House, 2012), 17; Charles Duhigg, *Smarter Faster Better: The Secrets of Being Productive in Life and Business* (New York: Random House, 2016), loc. 1890, Kindle.

8. Gabriele Oettingen, *Rethinking Positive Thinking: Inside the New Science of Motivation* (New York: Penguin, 2014).

9. Angela Duckworth, *Grit: The Power of Passion and Perseverance* (New York: Scribner, 2016); Angela Duckworth, "Grit: The Power of Passion and Perseverance," YouTube, May 9, 2013, https://www.youtube.com/watch?v=H14bBuluwB8.

10. Nir Eyal with Ryan Hoover, *Hooked: How to Build Habit-Forming Products* (New York: Portfolio/Penguin, 2014).

11. Winter, *The Motivation Hacker*, 76.

12. Nick Winter, "The 120-Hour Workweek Epic Coding Time-Lapse," November 2013, http://blog.nickwinter.net/the-120-hour-workweek-epic-coding-time-lapse.

13. Wisdom, "Comment," November 2013, http://blog.nickwinter.net/uid/84714.

14. Melanie Pinola, "Work Smarter and More Easily by 'Sharpening Your Axe,'" *Lifehacker* (blog), June 21, 2011, https://lifehacker.com/5814019/work-smarter-and -more-easily-by-sharpening-your-axe.

15. *43 Folders* (blog), "Productivity PrOn," 43FoldersWiki, March 21, 2005, http:// wiki.43folders.com/?oldid=769.

16. Merlin Mann, "43 Folders: Time, Attention, and Creative Work," *43 Folders* (blog), September 10, 2008, http://www.43folders.com/2008/09/10/time-attention -creative-work; Merlin Mann, "Better," September 3, 2008, http://www.merlinmann .com/better/; Matt Thomas, "Life Hacking: A Critical History, 2004–2014" (PhD diss., University of Iowa, 2015), 76.

17. Heidi Waterhouse, "Life-Hacking and Personal Time Management for the Rest of Us," March 8, 2015, https://youtu.be/gKAQtnbQ1-U.

18. Randall Munroe, "Is It Worth the Time?," XKCD, April 30, 2013, https://xkcd .com/1205/.

19. Mihir Patkar, "The Best Body Hacks to Boost Your Productivity at Work," *Lifehacker* (blog), September 2, 2014, https://lifehacker.com/the-best-body-hacks-to-boost -your-productivity-at-work-1629589572.

20. John Bohannon, "I Fooled Millions into Thinking Chocolate Helps Weight Loss. Here's How," *Gizmodo* (blog), May 27, 2015, https://io9.gizmodo.com/i-fooled -millions-into-thinking-chocolate-helps-weight-1707251800.

21. Open Science Collaboration, "Estimating the Reproducibility of Psychological Science," *Science* 349, no. 6251 (August 28, 2015), https://doi.org/10.1126/science .aac4716; Benedict Carey, "Many Psychology Findings Not as Strong as Claimed, Study Says," *New York Times*, August 27, 2015, https://www.nytimes.com/2015/08/28/sci ence/many-social-science-findings-not-as-strong-as-claimed-study-says.html; Ulrich Schimmack, "Replicability Report No. 1: Is Ego-Depletion a Replicable Effect?" *Replica-bility-Index* (blog), April 18, 2016, https://replicationindex.wordpress.com/2016/04/18/ is-replicability-report-ego-depletionreplicability-report-of-165-ego-depletion-articles/.

22. "The Downside of 'Grit' (Commentary)," Alfie Kohn, April 6, 2014, https://www .alfiekohn.org/article/downside-grit/; James Coyne, "Do Positive Fantasies Prevent Dieters from Losing Weight?," *PLOS Blogs: Mind the Brain* (blog), September 16, 2015, http://blogs.plos.org/mindthebrain/2015/09/16/do-positive-fantasies-prevent-dieters -from-losing-weight/; James Coyne, "Promoting a Positive Psychology Self-Help Book with a Wikipedia Entry," *PLOS Blogs: Mind the Brain* (blog), September 23, 2015, http:// blogs.plos.org/mindthebrain/2015/09/23/promoting-a-positive-psychology-self-help -book-with-a-wikipedia-entry/; Daniel Engber, "Angela Duckworth Says Grit Is the Key to Success in Work and Life: Is This a Bold New Idea or the Latest Self-Help Fad?," *Slate*, May 8, 2016, http://www.slate.com/articles/health_and_science/cover_story/2016/05/ angela_duckworth_says_grit_is_the_key_to_success_in_work_and_life_is_this.html.

23. Amy Cuddy, "Your Body Language Shapes Who You Are," TED.com, June 15, 2012, https://www.ted.com/talks/amy_cuddy_your_body_language_shapes_who _you_are.

24. Dana Carney, "My Position on 'Power Poses,'" University of California at Berkeley, September 2016, http://faculty.haas.berkeley.edu/dana_carney/pdf_My%20position %20on%20power%20poses.pdf; Amy Cuddy, "Amy Cuddy's Response to Power-Posing Critiques," *Science of Us* (blog), September 30, 2016, http://www.thecut.com/ 2016/09/read-amy-cuddys-response-to-power-posing-critiques.html; Susan Domi-nus, "When the Revolution Came for Amy Cuddy," *New York Times*, October 18, 2017, https://www.nytimes.com/2017/10/18/magazine/when-the-revolution-came-for -amy-cuddy.html.

25. Will Stephen, "How to Sound Smart in Your TEDx Talk," TEDx, January 15, 2015, https://youtu.be/8S0FDjFBj8o.

26. Benjamin Bratton, "We Need to Talk about TED," *Guardian*, December 30, 2013, https://www.theguardian.com/commentisfree/2013/dec/30/we-need-to-talk-about -ted; Houman Harouni, "The Sound of TED: A Case for Distaste," *American Reader*, March 2014, http://theamericanreader.com/the-sound-of-ted-a-case-for-distaste/; Chris

Anderson, "TED Isn't a Recipe for 'Civilisational Disaster,'" *Guardian*, January 8, 2014, https://www.theguardian.com/commentisfree/2014/jan/08/ted-not-civilisational -disaster-but-wikipedia.

27. Rebecca Mead, "Better, Faster, Stronger," *New Yorker*, September 5, 2011, https://www.newyorker.com/magazine/2011/09/05/better-faster-stronger; Sanjiv Bhattacharya, "Timothy Ferriss: The Time Management Master," *Telegraph*, December 2, 2013, https://www.telegraph.co.uk/culture/9791532/Timothy-Ferriss-the-time-management -master.html.

28. "Meet the Beeminder Team," Beeminder, April 1, 2014, https://www.beeminder .com/aboutus.

29. A. J. Jacobs and Noah Charney, "A. J. Jacobs: How I Write," *The Daily Beast* (blog), May 29, 2013, https://www.thedailybeast.com/articles/2013/05/29/a-j-jacobs-how-i -write.html.

30. "Beeminder FAQ," Beeminder, March 15, 2015, https://www.beeminder.com/ faq; Dreeves, "The Road Dial and the Akrasia Horizon," *Beeminder* (blog), August 31, 2011, https://blog.beeminder.com/dial/; Bethany Soule and Danny Reeves, email to author, November 7, 2017.

31. Sean Fellows, interview with author, July 13, 2015.

32. Winter, The Motivation Hacker, 77.

33. Winter, interview with author.

34. Winter, The Motivation Hacker, 40.

35. "Beeminder FAQ"; emphasis in original.

36. Nancy K. Innis, "Tolman and Tryon: Early Research on the Inheritance of the Ability to Learn," *American Psychologist* 47, no. 2 (1992): 190–197, http://emilkirke-gaard.dk/en/wp-content/uploads/Tolman-and-Tryon-Early-research-on-the -inheritance-of-the-ability-to-learn.pdf.

37. Robert Rosenthal and Kermit L. Fode, "The Effect of Experimenter Bias on the Performance of the Albino Rat," *Behavioral Science* 8, no. 3 (1963): 183–189, https://doi.org/10.1002/bs.3830080302.

38. Micki McGee, *Self-Help, Inc.: Makeover Culture in American Life* (Oxford: Oxford University Press, 2005), 12, 17.

39. Thomas, "Life Hacking," 46, 210.

40. Melissa Gregg, *Work's Intimacy* (Malden, MA: Polity, 2011), 2; Phoebe Moore and Andrew Robinson, "The Quantified Self: What Counts in the Neoliberal Workplace," *New Media & Society* 18, no. 11: 2775, https://doi.org/10.1177/1461444815604328.

41. Winter, interview with author.

42. Bethany Soule, "Bethany's Maniac Week," *Beeminder* (blog), June 6, 2014, https://blog.beeminder.com/maniac/.

5 Hacking Stuff

1. Tynan, *Life Nomadic* (Seattle, WA: Amazon Digital Services, 2010), loc. 56 of 2058, Kindle.

2. Tynan, *The Tiniest Mansion: How to Live in Luxury on the Side of the Road* (Seattle, WA: Amazon Digital Services, 2012), loc. 552 of 678, Kindle.

3. Tynan, *Life Nomadic*, loc. 690 of 2058.

4. Tynan, *Life Nomadic*, loc. 700 of 2058.

5. Henry David Thoreau, *Walden, and on the Duty of Civil Disobedience* (1854; repr., Project Gutenberg, 1995), http://www.gutenberg.org/files/205/205-h/205-h.htm.

6. Fred Turner, *From Counterculture to Cyberculture: Stewart Brand, the Whole Earth Network, and the Rise of Digital Utopianism* (Chicago: University of Chicago Press, 2006).

7. Stewart Brand, "The Purpose," *Whole Earth Catalog*, 1968, http://www.wholeearth.com/issue/1010/article/196/the.purpose.of.the.whole.earth.catalog.

8. Tim Ferriss, *Tools of Titans: The Tactics, Routines, and Habits of Billionaires, Icons, and World-Class Performers* (Boston: Houghton Mifflin Harcourt, 2016), xix.

9. Stewart Brand, "Introduction to Whole Earth Software Catalog," *Whole Earth Software Catalog*, 1984, http://www.wholeearth.com/issue/1230/article/283/introduction.to.whole.earth.software.catalog.

10. Stewart Brand, "We Owe It All to the Hippies," *Time* 145, no. 12 (Spring 1995), http://members.aye.net/~hippie/hippie/special_.htm; see also Theodore Roszak, *From Satori to Silicon Valley: San Francisco and the American Counterculture* (San Francisco: Don't Call It Frisco Press, 1986).

11. Richard Barbrook and Andy Cameron, "The Californian Ideology," Imaginary Futures, April 17, 2004, http://www.imaginaryfutures.net/2007/04/17/the-californian-ideology-2.

12. Kevin Kelly, "Amish Hackers," *The Technium* (blog), February 10, 2009, http://kk.org/thetechnium/amish-hackers-a/.

13. Kevin Kelly, "Cool Tools," *Cool Tools* (blog), January 30, 2013, http://kk.org/cooltools/.

14. Kevin Kelly, "Lifehacking, the Whole Earth Catalog Archive," *KK* (blog), 2015, http://kk.org/ct2/lifehacking-the-whole-earth-ca/; Kevin Kelly, "Over the Long Term, the Future Is Decided by Optimists," Twitter, April 25, 2014, https://twitter .com/kevin2kelly/status/459723553642778624.

15. Turner, From Counterculture to Cyberculture, 97.

16. Matt Thomas, "Life Hacking: A Critical History, 2004–2014" (PhD diss., University of Iowa, 2015), 22, 61, 93–94, 116; for parallels with feminine-inflected labor in social media, see Brooke Erin Duffy, *(Not) Getting Paid to Do What You Love: Gender, Social Media, and Aspirational Work* (New Haven, CT: Yale University Press, 2017).

17. Danny Heitman, "Thoreau, the First Declutterer," *New York Times*, July 4, 2015, https://www.nytimes.com/2015/07/04/opinion/thoreau-the-first-declutterer.html; Ephrat Livni, "Henry David Thoreau Was the Original Hipster Minimalist," Quartz, January 13, 2017, https://qz.com/884130/henry-david-thoreau-was-the-original-hipster -minimalist/; Thomas, "Life Hacking," 124.

18. Kathryn Schulz, "Why Do We Love Henry David Thoreau?," *New Yorker*, October 19, 2015, https://www.newyorker.com/magazine/2015/10/19/pond-scum; for a critique of Thoreau's opinion of the worker's shanty, see Lisa Goff, *Shantytown, USA* (Cambridge, MA: Harvard University Press, 2016), 11.

19. Rebecca Solnit, "Mysteries of Thoreau, Unsolved: On Dirty Laundry and the Meaning of Freedom," *Orion*, May 2013, http://www.orionmagazine-digital.com/ orionmagazine/may_june_2013?folio=18&pg=20#pg20.

20. Gini Laurie, "Homemaking Problems & Solutions," 1968, http://www.polioplace .org/sites/default/files/files/Toomey_j_GAZETTE_1968_OCR.pdf; Bess Williamson, "Electric Moms and Quad Drivers: People with Disabilities Buying, Making, and Using Technology in Postwar America," *American Studies* 52, no. 1 (2012): 8, https:// journals.ku.edu/index.php/amerstud/article/download/3632/4142.

21. Arwa Mahdawi, "Silicon Valley Thinks It Invented Roommates. They Call It 'Co-Living,'" *Guardian*, November 16, 2017, https://www.theguardian.com/comment isfree/2017/nov/16/silicon-valley-thinks-it-invented-roommates-they-call-it-co-living.

22. Aziz, "OH: SF Tech Culture Is Focused on Solving One Problem: What Is My Mother No Longer Doing for Me?," Twitter, May 4, 2015, https://twitter.com/ azizshamim/status/595285234880491521.

23. Nellie Bowles, "Food Tech Is Just Men Rebranding What Women Have Done for Decades," *Guardian*, April 1, 2016, https://www.theguardian.com/technology/2016/ apr/01/food-technology-soylent-slimfast-juice-fasting.

24. Rob Rhinehart, quoted in Lee Hutchinson, "Ars Does Soylent, the Finale: Soylent Dreams for People," *Ars Technica*, September 5, 2013, https://arstechnica .com/gadgets/2013/09/ars-does-soylent-the-finale-soylent-dreams-for-people/.

25. Kevin Kelly, "What Is the Quantified Self?," *Quantified Self* (blog), October 5, 2007, https://web.archive.org/web/20111101100244/http://quantifiedself.com/2007/10/ what-is-the-quantifiable-self/.

26. Maggie Delano and Amelia Rocchi, "QSXX Quantified Self Women's Meetup Boston," Meetup, March 5, 2015, https://www.meetup.com/QSXX-Quantified-Self -Womens-Meetup-Boston/; Amelia Greenhall, interview with author, December 17, 2014.

27. Amelia Greenhall, "The First Quantified Self Women's Meetup," *Quantified Self* (blog), July 16, 2013, http://quantifiedself.com/2013/07/the-first-quantified-self -womens-meetup/; recent books about productivity and QS by women include Gina Neff and Dawn Nafus, *Self-Tracking* (Cambridge, MA: MIT Press, 2016); Deborah Lupton, *The Quantified Self: A Sociology of Self-Tracking* (Malden, MA: Polity, 2016); and Phoebe V. Moore, *The Quantified Self in Precarity* (New York: Routledge, 2017), Kindle.

28. Emilia Greenhall, "Quantified Self at the Frontier of Feminism," ed. Emilia Greenhall and Shanely Cane, *Model View Culture*, no. 1 (April 2014): 73; Rose Eveleth, "How Self-Tracking Apps Exclude Women," *Atlantic*, December 15, 2014, https:// www.theatlantic.com/technology/archive/2014/12/how-self-tracking-apps-exclude -women/383673/; see also Deborah Lupton, "Quantify the Sex: A Critical Analysis of Sexual and Reproductive Self-Tracking Using Apps," *Culture, Health & Sexuality* 17, no. 4 (2015): 440–453, https://doi.org/10.1080/13691058.2014.920528; some also complain that Silicon Valley tends to solve problems that are overly simplified or nonexistent, for example, Evgeny Morozov, *To Save Everything, Click Here: The Folly of Technological Solutionism* (New York: PublicAffairs, 2014).

29. Debbie Chachra, "Why I Am Not a Maker," *Atlantic*, January 23, 2015, https:// www.theatlantic.com/technology/archive/2015/01/why-i-am-not-a-maker/384767/.

30. Joshua Fields Millburn and Ryan Nicodemus, "About Joshua & Ryan," *The Minimalists* (blog), August 6, 2015, https://www.theminimalists.com/about/.

31. Nicodemus, quoted in Taryn Plumb, "Like Henry David Thoreau, but with WiFi," *Boston Globe*, December 19, 2012, https://www.bostonglobe.com/lifestyle/ style/2012/12/19/like-henry-david-thoreau-but-with-wifi/AXbWgbzx9PLGwJ1jf/ geQvL/story.html.

32. Leo Babauta, "Zen to Done: The Simple Productivity E-Book," *Zen Habits* (blog), November 6, 2007, http://zenhabits.net/zen-to-done-the-simple-productivity-e-book/; Leo Babauta, *The Power of Less: The Fine Art of Limiting Yourself to the Essential—in Business and in Life* (New York: Hyperion, 2009); Leo Babauta, "Toss Productivity Out," *Zen Habits* (blog), September 6, 2011, http://zenhabits.net/un/; for a more complete history of digital minimalists and the subsequent backlash, see Thomas, "Life Hacking," chap. 2.

33. Colin Wright, "Minimalism Explained," *Exile Lifestyle* (blog), September 15, 2010, http://exilelifestyle.com/minimalism-explained/.

34. Dave Bruno, *The 100 Thing Challenge: How I Got Rid of Almost Everything, Remade My Life, and Regained My Soul* (New York: Harper, 2010).

35. Rita Holt, "Deleted Blog," *Deleted Blog* (blog), November 30, 2010.

36. Marie Kondo, *The Life-Changing Magic of Tidying Up: The Japanese Art of Decluttering and Organizing*, trans. Cathy Hirano (2011; trans., Berkeley, CA: Ten Speed, 2014).

37. Nick Winter, "99 Things," March 25, 2012, http://www.nickwinter.net/things; Everett Bogue, "Why I Live with 57 Things (and What They Are)," *Far Beyond the Stars* (blog), July 30, 2010, http://www.farbeyondthestarsthearchives.com/why-i-live -with-57-things-and-what-they-are/; Kelly Sutton, "Is It Possible to Own Nothing?," *Cult of Less* (blog), September 8, 2009, http://web.archive.org/web/20150816160313/ http://cultofless.tumblr.com/post/182833987/is-it-possible-to-own-nothing; Tynan, *Life Nomadic*, loc. 314.

38. "About," *Black Minimalists* (blog), December 16, 2017, https://blackminimalists .net/about/; Cameron Glover, "Is Minimalism for Black People?," *Pacific Standard*, November 15, 2017, https://psmag.com/social-justice/is-minimalism-for-black-pepo.

39. Courtney Carver, "Minimalist Fashion Project 333 Begins," *Be More with Less* (blog), October 1, 2010, https://bemorewithless.com/minimalist-fashion-project-333 -begins/; Courtney Carver, "Women Can Be Minimalists Too," *Be More with Less* (blog), January 13, 2015, https://bemorewithless.com/women/; Tammy Strobel, "Living with 72 Things," *Rowdy Kittens* (blog), October 4, 2009, https://www.rowdykittens .com/2009/10/living-with-72-things/.

40. Marie Kondo, quoted in Richard Lloyd Parry, "Marie Kondo Is the Maiden of Mess," *Australian*, April 19, 2014, https://www.theaustralian.com.au/news/world/marie-kondo -is-the-maiden-of-mess/news-story/bcf67ad21c7063456db7440b5afba67c.

41. Graham Hill, "Living with Less. A Lot Less," *New York Times*, March 9, 2013, https:// www.nytimes.com/2013/03/10/opinion/sunday/living-with-less-a-lot-less.html.

42. Thomas, "Life Hacking," 100, 141.

43. Alexei Sayle, "Barcelona Chairs," in *The Dogcatcher* (London: Scepter, 2001), 87–89, 98.

44. Rita Holt, interview with author, May 25, 2017.

45. Sarah Goodyear, "The Minimalist Living Movement Could Use a Different Spokesperson," CityLab, March 21, 2013, https://www.citylab.com/housing/2013/ 03/minimalist-living-movement-could-use-different-spokesperson/5040/.

46. Richard Kim, "What's the Matter with Graham Hill's 'Living with Less,'" *Nation*, March 13, 2013, https://www.thenation.com/article/whats-matter-graham-hills-living-less/.

47. Colin Wright, "Extremes Are Easy," TEDxWhitefish, July 14, 2015, https://youtu.be/AnCJn6BxCGo; Annie, "The Slavery of Extreme Minimalism," *Annienygma* (blog), January 4, 2011, https://web.archive.org/web/20110108024319/annienygma.com/2011/01/the-slavery-of-extreme-minimalism/; Dave Bruno, in Katy Waldman, "Is Minimalism Really Sustainable? It's Easy to Live with Very Few Things If You Can Buy Whatever You Want," *Slate*, March 27, 2013, http://www.slate.com/articles/life/culturebox/2013/03/graham_hill_essay_in_the_new_york_times_is_minimalism_really_sustainable.html; Anthony Ongaro, "Avoid This One Minimalism Mistake," YouTube, September 21, 2016, https://youtu.be/KrFz2qJmvrM; Kristin Wong, "Beware the 'Keeping Up with the Joneses' Trap of a Minimalist Lifestyle," *Lifehacker* (blog), February 15, 2017, https://lifehacker.com/beware-the-keeping-up-with-the-joneses-trap-of-a-mini-1792355551.

48. Greg McKeown, *Essentialism: The Disciplined Pursuit of Less* (New York: Crown, 2014), 7.

49. Charlie Lloyd, "Wealth, Risk, and Stuff," *Tupperwolf* (blog), March 13, 2013, http://vruba.tumblr.com/post/45256059128/wealth-risk-and-stuff.

50. Tynan, "The Less Fortunate," *Tynan* (blog), March 5, 2013, http://tynan.com/inocente.

6 Hacking Health

1. Kevin Kelly, "What Is the Quantified Self?," *Quantified Self* (blog), October 5, https://web.archive.org/web/20111101100244/http://quantifiedself.com/2007/10/what-is-the-quantifiable-self/.

2. Peter Drucker, quoted in Paul Zak, "Measurement Myopia," The Drucker Institute, July 4, 2013, http://www.druckerinstitute.com/2013/07/measurement-myopia/.

3. Marilyn Strathern, "'Improving Ratings': Audit in the British University System," *European Review* 5, no. 3 (July 1997): 308, https://doi.org/10.1017/S1062798700002660; Joseph Reagle, *Reading the Comments: Likers, Haters, and Manipulators at the Bottom of the Web* (Cambridge, MA: MIT Press, 2015), 56, http://reagle.org/joseph/2015/rtc/.

4. Gary Wolf, "The Data-Driven Life," *New York Times Magazine*, April 18, 2010, https://www.nytimes.com/2010/05/02/magazine/02self-measurement-t.html.

5. Gary Wolf, "WHY?," *Quantified Self* (blog), September 19, 2008, http://quantifiedself.com/2008/09/but-why/.

6. A survey of self-trackers discerned three main motives: improvement of (1) health and (2) other life areas and (3) having new life experiences (curiosity, fun, and

learning). See Eun Kyoung Choe, Nicole B. Lee, Bongshin Lee, Wanda Pratt, and Julie A. Kientz, "Understanding Quantified-Selfers' Practices in Collecting and Exploring Personal Data," in *CHI '14: Proceedings of the 32nd Annual ACM Conference on Human Factors in Computing Systems* (New York: Association for Computing Machinery, 2014), 1147, https://doi.org/10.1145/2556288.2557372; for a review of motivations, see Sara M. Watson, "Living with Data: Personal Data Uses of the Quantified Self" (MSc thesis, University of Oxford, 2013), 9, http://www.saramwatson.com/blog/living-with-data-personal-data-uses-of-the-quantified; see also Tamar Sharon and Dorien Zandbergen, "From Data Fetishism to Quantifying Selves: Self-Tracking Practices and the Other Values of Data," *New Media & Society* 19, no. 11 (2017): 1695–1709, http://dx.doi.org/10.1177/1461444816636090.

7. Kay Stoner, interview with author, January 26, 2015.

8. Charles Duhigg, *Smarter Faster Better: The Secrets of Being Productive in Life and Business* (New York: Random House, 2016), Kindle.

9. Tynan, *Superhuman by Habit: A Guide to Becoming the Best Possible Version of Yourself, One Tiny Habit at a Time* (Middletown, DE: Amazon Digital Services, 2014), Kindle; Tynan, Superhuman Social Skills: A Guide to Being Likeable, Winning Friends, and Building Your Social Circle (Seattle, WA: Amazon Digital Services, 2015), Kindle; Tim Ferriss, *The 4-Hour Body: An Uncommon Guide to Rapid Fat-Loss, Incredible Sex, and Becoming Superhuman* (New York: Crown Archetype, 2010); Tim Ferriss, *The Tim Ferriss Experiment,* iTunes, April 27, 2014, https://itunes.apple.com/us/tv-season/the-tim-ferriss-experiment/id984734983.

10. Julian Huxley, "Transhumanism," in *New Bottles for New Wine* (London: Chatto & Windus, 1957), 17, https://archive.org/stream/NewBottlesForNewWine/New-Bottles-For-New-Wine#page/n15/mode/2up; Huxley's approach was preceded by Ellen H. Richards, *Euthenics, the Science of Controllable Environment: A Plea for Better Living Conditions as a First Step toward Higher Human Efficiency* (1912; repr., Middletown, DE: Amazon Digital Services, 2011), Kindle.

11. Julian Huxley, "The Uniqueness of Man," 1943, 64–70, https://archive.org/stream/TheUniquenessOfMan/The%20Uniqueness%20of%20Man_djvu.txt.

12. Mark O'Connell, *To Be a Machine: Adventures among Cyborgs, Utopians, Hackers, and the Futurists Solving the Modest Problem of Death* (New York: Doubleday, 2017), 7.

13. Ray Kurzweil, *The Singularity Is Near: When Humans Transcend Biology* (New York: Viking, 2005).

14. *Wired* Staff, "Meet the Extropians," *Wired,* April 11, 1994, https://www.wired.com/1994/10/extropians/; Max More, "Transhumanism: A Futurist Philosophy," 1990, https://web.archive.org/web/20051029125153/http://www.maxmore.com/trans hum.htm.

15. Kevin Kelly, "Extropy," *The Technium* (blog), August 29, 2009, http://kk.org/thetechnium/extropy/.

16. Anna Wiener, "Only Human: Meet the Hackers Trying to Solve the Problem of Death," *New Republic*, February 16, 2017, https://newrepublic.com/article/140260/human.

17. Robert Crawford, "Healthism and the Medicalization of Everyday Life," *International Journal of Health Services* 10, no. 3 (1980), 365, https://www.ncbi.nlm.nih.gov/pubmed/7419309; see also Deborah Lupton, "Quantifying the Body: Monitoring and Measuring Health in the Age of mHealth Technologies," *Critical Public Health* 23, no. 4 (2010): 397, https://doi.org/10.1080/09581596.2013.794931.

18. Seth Roberts, "Seth Roberts on Acne: Guest Blog, Part IV," *Freakonomics* (blog), September 15, 2005, http://freakonomics.com/2005/09/15/seth-roberts-on-acne-guest-blog-pt-iv/.

19. Stephen J. Dubner and Steven D. Levitt, "Does the Truth Lie Within?," *New York Times*, September 11, 2005, https://www.nytimes.com/2005/09/11/magazine/does-the-truth-lie-within.html; Seth Roberts, "Self-Experimentation as a Source of New Ideas: Ten Examples about Sleep, Mood, Health, and Weight," *Behavioral and Brain Sciences* 27, no. 2 (April 2004): 227–262, https://doi.org/10.1017/S0140525X04000068; Seth Roberts, *The Shangri-La Diet: The No Hunger Eat Anything Weight-Loss Plan* (New York: G. P. Putnam's Sons, 2006); also see Robert Sanders, "Smelling Your Food Makes You Fat," *Berkeley News*, July 5, 2017, http://news.berkeley.edu/2017/07/05/smelling-your-food-makes-you-fat/.

20. Seth Roberts, "Effect of One-Legged Standing on Sleep," *Personal Science, Self-Experimentation, Scientific Method* (blog), March 22, 2011, http://archives.sethroberts.net/blog/2011/03/22/effect-of-one-legged-standing-on-sleep/.

21. Seth Roberts, "More about Pork Fat and Sleep," *Personal Science, Self-Experimentation, Scientific Method* (blog), July 14, 2012, http://archives.sethroberts.net/blog/2012/07/14/more-about-pork-fat-and-sleep/.

22. Seth Roberts, "Seth Roberts' Final Column: Butter Makes Me Smarter," *Observer*, April 28, 2014, http://observer.com/2014/04/seth-roberts-final-column-butter-makes-me-smarter/; Seth Roberts, "Arithmetic and Butter," *Personal Science, Self-Experimentation, Scientific Method* (blog), August 13, 2010, http://archives.sethroberts.net/blog/2010/08/13/arithmetic-and-butter/.

23. Roberts, "Seth Roberts' Final Column."

24. Richard Sprague, "Fish Oil Makes Me Smarter," Vimeo, June 21, 2015, https://vimeo.com/147673343.

25. Anthony Giddens, "The Trajectory of Self," in *Modernity and Self-Identity: Self and Society in the Late Modern Age* (Stanford, CA: Stanford University Press, 1997), 83.

26. Gina Neff and Dawn Nafus, *Self-Tracking* (Cambridge, MA: MIT Press, 2016), 85.

27. Roberts, "More about Pork Fat and Sleep."

28. Stoner, interview with author.

29. BrainQUICKEN, "Improve Your Mental Performance with the World's First Neural Accelerator," BrainQUICKEN/BodyQUICKEN, July 13, 2003, https://web .archive.org/web/20040401233359/http://www.brainquicken.com:80/index2.asp.

30. Tim Ferriss, quoted in Aaron Gell, "If You're Not Happy with What You Have, You Might Never Be Happy," *Entrepreneur*, January 5, 2017, https://www .entrepreneur.com/article/286674.

31. Jim Rohn, *7 Strategies for Wealth & Happiness: Power Ideas from America's Foremost Business Philosopher*, 2nd ed. (1985; repr., Harmony, 2013), 86, Kindle.

32. Tony Robbins and Tim Ferriss, "Tony Robbins—on Achievement versus Fulfillment," *4-Hour Workweek* (blog), August 10, 2016, at 30:00, https://fourhourworkweek .com/2016/08/10/tony-robbins-on-achievement-versus-fulfillment/; Tim Ferriss, "Cal Fussman Corners Tim Ferriss (#324)," *The Blog of Author Tim Ferriss*, June 30, 2018, at 25:00–50:00, https://tim.blog/2018/06/30/cal-fussman-corners-tim-ferriss/.

33. Dwight Garner, "New! Improved! Shape Up Your Life!," *New York Times*, August 15, 2016, https://www.nytimes.com/2011/01/07/books/07book.html.

34. Tim O'Reilly, Kevin Kelly, and Mark Frauenfelder, "Tim O'Reilly Interview," Cool Tools, October 10, 2016, 14:00, http://kk.org/cooltools/tim-oreilly-founder-of -oreilly-media/.

35. Although Seth Roberts endorsed some questionable hypotheses, he could, at the same time, rigorously critique others' questionable claims, as seen in Seth Roberts and Saul Sternberg, "Do Nutritional Supplements Improve Cognitive Function in the Elderly?," *Nutrition* 19, nos. 11–12 (November 2003): 976–978, https://doi.org/ 10.1016/S0899-9007(03)00025-X.

36. Rob Rhinehart, "What's in Soylent," *Mostly Harmless* (blog), February 14, 2013, https://web.archive.org/web/20130217140854/robrhinehart.com/%3Fp=424.

37. Rob Rhinehart, "How I Stopped Eating Food," *Mostly Harmless* (blog), February 13, 2013, https://web.archive.org/web/20130216102825/http://robrhinehart.com/ ?p=298.

38. Rob Rhinehart, "The Appeal of Outsourcing," *Mostly Harmless* (blog), August 5, 2015, https://web.archive.org/web/20150807071331/robrhinehart.com/%3Fp=1366.

39. Ron A., interview with author, March 2016.

40. Barry Schwartz, *The Paradox of Choice: Why More Is Less* (New York: Harper Collins, 2004); Reagle, *Reading the Comments*, 22.

41. Lee Hutchinson, "The Psychology of Soylent and the Prison of First-World Food Choices," *Ars Technica*, May 29, 2014, https://arstechnica.com/gadgets/2014/05/the -psychology-of-soylent-and-the-prison-of-first-world-food-choices/.

42. Tynan, "The Benefit of Automating Everything," *Tynan* (blog), April 7, 2017, http://tynan.com/automateit.

43. Colin Wright, *My Exile Lifestyle* (Missoula, MT: Asymmetrical, 2014), 69.

44. Chris Anderson, "'After Many Years of Self-Tracking Everything (Activity, Work, Sleep) I've Decided It's [Mostly] Pointless. No Non-Obvious Lessons or Incentives :(,'" Twitter, April 16, 2016, https://twitter.com/chr1sa/status/721198400150966274.

45. Stewart Brand, "Being Lazier Than Chris, I Only Lasted a Few Months Self-Tracking. Not All Mirrors Are Windows," Twitter, April 16, 2016, https://twitter.com/ stewartbrand/status/721366233170325504.

46. Kevin Kelly, "Over the Long Term, the Future Is Decided by Optimists," Twitter, April 25, 2014, https://twitter.com/kevin2kelly/status/459723553642778624.

7   Hacking Relationships

1. Neil Strauss, *The Game: Penetrating the Secret Society of Pickup Artists* (New York: ReganBooks, 2005); Tynan, "How I Became a Famous Pickup Artist—Part 1," January 18, 2006, http://tynan.com/how-i-became-a-famous-pickup-artist-part-1.

2. Tynan, *Make Her Chase You: The Guide to Attracting Girls Who Are "Out of Your League" Even If You're Not Rich or Handsome* (self-published, CreateSpace, 2008); Mystery, *The Mystery Method: How to Get Beautiful Women into Bed* (New York: St. Martin's, 2006).

3. Mystery, *The Mystery Method*, 2.

4. Paul Buchheit, "Applied Philosophy, a.k.a. 'Hacking,'" October 13, 2009, http:// paulbuchheit.blogspot.com/2009/10/applied-philosophy-aka-hacking.html.

5. Abraham Maslow, *The Psychology of Science* (New York: Harper & Row, 1966), 15–16.

6. Joseph Reagle, "Nerd vs. Bro: Geek Privilege, Triumphalism, and Idiosyncrasy," *First Monday* 23, no. 1 (January 1, 2018), https://doi.org/10.5210/fm.v23i1.7879.

7. Tristan Miller, "Why I Will Never Have a Girlfriend," *Logological* (blog), December 20, 1999, https://www.improbable.com/airchives/paperair/volume8/v8i3/AIR _8-3-why-never-girlfriend.pdf.

8. Ran Almog and Danny Kaplan, "The Nerd and His Discontent: The Seduction Community and the Logic of the Game as a Geeky Solution to the Challenges of Young Masculinity," *Men and Masculinities* 20, no. 1 (2017): 27–48, https://doi.org/

10.1177/1097184x15613831; Matt Thomas, "Life Hacking: A Critical History, 2004–2014" (PhD diss., University of Iowa, 2015), 203–206; Brittney Cooper and Margaret Rhee, "Introduction: Hacking the Black/White Binary," *Ada: A Journal of Gender, New Media, and Technology*, no. 6 (January 2015), https://adanewmedia.org/2015/01/issue6-cooperrhee/.

9. Eric Raymond, "Sex Tips for Geeks," catb, September 4, 2004, http://www.catb.org/esr/writings/sextips/.

10. Mystery, *The Mystery Method*, 8–9.

11. Eric Weber, *How to Pick Up Girls* (New York: Symphony, 1970), 85.

12. Weber, 1.

13. Joseph O'Connor and John Seymour, *Introducing NLP: Psychological Skills for Understanding and Influencing People* (San Francisco: Conari, 2011), xii.

14. Gareth Roderique-Davies, "Neuro-Linguistic Programming: Cargo Cult Psychology?," *Journal of Applied Research and Higher Education* 1, no. 2 (2009): 58–62, https://doi.org/10.1108/17581184200900014.

15. Scott Adams and Tim Ferriss, "Scott Adams: The Man behind Dilbert," *4-Hour Workweek* (blog), September 22, 2015, 2:03:45, https://fourhourworkweek.com/2015/09/22/scott-adams-the-man-behind-dilbert/; Scott Adams, *How to Fail at Almost Everything and Still Win Big: Kind of the Story of My Life* (New York: Penguin, 2013), 2.

16. Ross Jeffries, "'So Hard in Your Mouth'?," *Speed Seduction* (blog), May 18, 2011, http://www.seduction.com/blog/so-hard-in-your-mouth/.

17. Ross Jeffries, *How to Get the Women You Desire into Bed: A Down and Dirty Guide to Dating and Seduction for the Man Who Is Fed Up with Being Mr. Nice Guy* (self-published, 1992), http://www.maerivoet.org/website/links/miscellaneous/speed-seduction-book/resources/speed-seduction-book.pdf; Ellen Fein and Sherrie Schneider, *The Rules: Time-Tested Secrets for Capturing the Heart of Mr. Right* (New York: Warner, 1996).

18. Joseph Reagle, *Reading the Comments: Likers, Haters, and Manipulators at the Bottom of the Web* (Cambridge, MA: MIT Press, 2015), chap. 6, http://reagle.org/joseph/2015/rtc/.

19. Strauss, *The Game*, 161, 242.

20. Jason Comely, Rejection Therapy: Entrepreneur Edition, June 13, 2015, https://www.thegamecrafter.com/games/rejection-therapy-entrepreneur-edition.

21. Tynan, *Superhuman Social Skills: A Guide to Being Likeable, Winning Friends, and Building Your Social Circle* (Seattle, WA: Amazon Digital, 2015), loc. 20, 75 of 1567, Kindle.

22. Strauss, *The Game*, 20–21.

23. Randall Munroe, "Pickup Artist," XKCD, 2012, https://xkcd.com/1027/.

24. Tynan, "A Frame-by-Frame Rebuttal to XKCD's Pickup Artist Comic," March 9, 2012, http://tynan.com/xkcd.

25. Amy Webb, "Amy Webb: How I Hacked Online Dating," TED.com, April 21, 2013, https://www.ted.com/talks/amy_webb_how_i_hacked_online_dating; Amy Webb, *Data, a Love Story: How I Cracked the Online Dating Code to Meet My Match* (New York: Plume, 2013).

26. Kevin Poulsen, "How a Math Genius Hacked OkCupid to Find True Love," *Wired*, June 21, 2012, https://www.wired.com/2014/01/how-to-hack-okcupid/all/; Christopher McKinlay, *Optimal Cupid: Mastering the Hidden Logic of OkCupid* (Seattle, WA: Amazon, 2014), Kindle.

27. Tim Ferriss, "Mail Your Child to Sri Lanka or Hire Indian Pimps: Extreme Personal Outsourcing," *4-Hour Workweek* (blog), July 24, 2007, https://fourhourwork week.com/2007/07/24/mail-your-child-to-sri-lanka-or-hire-indian-pimps-extreme -personal-outsourcing/.

28. Ferriss.

29. Sebastian Stadil, "Looking for the One: How I Went on 150 Dates in 4 Months: My Failed Attempt at Engineering Love," *Medium* (blog), July 23, 2016, https:// medium.com/the-mission/looking-for-the-one-how-i-went-on-150-dates-in-4 -months-bf43a095516c.

30. Stadil.

31. Nick Winter, interview with author, July 7, 2015.

32. Ben Popken, "The Couple That Pays Each Other to Put Kids to Bed," *NBC News*, August 4, 2014, https://www.nbcnews.com/business/consumer/couple-pays-each -other-put-kids-bed-n13021; Faire Soule-Reeves, "Beeminder's Youngest User," *Bee-minder* (blog), November 21, 2015, https://blog.beeminder.com/faire/.

33. Bethany Soule, quoted in Popken, "The Couple That Pays Each Other to Put Kids to Bed."

34. Bethany Soule, "For Love and/or Money: Financial Autonomy in Marriage," *Messy Matters* (blog), April 13, 2013, http://messymatters.com/autonomy/.

35. Paula Szuchman and Jenny Anderson, *Spousonomics: Using Economics to Master Love, Marriage and Dirty Dishes* (New York: Random House, 2011).

36. Tim Ferriss and Esther Perel, "The Relationship Episode: Sex, Love, Polyamory, Marriage, and More," *The Tim Ferriss Show* (blog), October 26, 2017, 01:22:08, http:// tim.blog/2017/05/21/esther-perel/.

37. Luke Zaleski, "And Now, Here's What We Think of That Married Couple Paying Each Other to Do Chores," *GQ*, February 14, 2014, https://www.gq.com/story/married-couple-money-chores; the critiques I discuss fall within the eight categories recently delineated by John Danaher, Sven Nyholm, and Brian D. Earp, "The Quantified Relationship," *American Journal of Bioethics* 18, no. 2 (2018): 3–19, https://doi.org/10.1080/15265161.2017.1409823.

38. Sarah Gould, "The Sixth Love Language," *Catholic Insight* (blog), May 1, 2014, https://catholicinsight.com/the-sixth-love-language/.

39. Paulina Borsook, *Cyberselfish: A Critical Romp through the Terribly Libertarian Culture of High-Tech* (New York: PublicAffairs, 2000), 215.

40. Valerie Aurora, "Between the Spreadsheets: Dating by the Numbers," December 20, 2015, https://blog.valerieaurora.org/2015/12/20/between-the-spreadsheets-dating-by-the-numbers/.

41. Aurora.

42. David Finch, *Journal of Best Practices: A Memoir of Marriage, Asperger's Syndrome, and One Man's Quest to Be a Better Husband* (New York: Scribner, 2012), 217.

8 Hacking Meaning

1. Dale Davidson, "About the Project," The Ancient Wisdom Project, August 14, 2017, https://theancientwisdomproject.com/about/.

2. Davidson, "About the Project."

3. Tim Ferriss, *The 4-Hour Chef: The Simple Path to Cooking Like a Pro, Learning Anything, and Living the Good Life* (Boston: New Harvest, 2012), 626.

4. Seneca, *Letters from a Stoic: Epistulae Morales ad Lucilium*, trans. Robin Campbell (Harmondsworth, UK: Penguin, 1974), 37.

5. Seneca, *Letters from a Stoic*, 199; Seneca, *Moral Letters to Lucilius*, vol. 1, trans. Richard Mott Gummere, Wikisource (1917; repr., Loeb Classical Library, Cambridge, MA: Harvard University Press, 2009), letter 18, https://en.wikisource.org/wiki/Moral_letters_to_Lucilius.

6. Epictetus, *Discourses, Fragments, Handbook*, trans. Robin Hard (Oxford: Oxford University Press, 2014).

7. Marcus Aurelius, *Meditations*, trans. Maxwell Staniforth (New York: Penguin Books, 2005), sec. 5.28.

8. William B. Irvine, *A Guide to the Good Life: The Ancient Art of Stoic Joy* (Oxford: Oxford University Press, 2009).

9. Massimo Pigliucci, *How to Be a Stoic: Using Ancient Philosophy to Live a Modern Life* (New York: Basic, 2017).

10. Tim Ferriss, *Tribe of Mentors: Short Life Advice from the Best in the World* (New York: Houghton Mifflin Harcourt, 2017).

11. Tim Ferriss, "The Tao of Seneca," *4-Hour Workweek* (blog), January 22, 2016, https://fourhourworkweek.com/2016/01/22/the-tao-of-seneca/.

12. Ryan Holiday, "About," 2016, https://ryanholiday.net/about/; Robert Greene, *The 48 Laws of Power* (New York: Penguin, 2000).

13. Ryan Holiday, *Trust Me I'm Lying: Confessions of a Media Manipulator* (New York: Portfolio/Penguin, 2012); Ryan Holiday, *Growth Hacker Marketing: A Primer on the Future of PR, Marketing, and Advertising* (New York: Portfolio/Penguin, 2013).

14. Betsy Haibel, "The Fantasy and Abuse of the Manipulable User," *Model View Culture*, April 28, 2016, https://modelviewculture.com/pieces/the-fantasy-and-abuse -of-the-manipulable-user.

15. Ryan Holiday, *The Obstacle Is the Way: The Timeless Art of Turning Trials into Triumph* (New York: Portfolio/Penguin, 2014); Ryan Holiday, *Ego Is the Enemy* (New York: Portfolio/Penguin, 2016); Ryan Holiday and Stephen Hanselman, *The Daily Stoic: 366 Meditations on Wisdom, Perseverance, and the Art of Living* (New York: Portfolio/Penguin, 2016).

16. Alexandra Alter, "Ryan Holiday Sells Stoicism as a Life Hack, without Apology," *New York Times*, December 6, 2016, https://www.nytimes.com/2016/12/06/fashion/ ryan-holiday-stoicism-american-apparel.html.

17. Tynan, "Emotional Minimalism," January 27, 2017, http://tynan.com/minemo.

18. Tynan, "Becoming a Pro Poker Player," August 18, 2008, http://tynan.com /becoming-a-pro-poker-player; Tynan and John Sonmez, "Increasing Your Productivity as a Developer (with Tynan)," Youtube: Simple Programmer, May 20, 2017, 38:00, https://youtu.be/doGvF0k_4jA; for more on emotional management and poker, see Natasha Dow Schüll, "Abiding Chance: Online Poker and the Software of Self-Discipline," *Public Culture* 28, no. 3 (80) (August 24, 2016), https://doi.org/10.1215/ 08992363-3511550.

19. Tynan, email to author, November 17, 2017.

20. Irvine, *A Guide to the Good Life*, 7; see also Chiara Sulprizio, "Why Is Stoicism Having a Cultural Moment?," *Medium* (blog), October 12, 2015, https://medium .com/eidolon/why-is-stoicism-having-a-cultural-moment-5f0e9963d560.

21. Tim Ferriss, "Stoicism 101: A Practical Guide for Entrepreneurs," *4-Hour Workweek* (blog), April 13, 2009, https://fourhourworkweek.com/2009/04/13/stoicism-101 -a-practical-guide-for-entrepreneurs/.

22. Michel Foucault, *Technologies of the Self* (1982), in *Ethics: Subjectivity and Truth (Essential Works of Foucault, 1925–1984, Vol. 1)*, ed. Paul Rabinow, trans. Robert Hurley (New York: New Press, 1998), 226.

23. Nick Reese, "Cold Shower Therapy: How to Take Control of Your Business and Life," May 26, 2016, http://nicholasreese.com/exclusives/cold-showers/; Joel Runyon, "Why Do the Impossible?," *Impossible HQ* (blog), January 4, 2016, https://impossiblehq.com/why-do-the-impossible/; Dale Davidson, "What I Learned from Taking 30 Ice Baths in 30 Days," *Observer*, October 22, 2015, http://observer.com/2015/10/what-i-learned-from-taking-30-ice-baths-in-30-days/.

24. Tim Ferriss, "How to Cage the Monkey Mind," *4-Hour Workweek* (blog), July 24, 2016, 09:00, https://fourhourworkweek.com/2016/07/24/how-to-cage-the-monkey-mind/.

25. Ryan Holiday, "Stoicism 101: A Practical Guide for Entrepreneurs," *4-Hour Workweek* (blog), April 13, 2009, https://fourhourworkweek.com/2009/04/13/stoicism-101-a-practical-guide-for-entrepreneurs/.

26. Ferriss, "The Tao of Seneca."

27. Irvine, *A Guide to the Good Life*, 72.

28. Tim Peters, "PEP 20—The Zen of Python," Python.org, August 19, 2004, https://www.python.org/dev/peps/pep-0020/.

29. Jon Kabat-Zinn, *Full Catastrophe Living: Using the Wisdom of Your Body and Mind to Face Stress, Pain, and Illness* (New York: Bantam Doubleday, 1991).

30. Chade-Meng Tan, *Search Inside Yourself: The Unexpected Path to Achieving Success, Happiness (and World Peace)* (New York: HarperOne, 2012), 4–5.

31. Bill Duane, "Interview," Vimeo: Mindful Direct, 2014, 01:40, https://vimeo.com/89332988; Duane, quoted in Noah Shachtman, "Meditation and Mindfulness Are the New Rage in Silicon Valley," *Wired*, August 9, 2013, http://www.wired.co.uk/article/success-through-enlightenment.

32. Michael W. Taft, *The Mindful Geek: Mindfulness Meditation for Secular Skeptics* (Kensington, CA: Cephalopod Rex, 2015), 11.

33. *Silicon Valley*, "The Cap Table" episode, directed by Mike Judge, written by Carson D. Mell, aired April 13, 2014, on HBO, https://www.imdb.com/title/tt3668816/.

34. Kathleen Chaykowski, "Meet Headspace, the App That Made Meditation a $250 Million Business," *Forbes*, January 8, 2017, https://www.forbes.com/sites/kathlenchaykowski/2017/01/08/meet-headspace-the-app-that-made-meditation-a-250-million-business/.

35. Steven Novella, "Is Mindfulness Meditation Science-Based?," *Science-Based Medicine* (blog), October 18, 2017, https://sciencebasedmedicine.org/is-mindfulness

-meditation-science-based/; Inmaculada Plaza, Marcelo Marcos Piva Demarzo, Paola Herrera-Mercadal, and Javier García-Campayo, "Mindfulness-Based Mobile Applications: Literature Review and Analysis of Current Features," *JMIR mHealth and uHealth* 1, no. 2 (November 1, 2013): e24, doi:10.2196/mhealth.2733; Krista Lagus, "Looking at Our Data-Perspectives from Mindfulness Apps and Quantified Self as a Daily Practice," in *Proceedings: 2014 IEEE International Conference on Bioinformatics and Biomedicine (BIBM)*, ed. Huiru (Jane) Zheng, Werner Dubitzky, Xiaohua Hu, Jin-Kao Hao, Daniel Berrar, Kwang-Hyun Cho, Yadong Wang, and David Gilbert (November 2–5, 2014, Belfast, UK), doi:10.1109/BIBM.2014.6999287; MadhavanMani, DavidJ. Kavanagh, LeanneHides, and StoyanR.Stoyanov, "Review and Evaluation of Mindfulness-Based Iphone Apps," *JMIR mHealth and uHealth* 3, no. 3 (August 19, 2015): e82, https://www.ncbi.nlm.nih.gov/pmc/articles/PMC4705029/; John Torous and Joseph Firth, "The Digital Placebo Effect: Mobile Mental Health Meets Clinical Psychiatry," *The Lancet Psychiatry* 3, no. 2 (February 2016): 101, doi:10.1016/S2215-0366(15)00565-9.

36. Rich Pierson, quoted in David Gelles, "Inner Peace in the Palm of Your Hand, for a Price," *New York Times*, December 5, 2016, https://www.nytimes.com/2016/12/03/business/inner-peace-in-the-palm-of-your-hand-for-a-price.html; Alissa Walker, "Is Apple's New Meditation App More Full of Shit Than Deepak Chopra?," *Gizmodo* (blog), June 16, 2016, https://gizmodo.com/is-apple-s-new-meditation-app-more-full-of-shit-than-de-1781906778.

37. Annika Howells, Itai Ivtzan, and Francisco Jose Eiroa-Orosa, "Putting the 'App' in Happiness: A Randomised Controlled Trial of a Smartphone-Based Mindfulness Intervention to Enhance Wellbeing," *Journal of Happiness Studies* 17, no. 64 (October 29, 2014): 163–85, https://doi.org/10.1007/s10902-014-9589-1.

38. Thomas Joiner, "Mindfulness Would Be Good for You. If It Weren't So Selfish," *Washington Post*, August 25, 2017, https://www.washingtonpost.com/outlook/mindfulness-would-be-good-for-you-if-it-werent-all-just-hype/2017/08/24/b97d0220-76e2-11e7-9eac-d56bd5568db8_story.html.

39. Martin E. Héroux, Colleen K. Loo, Janet L. Taylor, and Simon C. Gandevia, "Questionable Science and Reproducibility in Electrical Brain Stimulation Research," *PLOS ONE* 12, no. 4 (April 26, 2017): e0175635, https://doi.org/10.1371/journal.pone.0175635; more generally, see Anna Wexler, "The Social Context of 'Do-It-Yourself' Brain Stimulation: Neurohackers, Biohackers, and Lifehackers," *Frontiers in Human Neuroscience* 11 (May 10, 2017), https://doi.org/10.3389/fnhum.2017.00224.

40. *Silicon Valley*, "The Cap Table."

41. Tim Ferriss, "How to Optimize Creative Output—Jarvis versus Ferriss," *4-Hour Workweek* (blog), May 13, 2016, 25:26, https://fourhourworkweek.com/2016/05/13/how-to-optimize-creative-output-jarvis-versus-ferriss/.

42. Tara Brach and Tim Ferriss, "Tara Brach on Meditation and Overcoming FOMO (Fear of Missing Out)," *Tim Ferriss Blog* (blog), July 31, 2015, 42:00–52:00, https://fourhourworkweek.com/2015/07/31/tara-brach/.

43. In late 2017, Ferriss began indicating that he was rethinking his instrumental approach to meditation; see Richard Feloni, "Tim Ferriss Realized He Was Successful, but Not Happy," *Business Insider*, November 21, 2017, http://www.businessinsider.com/tim-ferriss-how-to-be-happy-2017-11; Jack Kornfield and Tim Ferriss, "Jack Kornfield—Finding Freedom, Love, and Joy in the Present," March 5, 2018, https://tim.blog/2018/03/05/jack-kornfield/.

44. Shachtman, "Meditation and Mindfulness Are the New Rage in Silicon Valley."

45. Onthe1, "Has Mindfulness Lost That Loving Feeling?," Headspace, August 14, 2015, https://www.headspace.com/forum/viewtopic.php?f=7&t=1253; see also Meditator-B3UO2V, "Metta (Loving-Kindness) Meditation," Headspace, January 16, 2015, https://www.headspace.com/forum/viewtopic.php?f=8&t=560; meditator-LXR0TX, "Loving Kindness?," Headspace, June 19, 2015, https://www.headspace.com/forum/viewtopic.php?f=7&t=1159.

46. Alex Payne, "Meditation and Performance," February 24, 2015, http://al3x.net/2015/02/24/meditation-and-performance.html; also see Joiner, "Mindfulness Would Be Good for You. If It Weren't So Selfish."

47. Wisdom 2.0, "Wisdom 2.0 Conference 2014 On-Stage Protest," YouTube, February 24, 2014, https://www.youtube.com/watch?v=S_AHuOkwisI; Amanda Ream, "Why I Disrupted the Wisdom 2.0 Conference," *Tricycle*, February 19, 2014, https://tricycle.org/trikedaily/why-i-disrupted-wisdom-20-conference/.

48. Ron Purser and David Forbes, "Beyond McMindfulness," *Huffington Post* (blog), August 31, 2013, https://www.huffingtonpost.com/ron-purser/beyond-mcmindfulness_b_3519289.html.

49. Purser and Forbes.

50. Ron Purser and David Forbes, "Search Outside Yourself: Google Misses a Lesson in Wisdom 101," *Huffington Post* (blog), May 5, 2014, https://www.huffingtonpost.com/ron-purser/google-misses-a-lesson_b_4900285.html.

51. Rebecca Jablonsky, "The Qualified Self in Quantified Times: Translating Embodied Wellness Practices into Technological Experiences" (paper presented at the 4S: Society for Social Study of Science conference, Boston, August 2017), 6, http://rebeccajablonsky.com/wp-content/uploads/2017/09/RJablonsky_4S2017Draft.pdf.

52. Thanissaro Bhikku, "Lost in Quotation," Access to Insight, August 29, 2012, http://www.accesstoinsight.org/lib/authors/thanissaro/lostinquotation.html.

53. Dale Davidson, "Buddhism: Day 30 and Month 5 Wrap-Up," The Ancient Wisdom Project, November 8, 2014, https://theancientwisdomproject.com/2014/11/

buddhism-day-30-month-5-wrap/; Dale Davidson, "Islam Day 5—The Case against DIY Religion," The Ancient Wisdom Project, June 24, 2014, https://theancientwis domproject.com/2014/06/islam-day-5-case-diy-religion/; Dale Davidson, "Stoicism Is Lonely," The Ancient Wisdom Project, February 24, 2014, https://theancientwis domproject.com/2014/02/stoicism-day-13-stoicism-lonely/#comment-744.

54. Bhikku, "Lost in Quotation."

9   Blinkered

1. Tim Ferriss, "5 Morning Rituals That Help Me Win the Day," *4-Hour Workweek* (blog), September 18, 2015, https://fourhourworkweek.com/2015/09/18/5-morning -rituals/.

2. Shem Magnezi, "Fuck You Startup World," *Medium* (blog), October 12, 2016, https://medium.com/startup-grind/fuck-you-startup-world-ab6cc72fad0e.

3. Holly Theisen-Jones, "My Fully Optimized Life Allows Me Ample Time to Optimize Yours," *McSweeney's*, March 27, 2017, https://www.mcsweeneys.net/articles/ my-fully-optimized-life-allows-me-ample-time-to-optimize-yours.

4. James Altucher, "How to Break All the Rules and Get Everything You Want," *Altucher Confidential* (blog), October 31, 2013, https://www.jamesaltucher.com/2013/ 10/how-to-break-all-the-rules-and-get-everything-you-want/.

5. James Altucher, "How Minimalism Brought Me Freedom and Joy," *Boing Boing* (blog), April 15, 2016, https://boingboing.net/2016/04/15/how-minimalism-brought -me-free.html; Alex Williams, "Why Self-Help Guru James Altucher Only Owns 15 Things," *New York Times*, August 28, 2016, https://www.nytimes.com/2016/08/07/ fashion/james-altucher-self-help-guru.html.

6. James Altucher, "James Altucher's 100,000% Crypto Secret," jamesaltucher.com, October 16, 2018, https://signups.jamesaltucher.com/X403TA32; Erin Griffith, "A Debate about Bitcoin That Was a Debate about Nothing," *Wired*, February 12, 2018, https://www.wired.com/story/a-debate-about-bitcoin-that-was-a-debate-about -nothing/.

7. James Altucher, "How Being a Sore Loser Can Make You Rich (or Crazy)," *Altucher Confidential* (blog), January 27, 2011, https://www.jamesaltucher.com/2011/01/how being-sore-loser-can-make-rich-crazy/; James Altucher, "Life Is like a Game. Here's How You Master Any Game," *Altucher Confidential* (blog), October 2, 2014, https://www .jamesaltucher.com/2014/10/life-is-like-a-game-heres-how-you-master-any-game/; Altucher, "How to Break All the Rules and Get Everything You Want."

8. Maneesh Sethi, "The Sex Scandal Technique: How to Achieve Any Goal, Instantly (and Party with Tim Ferriss)," *Scott H. Young* (blog), February 2012, https://www .scotthyoung.com/blog/2012/02/06/sex-scandal-technique/; Tim Ferriss, *"The Tim*

Ferriss Experiment: How to Play Poker," YouTube, June 20, 2017, 00:30, https://youtu .be/YJE6zeMV2_Y.

9. Altucher, "How to Break All the Rules and Get Everything You Want."

10. BrainQUICKEN, "Improve Your Mental Performance with the World's First Neural Accelerator," BrainQUICKEN/BodyQUICKEN, July 13, 2003, https://web.archive.org/ web/20040401233359/http://www.brainquicken.com:80/index2.asp; James Altucher, "James Altucher Cracks the 'Crypto Code'," Choose Yourself Financial, April 18, 2018, https://pro.chooseyourselffinancial.com/p/ACT_cryptocode_1217/WACTU102/ ?h=true; Altucher, "James Altucher's 100,000% Crypto Secret."

11. Ross Levine and Yona Rubinstein, "Smart and Illicit: Who Becomes an Entrepreneur and Do They Earn More?" (working paper 19276, National Bureau of Economic Research, Cambridge, MA, August 2013), 20, http://www.nber.org/papers/w19276.pdf; Sandra E. Black, Paul J. Devereux, Petter Lundborg, and Kaveh Majlesi, "On the Origins of Risk-Taking" (working paper 21332, National Bureau of Economic Research, Cambridge, MA, July 2015), http://www.nber.org/papers/w21332; Aimee Groth, "Entrepreneurs Don't Have a Special Gene for Risk—They Come from Families with Money," *Quartz* (blog), July 17, 2015, https://qz.com/455109/entrepreneurs-dont-have-a-special -gene-for-risk-they-come-from-families-with-money/.

12. Jen Dziura, "When 'Life Hacking' Is Really White Privilege," *Medium* (blog), December 19, 2013, https://medium.com/p/a5e5f4e9132f.

13. Richard Barbrook and Andy Cameron, "The Californian Ideology," Imaginary Futures, April 17, 2004, http://www.imaginaryfutures.net/2007/04/17/the-californian -ideology-2.

14. "WEAR SPACE—Red Dot Award," Red Dot, April 24, 2017, http://www.red-dot .sg/en/wear-space/; Chris Ip, "Panasonic Designed Blinkers for the Digital Age," *Engadget* (blog), March 12, 2018, https://www.engadget.com/2018/03/12/panasonic -sxsw-blinkers/.

15. Steve Salerno, *Sham: How the Self-Help Movement Made America Helpless* (New York: Crown, 2005), 6.

Index